Special Thanks to Gary Craig, Gallo, Carol Look, Caroline Du. from ACEP and APEC, and all the others named in this book! Namasté

Contents

CONTENTS 2
   Contents 2
   Steve Wells Preface 5
STEVE WELLS PREFACE 5
   Clinical EFT Preface 9
CLINICAL EFT PREFACE 9
   THE BIRTH OF CLINICAL EFT 9
   THE BIRTH OF THE PROFESSIONAL FRENCH-SPEAKING NETWORK OF ENERGY PSYCHOLOGY AND CLINICAL EFT 11
   MAKING ENERGY PSYCHOLOGY A THERAPEUTIC MODALITY IN ITS OWN RIGHT 11
   THE CONSTRUCTION OF A REAL CLINICAL CURRICULUM FOR EFT 12
   PART 1: THE BASICS OF CLINICAL EFT 16
      I.   Introduction 16
      II.   Energy Psychology 17
      III. Significant dysfunctions of the energy system, correction and prevention 20
      IV. History of EFT 26
      V.   The principles of EFT – the "ZZZZZ" 28
      VI. Points used in EFT 30
      VII. Meridian points: psychological correspondence 34
      VIII. Evaluation scales 39
      IX. Indications 40
      X.   Focusing on the target 41

Contents

- XI. The basic EFT Tapping Sequence 44
- XII. Summary of the basic treatment steps 49
- XIII. Tapping points diagram and Tapping procedure 51
- XIV. The Movie technique 53
- XV. Description of aspects during tapping 56
- XVI. Finding the right target 62
- XVII. General protocol for deconditioning a simple trauma 70
- XVIII. The effect of the treatment 82
- XIX. Avoiding strong abreactions 83
- XX. Counter indications 93
- XXI. Surrogate treatment 94
- XXII. Borrowing Benefits 96
- XXIII. The introduction of the positive statements in EFT 97
- XXIV. EFT and the physical sensations 108
- XXV. Treatment algorithms and shortcuts 116
- XXVI. The Palace of Possibilities 127
- XXVII. The Volcano technique 129
- XXVIII. The treatment of conflict 130
- XXIX. EFT and children 133
- XXX. Seven other therapeutic approaches 138

PART 2: ADVANCED CLINICAL EFT 140
- I. Introduction 141
- II. Prerequisites and preparation 143
- III. Simple trauma: phases of the treatment 245
- IV. Complex traumas 307
- V. Summary: How to build a treatment plan for simple or complex traumas 339

APPENDIX 1: DISSOCIATION 353

I.	*Historical background*	*353*
II.	*Dissociative disorders*	*354*
III.	*Theory of the structural dissociation of the personality*	*356*

BIBLIOGRAPHY AND RESEARCH 370
  EMDR PROTOCOLS 370
  PROVOCATIVE THERAPY..370
  ENERGY PSYCHOLOGY 370
OTHER RESOURCES 375

Steve Wells Preface

I am very pleased to be asked to write an introduction to the English version of this excellent book written by my friends and respected colleagues Brigitte Hansoul and Yves Wauthier-Freymann.

I am also excited to introduce their insights on acupoint tapping and Clinical Emotional Freedom Techniques (EFT) to my English-speaking colleagues. There is a great deal of value here for those who read and apply the useful information contained within these pages.

The authors are at once the most serious and rigorous of researchers, clinicians, and trainers, and also the most soft and gentle of souls, with hearts of gold. Their insights deserve to be read and shared widely among serious students of EFT, as well as those seeking self-help.

I highly recommend a detailed study of their work to anyone who wants to go deep in learning this approach, with this book as your starting point.

Emotional Freedom Techniques (EFT) is a user-friendly and gentle approach to tapping on acupressure points developed by Gary Craig in the mid-1990's. This process often leads to surprisingly positive and enduring results.

Over the past 30-plus years since its inception and evolution from the earlier Thought Field Therapy (TFT) tapping approach developed by Roger Callahan, there has been a significant amount of research conducted on EFT. That research now comprehensively demonstrates the power of these techniques in providing rapid, effective, and lasting relief from a number of psychological conditions, including anxiety, depression, PTSD, food cravings, and more.

Apart from the scientific research, what's most impressive about EFT is its rapid results in relieving suffering for now millions of people worldwide. This is something I have experienced personally and also witnessed numerous times. Each time the results are striking.

I tell everyone who will listen that EFT is one of the few things I have learned in all my years of psychology training, personal development and research that actually works at home! I use it, my wife uses it, we have used it with all of our children, and shared it with many friends, colleagues, and (in my case) clients. Very few techniques have that kind of universal positive and practical utility for changing one's life for the better.

A very dramatic example of the power of EFT was when my good friend Dr David Lake was treated for his lifelong public speaking phobia in a single 38-minute EFT treatment with Gary Craig, in front of an audience of 75 professional people from all over the world.

We were attending an advanced training in EFT and David volunteered to go out on stage with Gary and work on his lifelong public speaking phobia using EFT.

Up on stage as David and Gary addressed each of the aspects of David's phobia, and applied this simple acupoint tapping process to them, in place of the ashen faced, drawn and tentative individual who started out on stage, I saw the real David Lake emerge. It was literally just minutes from when David started dry-mouthed, with his heart jumping out of his chest, to when he was able to laugh and joke with the audience, just as he had with those of us who went to dinner with him the night before. His phobia was nowhere to be seen.

A few short months later, I invited David to join me in teaching EFT to a group of professionals in a workshop. I'll never forget the moment when he introduced himself to the 40 professionals in the room, then turned to me with a look of awe and said, "I can't believe it, I don't feel any of it!" His previous life-long phobia was gone, replaced by a beautiful calmness.

It wasn't long before David and I were travelling to other countries and teaching EFT, followed by teaching our own developments to the approach. It was on one of those world trips that we met the authors of this book, in Belgium, and a beautiful friendship was formed.

Clinical EFT is a term originated by the authors, stemming from their desire to focus attention on the clinical uses of EFT, both to provide a focal point both for developing a curriculum for the serious clinician and to focus research efforts. The term Clinical EFT has now been adopted by many others, notably prolific EFT researcher Dawson Church, it has subsequently developed its own significant research base, and is being used by many thousands of therapists worldwide.

Steve Wells Preface

Here in this great book, the authors review the essential elements of Clinical EFT and provide an essential guidebook for serious therapists who want to learn the approach and get excellent results in using Clinical EFT with their clients.

If you are looking for a comprehensive introduction to Clinical Emotional Freedom Techniques (EFT) and how to apply it to relieve suffering, this is it. All the elements are here to support the clinician in using this unique "psychological acupressure" approach to get better results for their clients.

This is all part of a complete curriculum created by the authors, designed to produce competent practitioners who go way beyond the basic mechanical components of the EFT technique, and develop the skills required for those same therapists to obtain excellent results with their clients.

Many people approach learning and using EFT as if it is a very simple technique, which it is. However, without the depth of understanding of various clinical issues such as complex trauma, together with an understanding of important factors in using EFT to treat clinical issues, such as the importance of aspects, and testing, and more, the results practitioners of the approach can get with their clients will be limited. The fact that this guidebook covers all of these areas in depth is one of the things that makes it stand out among the myriad of EFT books out there.

Here you will see the authors have taken this more deeply and treated the whole enterprise of helping others using Clinical EFT with the seriousness it deserves.

Additionally, since EFT is still considered unconventional and seen as an alternative technique it has had some challenges in gaining acceptance among conventional therapists and counsellors. I think had many of the detractors been given a copy of this guide they might have been more willing to consider the value of finding out more about these techniques, as the authors are able to speak the language of the conventional therapists whilst simultaneously appealing to those who are attracted to the approach because of its different and alternative nature.

As well as being a very practical introduction to the key elements of the Clinical EFT approach, this is also a helpful guide on how to apply this approach with various conditions. Hansoul and Wauthier show the serious practitioner how to get results with even severe and complex issues using Clinical EFT, and this is another aspect which makes this book stand out from the majority of current EFT literature. There are separate sections on working with simple trauma and working with complex trauma, something which co-author Yves Wauthier, is very experienced and qualified in. This information alone makes this book a valuable addition to the library of the professional helper. And yet there is so much more.

This very practical and comprehensive guide to using Clinical EFT to relieve suffering is an excellent introduction to the state of the art of using these powerful methods and will become an important part of the toolkit of the serious practitioner of these methods. I commend it to you.

Steve Wells
Registered psychologist (Australia)
January 2022

Clinical EFT Preface

There are adventures in which it is inspiring to participate, and the development of EFT and Energy Psychology in general is certainly one of them. If you're reading this book, you're probably already on board!

Consciousness is in full evolution; we see its effects through different movements on a planetary level. This Consciousness transcends us and it manifests itself through what inspires or attracts us. Looking back on what led Yves and I to contribute to the field of Energy Psychology and EFT in particular, everything seems to have been perfectly orchestrated. Our respective capacities and expertise have been put at the service of these powerful healing modalities demonstrating that suffering is not inevitable, and that consciousness can heal from its identifications.

The birth of Clinical EFT

After years of career as a clinical psychologist, psychotherapist with a psychoanalytical orientation and head of a unit in a psychiatric hospital, I was seduced by the practice of other, newer or unconventional, therapies. After hypnosis and EMDR, I discovered EFT, then the whole emerging field of Energy Psychology. The speed and effectiveness of these methods amazed me, as I had had a long experience of classical speech therapy and could fully appreciate the rapid help these methods provided to my patients to free themselves from certain disorders or beliefs. The spontaneous healing capacity that these approaches revealed changed profoundly my vision of psychic functioning, which I thought I knew after nearly fifteen years of training in psychology and psychoanalysis. The field of EFT was full of creativity and many experts provided inventive and effective ways of doing things, so Yves and I devoured all these contributions with enthusiasm.

On the other hand, the contrast with my previous training was great, as I discovered at my first contacts with EFT. I was used to a depth and clinical structure that was sorely lacking in the way EFT was taught. By attending the annual congress of these methods in the United States, Yves was able to see that there was indeed no such clinical structure in the proposed training courses.

As a clinician, I immediately saw the potential to nurture this emerging field of Energy Psychology with the protocol and structural aspects that I was familiar with through my long training in EMDR, a method specialized in trauma treatment and in some respects a cousin of EFT. EMDR, whose practice is reserved for qualified clinicians, developed in a much more clinical field than EFT, which was born in the non-academic field of personal development. EMDR benefited from the contribution of high-flying clinicians and rigorous protocols. Through its simplicity and inclusive practice, EFT was gaining momentum exponentially and it was urgent to allow its practitioners to have real clinical training in their practice.

To provide a framework for the training Yves and I offer in EFT and other Energy Psychology methods, we founded Therapeutia, a training institute in Belgium.

First, I started to introduce into our EFT training courses standard protocols to find targets and their causes, and to treat them more effectively and clinically, using for example the worst image rather than the movie as taught by conventional EFT. I also introduced stabilisation techniques for patients who are very disturbed or at risk of presenting abreactions, such as the Safety Place and the Safe box: protocols to which Yves later added the Quick REMAP©. Yves has also gathered the contributions of classical EFT from a wide range of sources, as well as the lessons from his DCEP training in Energy Psychology at ACEP, USA. These protocols are the first part of this book called "Foundations of Clinical EFT"; they were partially published in our first EFT book *Tapping and Energy Psychology* published by Dangles in 2010 and are used in APEC-recognized EFT trainings and within Therapeutia.

The birth of the professional French-speaking network of Energy Psychology and Clinical EFT

In the meantime, after his visit to the United States in 2006, Yves' great ability to create networks and to federate has been used by the Consciousness to expand the recognition and diffusion of Energy Psychology. Together with some French-speaking American colleagues and some French colleagues, we founded APEC, the French-speaking Association of Clinical Energy Psychology, which aims to disseminate Energy Psychology in a clinical way and to guarantee the quality of training for practitioners. Yves has become the Belgian representative of ACEP, the Association for Comprehensive Energy Psychology, which is the American professional association of practitioners of the different currents of Energy Psychology, aiming to have this branch recognized and to bring together research.

As for the early days of Clinical EFT, I remember that we met our friend Dawson Church in the lounge of a Parisian hotel during EFT training sessions. Dawson was a research director for ACEP, the Association for Comprehensive Energy Psychology, and has contributed enormously to the development of EFT research and recognition in the United States. In particular, he was the mainspring for the development of the Veterans Stress Project (2008), which enables war veterans suffering from post-traumatic stress disorder (more than 300,000 individuals in the United States) to be supported by these state-of-the-art tools. A brilliant mind, he interviewed experienced EFT practitioners around the world to share his knowledge with others through publications. When we found ourselves in that hotel in Paris, Dawson was eager for everything we could teach him about the topic. We shared with him our efforts to raise community awareness of Clinical EFT, as well as the various clinical contributions we were already making in our EFT training. Convinced of the usefulness of giving EFT a status by developing Clinical EFT, Dawson adopted this term and is at the root of its dissemination in the United States, where he recently published the collective book *Clinical EFT Handbook* in which we wrote an article on the Affect Bridge (the advanced version of which, the "regression bridge", is called "floatback" in this book).

Making Energy Psychology a therapeutic modality in its own right

At Therapeutia and APEC, we trained many EFT practitioners who did not have basic training in the therapist profession. Many of them realized that their EFT training did not turn them into therapists. They agreed with the unanimous position of the professional community that it is not enough to practice techniques or take short courses to be a therapist. Making the relationship with the other one's job requires solid professional training.

When the people we were training at EFT asked us how and where to learn the basics of the therapist profession, we realized that there was no training institute that could provide them with what they needed. Institutes providing long-term courses trained their participants in a specific therapeutic method that our participants were not necessarily eager to learn, and their curriculum was organized around it. There was a lack of an institute that could provide professional training as a therapist and would integrate or be compatible with EFT techniques and/or other Energy Psychology methods. Our ambition was to achieve one day that the current Energy Psychology be recognised in Europe and that therapists could have an official status when they were trained at it. This required a long training course (therapy courses usually last three to four years) integrating theoretical courses, training in the therapeutic relationship between therapist/client, solid clinical training in Energy Psychology and the self-help work required for any therapist training.

Therapeutia's training comprising a three-year course was developed to enable those people who did not have formal training (such as psychologist training, for example) to become competent and reliable therapists.

The existence of this long-term training is an important step for the future of Energy Psychology in Europe, but the work is far from over. Yves tirelessly continues his work of associative construction to approach an official recognition of Energy Psychology.

The construction of a real clinical curriculum for EFT

The difference between an EFT practitioner, even an expert, and an EFT therapist trained on a complete clinical journey is a difference on many levels.

One is the therapist-patient relationship and that is why the therapist training at Therapeutia contains an in-depth teaching on this level, which

Clinical EFT Preface

Chantal Bailly has developed over the years and called the TRPE. It combines a solid classic Rogerian approach with recent tools to work throughout the three years on the presence of the therapist, the connection to the Self and the work with the parts of the Self of the therapist and the patient (inspired by the Internal Family Systems), the aspects of transference and countertransference, etc. The students are invited to turn their gaze inward as much as towards the inner world of those they help. At the end of the course, this allows the therapist himself to be the first and best professional tool in his practice. These contributions are not the subject of this book which focuses on clinical training applied to EFT and Energy Psychology, an aspect that has been developed at length in this therapist training.

The most important part I have integrated into the EFT clinical curriculum of the therapist training is the treatment plan. Indeed, the frequent limitations of an EFT practitioner lie in the lack of a general vision of the patient's case. Many EFT therapists rush to what the patient brings, which is often only the tip of the iceberg or a symptom of underlying problems. The practitioner therefore limits himself in each session to flickering from target to target according to what has happened to the patient on a daily basis. This is sufficient for simple "EFT sessions", but not as part of a real therapy where the aim is to have a more clinical and structured vision.

All EFT practitioners have experienced the limitations of "iceberg EFT" which is limited to dealing with what is apparent in the patient's daily speech. In one type of cases, the practitioner takes the problem brought by the patient literally and treats it in such a way that the symptom disappears. But, with this problem gone, the patient is not necessarily better off, because this surface problem was not the cause of the underlying distress. The other case that all clinicians will recognize is that of the patient who presents a general picture of insecurity or lack of self-confidence, for example, plunging his roots into chronic childhood situations. If the practitioner takes these symptoms as difficulties like any other and treats them as such, he quickly realizes that, although at each session the target is relatively well treated and gives an impression of progress, the underlying problem is not much improved. Finally, there is the most damaging case: patients with very heavy childhood situations that they do not necessarily talk about, and for whom the treatment of an emotional target from the present or recent past may lead to a heavy trauma from the past (such as abuse, for example). The EFT practitioner is always enthusiastic about being able to "do his magic" on a trauma, as it is true that it works wonderfully for simple cases. But in complex cases that are not identified as such, the attempt to treat this trauma will not only lead to failure, but also to a more intense reactivation of the associated distress.

All these cases require a specifically adapted treatment plan instead of an "iceberg EFT". I had made this observation myself years earlier, as my expertise brought me patients with increasingly severe disorders. For years, I have done many specialized training courses in the management of patients with complex traumas and attachment disorders. These were often EMDR training courses since it is a technique used massively in psycho-traumatology.

For the Therapeutia curriculum, I have gathered my expertise on these topics as well as on the establishment of a clinical treatment plan and essential resources, and I have converted them into protocols applied to EFT and Energy Psychology as you will discuss them in the chapters of the second part called **"Advanced Clinical EFT"**. Although they address complex trauma and very fragile patients, I quickly realized that these protocols were not only useful for heavy cases, **but also for the rest of the patients who came to us.** Indeed, they combine positive work with negative treatment and are wonderful tools to help all patients progress on the path of life.

Yves' advanced levels of EFT have benefited from the integration of traditional Chinese medicine and his deep knowledge of meridians and related emotions to accelerate the results of this tool. He also continued his research work on complex traumas and attachment disorders and integrated the benefits of the Internal Family Systems and Compassion Focused Therapy as well as cardiac coherence into training. These contributions, which combine EFT, REMAP and clinical adaptations of Tonglen Buddhist compassionate meditation, have further changed the clinical application of EFT and have opened the doors to an effective and stable reprocessing of the heaviest cases where the treatment plan becomes just as vital as the presence and professionalism of the therapist.

Clinical EFT Preface

Through these protocols, at the end of their three-year training, the trained therapists not only integrate different Energy Psychology tools, but also acquire the clinical and rigorous spirit of structured practice.

In this book, we have compiled the courses given at the Therapeutia Institute on these subjects, as well as the latest more specialized extensions proposed by IIPECA (International Institute of Energy Psychology and Applied Clinical Psychology); the Therapeutia courses have served as the basis for APEC and IEPRA trainings where you can take them as well.

Brigitte Hansoul - Yves Wauthier-Freymann

Part 1: The Basics of Clinical EFT

I. Introduction

This first part, "**The Basics of Clinical EFT**", summarizes the clinical contributions of our EFT training before the creation of the complete therapist training program. This involves practicing EFT clinically on a specific subject or in isolated sessions. The overall vision of a treatment plan necessary for more consistent support is discussed in the second part, "**Advanced Clinical EFT**".

Part 1: The Basics of Clinical EFT

II. Energy Psychology

Energy Psychology (EP) is a movement of modern psychology that brings together techniques that act on the psyche through the body's energy field. The term itself was proposed by Fred Gallo, PhD, and adopted by the Association for Comprehensive Energy Psychology (ACEP). This federation brings together practitioners, therapists, psychologists and psychiatrists who use either of these modalities.

In energetic psychology, we act by stimulating what the East commonly calls the "vibratory matrix" (or vital energy "Ki" - "Chi", prana). The human brain seems to be neurologically wired in such a way that such stimuli simply heal psychological wounds (David Feinstein Ph. D., Fred P. Gallo Ph. D., Bruce H. Lipton Ph. D.).

The results are particularly fast and effective because they combine deconditioning work and information reprocessing that brings them closer to cognitive-behavioural therapies and also to the activation of meridian points used in traditional Chinese medicine (or chakras in Ayurvedic medicine, or even biofield). The results of these techniques have been clinically proven to be effective in a wide range of psychological conditions and have currently been the subject of more than 50 successful publications (see the "resources" tab of the Association for Comprehensive Energy Psychology www.energypsych.org).

These therapies work on the global circulation of energy in the body, but also, depending on their specificity, on energy systems such as meridians, chakras, etc.

Most of these approaches assume that the flow of our electromagnetic field has "frozen" or has been "frozen" by traumatic events. This immobilization of our energy field causes a series of disruptions that can result in a series of post-traumatic stress symptoms or greater activity of the sympathetic system regulating the reflex that is responsible for our survival (the so-called Fight-Flight-Freeze response). EFT is one of these meridian therapies based on the stimulation of acupressure points as determined in traditional Chinese medicine.

EFT is the most popular and best known of these approaches. This popularity, however, has made it "the child pointed at" as its very simplicity may have set up a trap. Some people have established themselves as EFT therapists after a few days of training - often less than two, four or six - and have called themselves EFT "experts".

It is true that the tool is simple and effective for all the "bumps" of everyday life, but it is nevertheless true that dealing with complex traumas (the dissociation levels) or identifying whether you are dealing with simple or complex traumas also requires a good basis in psychotherapy.

This will have a direct influence on the results that you will obtain and on their maintenance. If you allow me this comparison: I don't think you're learning to drive a city car or a Formula One vehicle in the same way. Nor do I think that your results will depend on a single tool, but also on a series of quality tools to be developed through work on oneself and knowledge of the Other. The notions of presence, compassion, consciousness and management of human mechanisms such as transference or countertransference, dissociation or different types of dissociation, abreactions, other defence mechanisms such as denial, avoidance, hyper-vigilance, amnesia, addictions, OCDs, etc - all this requires knowing and recognizing what we are addressing and how to work with it so that we choose and maintain the most ecological and comfortable approach for our customers.

This is part of an ethical and deontological framework. It is also part of a sense of responsibility that will lead us as therapists to continue our personal work or supervision. All this equipment is there not only to protect our customers, but also to bring us to a better awareness of the human being, of our interpersonal relationships and their impact in our professional life or in our private sphere.

All of these methods have various common aspects, including an emphasis on what are commonly referred to as the patient's "resistances" - that is, emotional roots that block the progress of treatment. Underneath these resistances are hidden energy imbalances such as Neurological Disorganization (ND) or Psychological Reversals (PR), which will be discussed later.

Part 1: The Basics of Clinical EFT

All these methods have been known in Europe for the last twenty years for the oldest and only for a few years for the most recent of them.

Energy Psychology represents a holistic humanistic treatment that brings together the western and eastern therapeutic intervention pathways.

Useful websites:

- Practitioners of the different currents of Energy Psychology are grouped in the frames of ACEP (Association for Comprehensive Energy Psychology): www.energypsych.org
- APEC (French-speaking Association of Clinical Energy Psychology) is a French-speaking association, founded in 2005, whose objective is to disseminate Energy Psychology in the French-speaking world and to guarantee the quality of training for practitioners. It offers certification and the possibility of being on a list of certified practitioners. Its website www.energypsy.org aims to gather French-speaking documents on Energy Psychology: protocols, descriptions, studies, practitioners, etc. The site is managed by Yves Wauthier-Freymann, info@yves-wauthier.com
- IEPRA's website: https://www.iepra.com – this is the training institute for whose programs we created the protocols in this book. It is the only training institute in Europe to offer integrative and clinical training in different methods of Energy Psychology as part of a long-term training as a therapist. You will find videos illustrating some of the protocols in this book.
- The website of Gary Craig (founder of EFT): https://www.emofree.com. There are also other professional certifications such as EFT Universe https://www.eftuniverse.com, which are taken over by Dawson Church Ph. D.
- The website of IEPRA https://academy.iepra.com/ offers thematic training courses in Energy Psychology (EFT, TAT, REMAP, SEB, etc.)

III. Significant dysfunctions of the energy system, correction and prevention

A. ND: Neurological Disorganization

1. Definition

This is a concept whose need for correction, prior to any therapeutic session, is disputed within this movement itself. Some tools actually do not deal with this disorganization. It could be seen as a loss of information due to a dysfunction of the body and the defective or incomplete transmission of information from the brain to the cells or organs concerned.

Tools or models such as TAT® (Tapas Acupressure Technique) or Logosynthesis® are not really interested in it or simply consider it as one of the targets to be addressed during the session itself.

For more details on neurological disorganization, you can attend the seminar "The Foundations of Energy Psychology" given at APEC (French speaking mainly) or ACEP (https://www.energypsych.org).

Neurological disorganization (ND) is an energetic disruption of brain function that may be due to specific psychological reasons, more general stress or fatigue.

If the brain is in neurological disorganization, it is no longer able to function properly, sometimes to the point of preventing healing. It is therefore essential to be able to identify and process it.

B. The Psychological Reversal

1. Definition

A Psychological Reversal (PR) is a disruption of the energy system due to negative and self-destructive thoughts. The result is an unconscious (sometimes partly conscious) propensity to keep the problem from being treated rather than to cure it. Physiological reversal (reversal of electrical

Part 1: The Basics of Clinical EFT

polarities) results in a psychological reversal (tendency to keep suffering rather than to go towards happiness).

It is never a question of resistance of "bad will". At the origin of a Psychological Reversal, there is most often a fear.

For example:

"If I heal, I will no longer be pitied or cared for" (case of physical illness, depression...).
"If I heal my pain from my mother's death, it would mean that I didn't love her enough."
Because of this fear, the energy system reacts negatively to the idea of change: it is blocked or even reversed (in terms of polarities).

Gary Craig, the inventor of EFT, uses the comparison with a battery:

"Here's another similarity that might enlighten you. Let's say you have a small tape recorder that uses batteries. You may have noticed the small symbols "+" and "-" that indicate the *polarity* on the batteries. If you align these polarities correctly, the electrical current flows and your device works perfectly. But what happens if you reverse the batteries upside down? The tape recorder would no longer work. This is exactly what happens when there is a reversed polarity in the energy system. It's like your batteries are upside down. I'm not saying you stop functioning all at once... but your behaviour is disturbed at some levels.

This reversed polarity is called **"Psychological Reversal"**. Therefore, some diseases are chronic and respond poorly to conventional care. This is also the reason why some people are unable to lose weight or give up their addictions. This is really the cause of auto-sabotage.

Psychological Reversal is due to negative and self-destructive thoughts that occur in the subconscious mind. This reversal is found in 40% of cases. Some people never suffer from it (which is rather rare), while others are almost always reversed (also rather rare). Most people fall between these two extremes. You don't feel it internally, so you can't know if this reversal is present or not. Even the most positive people can have such a reversal. If the reversal is present, it stops all attempts at healing, including EFT, altogether. **It must therefore be corrected for the treatment to be successful.**"

Many Psychological Reversals are often found in cases of depression or addiction.

Depending on the type of thinking behind Psychological Reversal, it can be classified into different categories: massive, specific, identity, loyalty, capacity, merit, shame, guilt, etc. (see also the seminar "The Foundations of Energy Psychology").

2. Corrections of Psychological Reversals (PR)

Psychological Reversals are like barriers that prevent the treatment train from moving forward. The proposed corrections allow this barrier to be temporarily removed so that the train can pass.

This barrier can be reinstalled an hour, a day, a week later. That's why we correct the reversal, then we treat the target problem in the process. However, some reversals, once corrected "temporarily", do not reappear.

If we want to be sure that a reversal is treated sustainably and will not block further therapeutic progress, it may be necessary to do some in-depth work on it. A distinction is therefore made between (temporary) correction and (long-term) treatment.

3. Types of Psychological Reversals

a. MPR: Massive Psychological Reversal

(1) Definition

Massive Psychological Reversal is a kind of resistance to any positive change, in all areas of life. The MPR is therefore not related to the perspective of addressing a problem.

(2) Diagnosis and corrections

See seminar "The Foundations of Energy Psychology"

b. Specific Psychological Reversal

(1) Definition

The Specific PR (which is abbreviated as PR by generalization) is related to a specific problem - the MPR was a general reversal of the perspective of

Part 1: The Basics of Clinical EFT

getting better; the Specific PR concerns the healing of a specific target. From this perspective, the energy system is reversed. It is this reversal that Gary Craig has chosen to systematically correct in the Standard EFT Protocol.

(2) Diagnosis and corrections

See seminar "The Foundations of Energy Psychology".

4. Practical advice

Before starting the session, and most certainly if you are a beginner, there are some tips to follow:

Check if there is a Specific or Massive Psychological Reversal (I want a happy life, a miserable life).
We tap, if the emotions go down, we continue.
If the emotions do not move, or even rise, we will check if we have a specific Psychological Disorganization or Reversal (a "yes, but").
If it's a Neurological Disorganization, we do Cook's Hook Up.
If you feel that emotions are starting to drop again, you keep tapping until you are at zero.
If we see that the emotions do not move or even rise, we will go check, do the energy routine, we will do Cook again, we tap, and we continue until the SUD drops to 0.

If it is not a Neurological Disorder, but a specific Psychological Reversal (a limiting or blocking belief, therefore "yes, but"), rub the Neurolymphatic Reflex point and tap until 0.

If the emotions do not move or rise, we do Cook again and we check if the emotions decrease. If they drop, we tap to 0.

If they do not move or rise, check for a disorganization that might have occurred anyway, then repeat the energy routine and Cook's exercise and tap at the same time.

You can also look for the Psychological Reversals specific to the problem brought about and work on the other Specific Psychological Reversals by massaging the sore spot and tapping.

When I have a problem, I work on my problem. I have chosen my target well, so that it is specific. If I observe that the SUD does not move, I must have in mind the reflex to ask myself: "Why doesn't it move? Am I on the right target? Or maybe I didn't choose the right emotion for the target?" Therefore, I check Emotion, Sensation, Situation, Person /Past, Present, Future/, Conscious and Unconscious mind, and I tap.

If I see that it doesn't move, I have to ask myself some questions: "Does the information pass when I tap or do I see my hands going in all directions, to all points?" If I see that they go off in all directions to all points in an arrhythmic way, it's probably a sign of Psychological Disorganization. It is better to correct it first as the EFT point stimulation will not work out correctly because of this loss of information, but if EFT does not work, I could try to do TAT® or REMAP® by stimulating the points, staying right on the points that are most activated and related with the problem (following the Traditional Chinese Medicine).

If it is not a Psychological Disorganization but a sign of the presence of Psychological Reversals, then they must be detected and identified. Either they will be complete reversals, or mini ones like "I have to keep my problem a little bit". If I did the muscle testing, I would find that the person answers "yes" and "no" to my reversal. Do you remember that in muscle testing the body will normally move always in the same side when it is a "yes" answer or a "no" answer to the question you asked? Here the testing would be both strong/strong or weak/weak, for example. It is the manifestation of one part that wants to keep "a little bit" of the problem and of another part that wants to give up a little bit of the problem. So, in order to reprocess this one, we would say: "Even though I want to keep my problem a little bit, I accept and respect myself" if we must correct it following the muscle testing result.

In my practice, I don't often do muscle testing. I simply detect during the session if the person becomes disorganized while tapping on a specific point or not. This is a clear indication that this meridian is more impacted than the others and I will therefore insist more on this meridian by staying there longer, for example. Eventually, I will hold or rub it, or do "Touch and Breathe" so that the point is well stimulated.

This can also give indications in relation to the emotions that are present. For example, if it is at the level of the liver (under the breasts or pectorals in EFT), there is anger. Then we can include the phrase "all my anger". We do it even if the person has not spoken clearly about it and we will often observe that there is a resonance. It was the body that spoke, and it never lies...

If a Specific Psychological Reversal does not move, it is because there is certainly another reversal behind it. For example, if we can't remove "I don't deserve...", there may be another reversal or belief behind it such as "I would lose my identity", "I have built myself upon this guilt or all of that". Sometimes you must remove the strongest reversal so that the others can leave. We have a series of classic Psychological reversal families: I don't deserve, I'm guilty, I'm ashamed, I'd lose my identity, I'll never get there, I'm not capable... There are six to ten beliefs that come up often and we check these first.

If it still doesn't move and the SUD doesn't evolve, then check if the customer is sufficiently connected to the targeted problem and not dissociated from it. And if it still does not move, it is because the targeted problem is not sufficiently specific or correctly targeted (specific situation; emotions, sensations and cognition with the worst image of the situation), or because there is such a disorganization that the information and the stimulation of the points are not enough to trigger the desensitization work.

C. The daily energy routine

When used preventatively or as an "energy hygiene", this routine helps to keep the energy system "in good working order". In case of severe neurological disorganization, it may be necessary to perform it every day for a few days or (rarely) weeks to correct it.

For a complete description of the routine, it is useful to refer to the EP seminar *"The Foundations of Energy Psychology"* or Donna Eden's book *Energy Medicine* published by Ariane.

IV. History of EFT

A. TFT - Thought Field Therapy (evidence based)

The TFT was created by Roger Callahan, an American psychologist.

He introduced the notion of the *thought field:* any thought is translated by (a modification of) a body energy field. Any negative or false thinking results in an imbalance of the body's energies.

TFT is the first psychotherapeutic method to offer treatment of emotional disorders by tapping acupressure points.

Callahan's protocol includes research (through Muscle Testing) and treatment of Psychological Reversals, as well as diagnosis (through MT - muscle testing) of alarm points and treatment points (acupuncture points to be stimulated to solve the problem).

Roger Callahan has also empirically identified the specific algorithms for the treatment of different disorders where he specifies the order of the used points.

Roger Callahan passed away in November 2013. He is and will remain one of the most important pioneers of this trend.

B. EFT - Emotional Freedom Techniques

EFT was created by Gary Craig, an engineer from Stanford in the United States.

By simplifying TFT, he has developed EFT - a single procedure for all disorders, including:

- the correction of the Specific Psychological Reversal related to the problem treated: no need to look for whether or not it exists, it is automatically treated;
- tapping all the points used in TFT: no need to select the points useful for processing, nor to know their sequence - an arbitrary (mnemonic) order is used.

Part 1: The Basics of Clinical EFT

V.   The principles of EFT – the "ZZZZZ"

"Any emotional disturbance **is due** to an energy imbalance in the body."

Correction is done by light tapping with the fingertips on a series of points on the face, upper body and hands, while keeping your attention focused on the physical or psychological pain you want to treat. By restoring the energetic balance, we obtain the healing of the disorders.

Gary Craig, in his EFT manual, has his own way of explaining why and how EFT works:

> "I invite you to compare the energy flow in your body to that in a TV set. As long as electricity normally travels through the TV, the sound and picture are clear. But imagine taking off the back of the TV and pricking these "electronic spaghetti" with the tip of a screwdriver. What is happening? Of course, as you have deregulated or diverted this flow of electricity, an electrical "zzzzzt" occurs. The picture and sound become unstable and the TV would show you its version of a "negative emotion".
>
> Similarly, when our energy systems become unbalanced, the same energy "zzzzzzzt" occurs within us. Align this "zzzzzzzt" (by tapping - and sometimes you should possess the art of EFT... see the videos) and the negative emotion disappears. [...]
>
> Everything becomes clear and you begin to recognize the gaps in other methods. For example, in the light of these discoveries, the falsity of the method explained earlier - treating the memory - becomes obvious. It is assumed in this method that a traumatic memory is the direct cause of the emotional disturbance in a person. That is not true. There is an intermediate step - the missing piece - between memory and emotional disturbance. And this intermediate step, of course, is the disruption of the body's energy system. It is this disturbance, this "zzzzzzzt", that is the direct cause of the emotional disturbance.
>
> Note that if the second step, the intermediate step, does not occur, there is no third step. In other words, **if the memory does not cause disruption in the body's energy system, the negative emotion cannot occur**. This is why some people are bothered by their memories, while others are not. The difference is that some people's energy systems tend to let themselves be unbalanced by such memories.
>
> Considering this, it is easy to see how the "treat-the-memory" method misses the target. It takes the first step and ignores the second. This is also the reason why

people often go from bad to worse when conventional psychology focuses on the memory and not on its cause (the energy disruption). Addressing the first step, requiring the person to relive a traumatic memory, produces more disruption in the energy system. This increases the pain instead of decreasing it. This can often aggravate the problem. If the second step were addressed rather than the first, there would be very little pain. The energy system would be harmonized (through tapping) and inner calm would take the place of negative emotion. The person would quickly be relieved because the real cause would have been addressed. This is what happens constantly with EFT.

Let's go back to our discovered affirmation. See how global it is: *The cause of ANY negative emotion is a disruption of the body's energy system*. This includes: fears, phobias, anger, grief, anguish, depression, traumatic memories, PTSD, worry, guilt, and all limiting emotions in the field of sports, business, performing arts, etc.

This means that all these negative emotions have only one cause... an electric zzzzzt in the body. This also means that **they can all be relieved in the same way**. Thus, grief has the same cause as the baseball player's trauma, guilt, fear and series of missed shots. The same basic method can be used for all these problems. This is also a real blessing for mental health professionals. They are used to hearing endless and constantly changing explanations for their clients' countless emotional concerns. How their work could be simplified if they learned that there is only one cause." (See Gary Craig's *EFT manual* or the one adapted in collaboration with Dawson Church - Dangles Editions, 2012).

For more scientific explanations of how EFT works, see our first French book *EFT, Tapping and Energy Psychology*, Dangles, 2010 or *The EFT Manual* by Gary Craig.

VI. Points used in EFT

A. Definition of an acupuncture point

An acupuncture point is a point on a meridian that has a lower resistivity, i.e. a higher conductivity. In other words, the current flows more easily there than elsewhere in the meridian.

B. Acupuncture points on the meridians

The points are preceded by the respective abbreviations given below:

EB: Eyebrow: the point is at the beginning of the eyebrow on the nose side.

SE: Side of the Eye: the point is on the orbit bone at the outside corner of the eye.

UE: Under the Eye: the point is on the orbit bone under the eye, at the vertical line of the pupil when looking straight ahead.

UN: Under the Nose: the point is in the centre of the space between the nose and the upper lip.

CH: Chin: the point is in the hollow between the lower lip and the hump of the chin.

CB: Collarbone: the point is to the right and to the left of the central "U" that joins the two clavicles, just under the bone. Put your fingers on the bumps that form the U in the middle where the clavicles meet at the base of the neck. Using the tips of the five fingers, you strike this point more strongly than anywhere else.

UA: Under the Arm: the point is about ten centimetres under the armpit, vertically under the arm, where the side band of a bra is placed. You can tap this point with the tips of your five fingers or even with the palm of your hand.

UB: Under the Breast: the point is just below the nipple (2.5 cm) for men, and for women it is in the same axis under the breast mass (just below the bra, therefore).

Part 1: The Basics of Clinical EFT

N.B. This point can be replaced by its equivalent **IK: Inner face of the Knee**. The point is located in the middle of the fold formed at the inner face of the bent knee - towards the inside. You can tap with the palm of your hand.

Th: Thumb: The point is on the edge between the nail and the flesh on the outer side of the finger.

IF: Index Finger: the point is on the edge between the nail and the flesh on the side facing the thumb.

MF: Middle Finger: the point is on the edge between the nail and the flesh on the side facing the thumb.

LF: Little Finger: the point is on the edge between the nail and the flesh on the side facing the thumb.

KC: Side of Hand/Karate Chop: the point is on the side of the hand, between the base of the little finger and the beginning of the wrist. This point is to be vigorously tapped with the flat fingers of the other hand.

G: Back of the Hand - Gamut point: it is located on the back of the hand, in the "V" between the metacarpals forming the extension of the little finger and the ring finger. This area is to be tapped with the fingertips of the other hand, along the Gamut point range, which is carried out as follows:

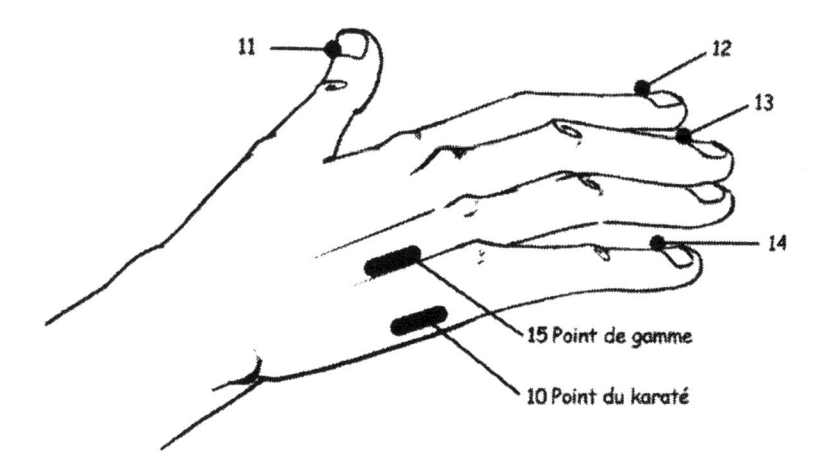

Illustration Tibo3D
www.tibo3d.com

C. Other points

NLR Sore Point

Neurolymphatic Reflex point whose congestion is responsible for the sensitivity felt when pressing on it (a sensitivity that disappears with use). Similarly to the Karate point (sometimes even more effective), its stimulation dissolves Psychological Reversals.

Location: see diagram or on YouTube: *"Présentation des points de l'EFT (Emotionnal Freedom Techniques) par Yves Wauthier"*

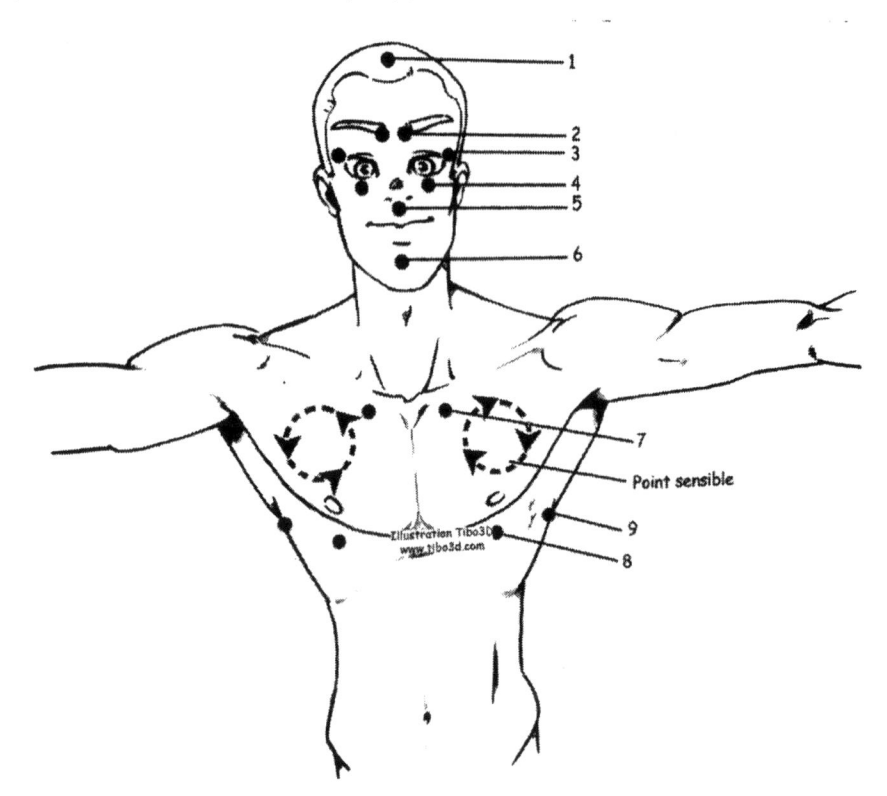

Top of the head (TH) - GV 21

This point and the following one were added by Gary Craig later. They are not part of the basic sequence.

Wrist (Heart 7)

Part 1: The Basics of Clinical EFT

Location: at the base of the wrist, on the inner side. As there are other points at the wrist fold, they can all be stimulated by tapping with the palm of the hand on the wrist fold.

D. Stimulations

In EFT the points are stimulated by tapping. In other EFT-related methods or in EFT itself when needed (if a point is too painful, for example), the points can be stimulated by rubbing, by simply touching, or even mentally.

Research has shown that it is just as effective to "imagine" tapping as it is to actually do it. If you are stuck, immobile and anxious, in an MRI machine or stuck on the chair at the dentist, it is a solution. Imagine tapping your EFT sequence. The effects will be the same.

VII. Meridian points: psychological correspondence

A. Bladder 2: Eyebrow (EB)

Dissipates:

- the emotional aftermath of difficult events;
- the lack of ambition, the lack of enthusiasm to do things;
- stagnation in any area of life.

Develops:

- the perception of emotions and intuition;
- the inner strength;
- the courage to make the changes you know are necessary.

Emotions: trauma, frustration, fear, impatience, restlessness

N.B. **Bladder 1**: Inner Side of the Eye (ISE), generally not used in EFT.

B. Gall bladder 1: Side of the Eye (SE)

Dissipates:

- obsessive rancours;
- feelings of rage and hatred;
- the need for revenge.

Develops:

- an accurate view of the overall situation;
- constructive expression of anger;
- the well-thought-out implementation of ideas and dreams.

Emotions: rage, power, blockage, anger, wrath.

C. Stomach 1: Under the Eye (UE)

Dissipates:

Part 1: The Basics of Clinical EFT

- obsessive worries and fixed ideas;
- excessive needs of attachment;
- the emptiness that we carry within us.

Develops:

- proper assimilation of experiences;
- ability to give and receive in a balanced way;
- feelings of contentment and fullness.

Emotions: anxiety, fear, phobia, hunger, deprivation, bitterness, disappointment, greed.

D. Governing Vessel 26: Under the Nose (UN)

Dissipates:

- shyness, awkwardness, shame of oneself;
- fear of asserting oneself, imposing oneself or saying "no";
- fear of speaking in public, fear of taking an exam.

Develops:

- personal originality;
- social comfort;
- acceptance of the current state of self.

Emotions: embarrassment, helplessness, despair.

E. Conception Vessel 24: Chin (CH)

Dissipates:

- feelings of guilt, remorse and regret;
- overwhelm, desolation and torment;
- the need to repress those who have harmed us;
- the need to punish oneself.

Develops:

- the possibility to forgive and forget, including towards oneself;
- the ability to accept things from the past as they are;
- the willingness to move forward by turning the page.

Emotions: shame, indignity, defectiveness, uselessness.

F. Kidney 27: Collarbone (CB)

Dissipates:

- fears, terrors, panic attacks;
- panic and agitation due to the felt horror;
- phobias (fear of loneliness, heights, going out of the house, driving, flying, etc.).

Develops:

- sense of safety in all places, inner calm;
- desire to do things that were previously unthinkable;
- desire to move forward in life.

Emotions: fear, indecision, cowardice, lack of sexual interest, lack of self-confidence.

G. Spleen 21: Under the Arm (UA)

Dissipates:

- the internal prohibitions that prevent people from enjoying life;
- feelings of boredom, renunciation, bitterness;
- defeatist point of view, lack of originality.

Develops:

- personal assurance through the free expression of innate abilities;
- the desire to increase one's intellectual knowledge, to undertake new things;
- feelings of well-being and contentment in life.

Emotions: anxiety for the future, worry, craving in case of dependency.

H. Liver 14: Under the Breast (UB)

Dissipates:

- feelings of frustration, inner confusion;
- procrastination, irresolution, narrow-mindedness;

Part 1: The Basics of Clinical EFT

- indolence and lethargy.

Develops:

- the dynamism and enthusiasm necessary to pursue ambitions;
- confidence in one's own judgment and perspective on things;
- the desire to express one's innate talents and personal skills.
- Emotions: anger (excessive, generalized), lack of joy, resentment.

Emotions: anger (excessive, generalised), lack of joy, resentment.

I. Lung 11: Thumb (Th)

Dissipates:

- sadness.

Develops:

- detachment;
- inhalation and exhalation;
- destiny.

Emotions: grief, sadness, intolerance, contempt, prejudice, disdain.

J. Large Intestine 1: Index Finger (IF)

Dissipates:

- the need for control.

Develops:

- letting go.

Emotions: guilt, relationship or contact problems.

K. Heart Master 9: Middle Finger (MF)

Works on the neglect of emotional needs, difficulty in making choices.

Emotions: jealousy, regret, sexual tension, stubbornness.

L. Heart 9: Little Finger (LF)

Works on heartache, love for oneself or others.

Emotions: anger (specific).

M. Small Intestine 3 (and Heart 8): Karate Chop (KC)

Dissipates:

- the possible oppositions of the subconscious mind to the achievement of our objectives;
- dark thoughts, lack of self-confidence and fear of failure (or success).

Develops:

- intellectual abilities, insight, physical ability;
- performance in any field (sports, sexual, academic, professional, etc.).

Emotions: vulnerability, compulsion, obsession, sadness.

N. Triple Heater 3: Gamut point (BH - Back of the Hand)

Works on the notion of survival, sense of security or insecurity.

Emotions: depression, physical pain, despair, sadness, grief, despondency, discouragement.

Part 1: The Basics of Clinical EFT

VIII. Evaluation scales

A. The SUD

SUD is a scale for measuring the negative disturbance felt when thinking about something. The disturbance can be felt emotionally or physically.

SUD: Subjective Units of Disturbance (subjective scale of emotional disturbance).

0 = neutral (no negative disturbance).

10 = the biggest possible disturbance for this event.

B. The VOC

VOC is a scale of cognitive (not emotional) measurement of the strength of an idea. It is used particularly to estimate the strength of negative beliefs, especially when no SUD can be associated with them.

VOC: Validity of Cognition.

0 = the idea sounds completely wrong.

10 = the idea sounds quite true.

IX. Indications

EFT has the merit of being simple, fast, effective and gentle. It can be used with almost anything. With most of the simple emotions or those related to a single, specific event, relief is achieved in less than five minutes. Treating complex issues, such as negative beliefs about oneself or childhood traumas that have occurred for years, takes several sessions.

It can also be used as self-treatment for a variety of things: to get rid of a difficult memory, to free one's energy system from the stress caused by certain aspects of family life, emotional life or professional activity; or to soothe certain emotion, anxiety, pain, tiredness, etc.

Gary Craig is used to saying, "Try it on everything."

In this book, which will discuss the more clinical applications of EFT, we intend to help you better target and recognize what you are working on, because a simple trauma is not treated in the same way as a complex trauma.

Part 1: The Basics of Clinical EFT

X. Focusing on the target

By Brigitte H.

The first thing is to focus on the event that has been identified as the source of the problem. The objective is to connect the person to the mental field associated with this event. A powerful way to do this is to associate the person with different aspects of the scene and the experience, which are then desensitised by tapping.

There are different ways to do this:

- the classic EFT way: by making a movie out of the memory;
- the technique of the Worst Image: this is not a classic EFT technique, but it enhances and considerably accelerates the processing of the target. On the other hand, as it is more powerful, it should be handled with caution or even avoided when the memory is difficult to bear.

A. Making a Movie

Original EFT technique by Gary Craig.

There are four elements that specify the target:

- the worst image;
- the emotion;
- the physical sensation;
- the SUD.

The clinical EFT will prefer to begin by examination of the worst image, the sensation (in order to make sure that there is no dissociation), the emotion and the cognition, as well as the SUD scale on all of these 4 elements.

1. The Movie

If you manage to make a short mental movie out of a situation, it is because the event is short and precise, a real element and not a concept.

The movie should have a beginning and an end, and should include specific characters. If it lasts too long, it should be split into shorter episodes.

Ask the patient to give the movie a **title**. This title can be freely chosen; it must essentially be powerfully evocative for the patient (and not necessarily for you).

2. The SUD

Ask the patient the level of SUD he/she feels when thinking about this movie in a global way.

B. Finding the worst image (the image associated with the worst moment)

Technique borrowed from EMDR.

There are four elements that specify the target:

- the worst image;
- the physical sensation (first sensation to check if there is no dissociation or mental part trying to control the system);
- the emotion;
- the SUD.

1. The worst image

This is **the visual image associated with the worst part** of the event/movie. Generally, the strongest trace (what we remember the most from an event) is what we see when we think about the event.

More rarely, it is not the visual image that is important, but rather the auditory memory of words that have been spoken, or noises (in an accident, etc.), or the physical feeling that has been imprinted in us.

In this case, try to find the image that accompanies the auditory or kinaesthetic memory, and focus on both.

Then give a title to this image.

You can immediately look for the worst image or use the (less accurate) movie in the first round and focus on the worst image(s) in subsequent rounds.

Part 1: The Basics of Clinical EFT

2. Specifying the emotion

Fear, anger, anguish, worry, guilt, frustration, discouragement, shock, etc. - there may be several emotions.

Be careful, there may be the reminiscence of an emotion from the past and/or a current emotion that is not present in the past.

3. Specifying the physical sensation

Focus on your stress and note the physical aspects: headache, lump in the throat, knot in the stomach, discomfort in any part of the body, etc.

4. The SUD - emotional units of distress

On a scale from 0 to 10, score SUD: 0 = neutral; 10 = maximum disturbance.

Be careful, it is about the **current** emotion that you experience when you think back of the past event.

XI. The basic EFT Tapping Sequence

A. The Setup statement - correction of the Reversal

Called "Setup" or "Start-up phrase", this is about correcting the Reversal.
It is a preparatory step that serves to clearly communicate to your unconscious mind your intentions to free yourself from your problem, thus dispelling any opposition.
This statement is made by repeating three times in a row:
"Even though... (say the short sentence describing your problem), I deeply and completely accept myself." (I would add "more or less" if there is complex trauma or attachment disorder, so as to ease the client in pronouncing this phrase).
Meanwhile you are either stimulating the Karate Chop or rubbing the sore point in circles, as you prefer (see the tapping points diagram on p. 51).

The Karate Chop is located on the edge of the hand, between the base of the little finger and the beginning of the wrist; in martial arts we use this area of the hand to cut an object with a sharp blow. This point is to be tapped with the flat fingers of the other hand.

The Sore Point: put your hand at the base of your neck, descend a few centimetres, then search for this point on the left or right. You will notice a sensitive area when pressing on it. Rub this area in circles, moving outwards as you go up and inwards as you go down. **N.B.** Sore points are situated lower and more distant from each other than the Collarbone points (see below).

B. The Tapping Round

As you will see below, there is a long version and a short version of the Tapping Round. The one most often used is the short version which is usually enough to solve all problems.

To do your tapping, you can use the hand of your choice or even change hands in the middle of the round and stimulate the points on the side of the body that suit you best, and even change sides along the way if you feel like it.

Part 1: The Basics of Clinical EFT

1. The Long version

The long version of EFT is presented as a sandwich:
- a) Top slice of bread: a series of tapping.
- b) Filling : the 9 Gamut Procedure (on the Gamut point - BH).
- c) Bottom slice of bread: the same series of tapping as in a).

a. First series

Illustration of the tapping points: see the Tapping points diagram and Tapping procedure on p. 51.

EB: Eyebrow

SE: Side of the Eye

UE: Under the Eye

UN: Under the Nose

CH: Chin

CB: Collarbone

UA: Under the Arm

UB: Under the Breast

Th: Thumb

IF: Index Finger

MF: Middle Finger

LF: Little Finger

KC: Hand edge / Karate Chop

b. The 9 Gamut Procedure

This is used to balance the two brain hemispheres, so that the round of tapping could dissolve more easily an eventual energy blockage in case of resistance. It is carried out on the following point:

BH: Back of the Hand - Gamut point: you tap on it with the fingertips of the other hand while doing the Gamut point sequence (or the 9 Gamut procedure) which is carried out as follows:

1) Close your eyes.
2) Open your eyes.
3) Keeping your head still, look down to the left.
4) Keeping your head still, look down to the right.
5) Roll your eyes in a full circle without moving the head.
6) Roll your eyes in the opposite direction without moving the head.
7) Hum about 3 seconds of a well-known tune.
8) Count quickly from 1 to 5.
9) Hum the same tune again for 3 seconds.

In Clinical EFT, we prefer not to do the 9 Gamut procedure and we replace it by an alternate and bilateral stimulation of the points during all the tapping (like EMDR bilateral stimulation – see below the rhythms of tapping)

c. First series (second time)

Once the 9 Gamut procedure is complete, you repeat the first part, stimulating again the same points as in the first part of the round, from EB to KC.

2. The Short version

The short round includes only the intervention points that go from the face to the point under the arm (7 points), or under the breast (8 points).

As all meridians are interdependent, stimulating one engages the others as well, and those of the fingers are also stimulated since they serve as tapping instruments.

We go around the 7 or 8 points several times in a row, even though a single round of the short series is often enough to lower the SUD, if there is no Psychological Reversal. If there is no change, it is because there is a PR or other energy problem, or the target is not well specified.

N.B. Additional point: you can start or end the round by tapping on your head (the Crown chakra). This point is not yet part of the EFT round as officially noted on Gary Craig's manual, although you can often see him using it during his filmed demonstrations. The same applies to the wrist point.

Part 1: The Basics of Clinical EFT

3. The Reminder Phrases

While tapping on the different points, the mind must be connected to the emotions and the negative sensations associated with the target. This is the concept of the "mental field": by evoking the psychological and physiological stress associated with the target, the tapping eliminates this stress.

To help the mind focus on the target, the tapping is done while repeating a reminder phrase at each tapping point. Note that some therapists have the experience that this is not necessary, but Gary Craig advocates it.

The reminder phrase can be the title of the movie or the worst image, or the name of the emotion, or a word/short sentence that summarizes the problem.

Part 1: The Basics of Clinical EFT

XII. Summary of the basic treatment steps

A. Specify the target

You need to specify:

- the movie and the SUD

or

- the worst image

We use 4 criteria: image, emotion, sensation, SUD.

B. Correct the Reversal

"Even though" phrase while tapping on **NLR or K**a**rate** Chop point.

C. Do the Long version (the sandwich)

By repeating the reminder phrase.

D. Re-evaluate the SUD

Now focus your attention on your problem and note the intensity of your suffering. How do you feel after that tapping round? Quite well or not really well? Even worse than before? Has your suffering decreased and how much? Have your feelings changed? Has your anger become sadness? Has your shoulder pain gone elsewhere? Maybe you have a sore throat now? All you must do is continue your tapping rounds.

E. Do the following rounds

1. The Aspects

Sometimes, after one or two rounds of EFT, the stress level does not seem to decrease. In fact, it is often because there are several aspects to the problem and we have focused on one of them, often the strongest, in the tapping series. Then the decreasing of this aspect is masked by the fact that another aspect is now predominant.

Example: At first, the main emotion (strong at 8/10) is anger. There is also sadness at 7, but we don't think about it. Anger then drops to 2/10, but the person feels some stress of 7/10, due to sadness. Indeed, it is the aspect on which we focus that mainly decreases.

Aspects can be emotions, but also any other partial aspect of the target.

Note that if you take the emotion as a reminder phrase, it may become obsolete during tapping.

After each round, evaluate: "What do I feel is the most disturbing aspect now?" (possibly "re-evaluate the SUD") and continue tapping on it. The fact that the SUD does not decrease is either an indication of a PR or a ND, or that the aspects have not been identified and addressed. These aspects may also hide PRs.

2. The Remaining issues

For the following rounds, we focus on the remaining aspects, detailing them.

If it is the same aspect or aspects, but attenuated, you can indicate to the Unconscious to finish the treatment by saying:

- during setup: "even though **there is still some**...";
- in a reminder phrase: "**the remaining...**"

Part 1: The Basics of Clinical EFT

XIII. Tapping points diagram and Tapping procedure

In this diagram, the point under the breast has been tactfully removed of the image, but you can still use it (normally it follows the point under the arm).

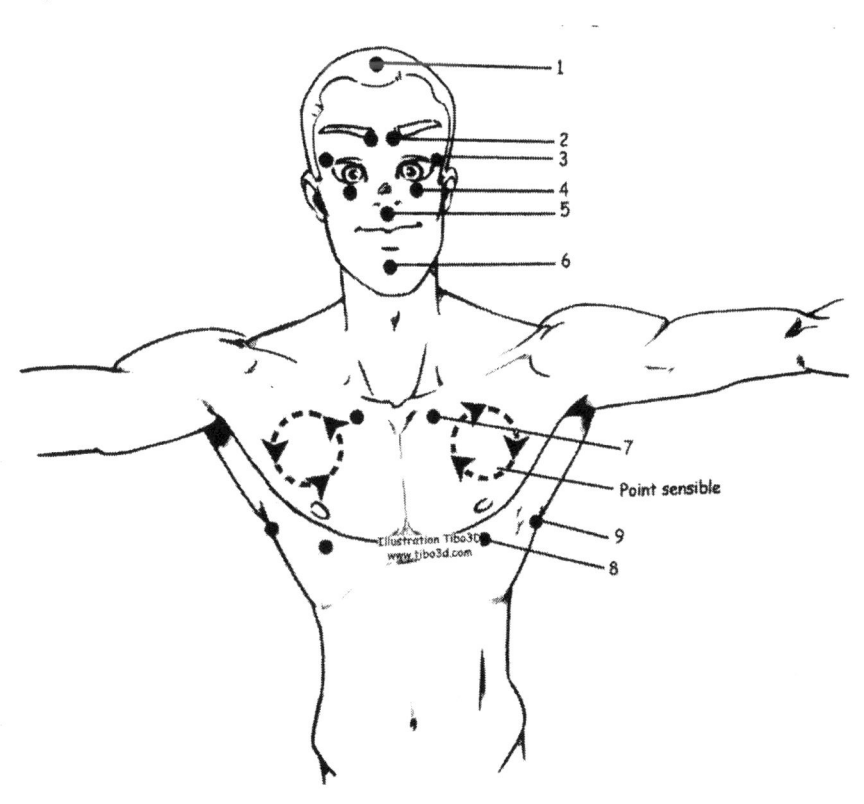

11

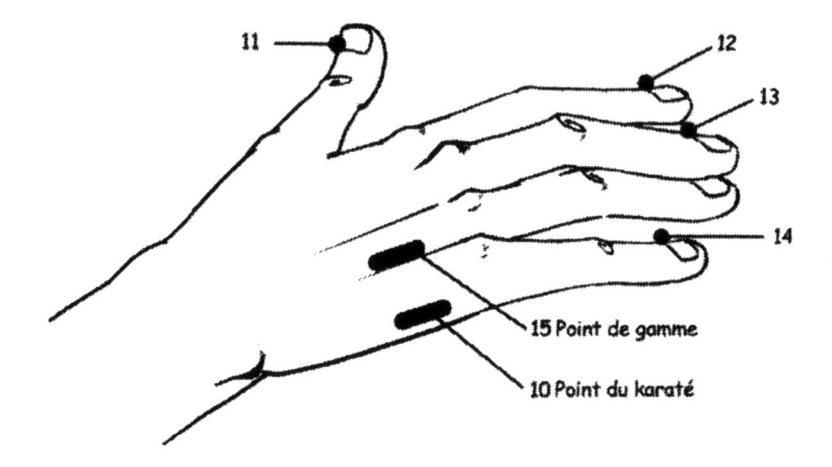

12

13

14

15 Point de gamme

10 Point du karaté

Illustration Tibo3D
www.tibo3d.com

Part 1: The Basics of Clinical EFT

XIV. The Movie technique

Adapted from the text of our friend and colleague *Marion Blique*.

This standard EFT technique is ideal for addressing specific events, which is very important for achieving results with EFT and bringing back elements from the past into the present. The Movie technique uses specific words, actions and emotions, and includes a beginning and an end. The elements are therefore contained within a very specific framework (which is essential in cases of severe trauma). The idea is to tell an unpleasant memory as if you were telling a movie, but you have to stop and apply EFT at certain moments of the movie, those that cause anxiety or trigger emotional intensity. Once the intensity has been neutralized using EFT, "rewind" the movie and tell it again, until you are able to play the whole movie without feeling any intense emotion.

You will see that the movie technique also facilitates the search for the specific event and makes it easier to understand a painful event because it is cut into sequences.

A. Ask the patient to identify a difficult memory. Tell him that he's going to imagine projecting the short movie of this painful event on the wall.

You will ask several questions before you begin. And most importantly, don't let your client start telling the story right away, which is quite common. Several key issues should be discussed first.

B. How long does your short movie last?

If the answer is "a few minutes", it is a specific event. By answering "a few days", the client is much too global. If he has problems with the duration of the "film", ask him to mention only the most intense part.

C. Ask him to give the movie a title. The title of the movie can be very evocative, surprising and revealing. Help your client find the title that relates to him and resonates with him the most.

D. Now let the patient visualise the movie in his head and ask him to measure his (imaginary) anxiety level on a scale of 0 to 10 (SUD).

Make sure that the patient is not "caught" in the movie too quickly. If the memory is too painful, ask him to use the statement: "Even though I am too anxious to talk about (title of the film), I accept myself and I am safe." If the patient is obviously beginning to feel anxious, use the softer technique mentioned below in this section. You can help your patient by telling him to divide the content of the movie into several sequences and measure their peaks of intensity. How many sequences are there and what is their intensity from 0 to 10? (This allows the therapist to have an idea of what he or she will have to manage.)

E. Ask the patient to start telling the story, starting at the beginning until he or she encounters a sequence that induces anxiety or emotional intensity, and then use EFT.

Sometimes the patient does not stop to tell you that he or she feels this anxiety inside of them. However, pay attention to the expression on his or her face, which tends to change when the person feels an intense emotion. When you notice a change in expression, tears rising to the eyes, redness on the face, an acceleration of the heartbeat, shortness of breath, tight jaws, ask him how he feels when describing this part of the film, and tap on these specific emotions, as well as on all aspects of the movie that cause these emotions (essential in trauma treatment): visual, auditory, olfactory, proprioceptive: everything that is present in this movie sequence.

F. Rewind the movie back to the beginning and let the patient retell it; make sure there is no more emotional intensity (according to the SUD scale) where there was previously a peak of intensity and continue until you reach a new peak of intensity.

Make sure at the end that the patient is able to tell the whole movie without any anxiety or intense emotion.

Note : Sometimes, when using the technique of the short movie in the treatment of severe or complex traumas, some sequences may emerge in the middle of the movie that were not anticipated at the beginning but resurface in the client's memory. It is important to treat them timely with EFT.

Very important : when dealing with a trauma, the client tends to get carried away and wants to speed up the movie process to get to the traumatic element or sequence. To avoid shortcuts, it is up to the therapist to slow down this process and ensure that emotions remain manageable. It is important to tap well on all the elements, even the less intense ones, to lower the general SUD before approaching the more intense parts.

G. At the end, the patient is able to view the entire movie in detail without any intensity.

He will often express a detachment from the treated scene that he now finds to be distant or that he reframes by himself in a different context.

Sometimes one session is not enough to finish the film. Put it in the imaginary Safe box and pick it up again at the next session.

XV. Description of aspects during tapping

Once you have mastered the basic procedure that uses a single Setup statement and a short Reminder phrase, you can move on to a more precise practice of EFT.

A. Changing the Setup Statement

During the setup, we will then say a whole series of statements that aim to cover the different reversals that could affect the problem. As these reversals are caused by negative beliefs, among other things, we take the ones we have identified by that time.

E.g.: "Even though I have lacked love and I am convinced that there is no cure for that, I accept myself deeply."

"Even though I think I deserve this disease, I accept to be here for the time being."

B. Modification of phrases during tapping

After each round, ask for the SUD and a description of "what is left".

Patients tend to describe what is better rather than what is not yet resolved, so it is useful to help them identify "what is left" as follows:

Ask them "This 3 (SUD) that remains, what is it made of? Why do you say 3 and not 0? Is that what you feel or do you want to say something? What is it?"

Tap on it, repeating the sentences your patient has formulated in response to your questions about the remaining negative residue.

C. Example of a session

By Yves W.

Respect the patient's rhythm

YVES : How are you feeling right now?
LAURA : He still doesn't listen to me, but now it's done, I saw him three days ago....

Part 1: The Basics of Clinical EFT

Y : And what do you feel?

L : He behaves like the teacher who advises me to do things, every time he sees me he advises me and then he lectures me, and he doesn't hear what I say; for me, it doesn't make sense to continue having a relationship like that with my father...

Y : And what is the emotion that is present for you?

L : I am not being listened to.

Y : Last week, you were very angry and now you don't seem too angry, what is that, frustration? Disappointment?

L : I don't really care, actually. I don't really like the word "frustration" or I'd rather call it "disillusionment", but that was more like last week, since apparently there's nothing he can do to understand that he's not the king... that he's just a father, that he's not the teacher, he's just a father with his daughter, period! And he doesn't understand it. I'm thinking to myself that I must stop wanting to change him because it won't work anyway. I've been working on this for years and it's been like this for years.

Y : And so, you are thinking to yourself: I must stop wanting to change him...

L : For example, he offered me to go to the museum and since July he hasn't found the time, I told him "you're retired, there's more to life than going to the university", because he keeps going there, then he gives excuses that are not valid for me, he has to take care of his stuff there... and I told him, going to the museum with your daughter is not going to change things.
And he blames me: "since July, I haven't heard from you..." He exaggerates! His childishness annoys me, I don't need it in my life. For the moment, I'm focused on learning how to walk again, nothing else.

Y : If you think about your father and this irritation, how much would it be on the scale between 0 and 10 (10 is unbearable)?

L : When I don't see him, it's fine, but when I see him, I would say it's 9.5.

Y : What if you think about your last meeting?

L : Right now? 5.

Y : We'll take that. Do you have an image that would be the worst of this meeting? Or is it the whole situation?

L : It's easier to take the pain than just one feeling....

Y : If you look back at the movie of your encounter, is there a moment that seemed more distinctive to you? More symbolic? When you think "here he is, he's not listening to me"?

L : In addition, he tells me that I see charlatans and he knows absolutely nothing about who I see... He tells me: you have to go to a pain centre, and I don't care about going to a pain centre, where I see people who are in a worse state than me, who complain all day...
Y : So, this pissed you off - he doesn't accept what you do, what you're going through...
Do you see a worst image? Is that when he tells you that you see charlatans? Do you see his face as he says it?
L : No, I was in the kitchen, I couldn't see him....
Y : On the physical level, do you feel something right now?
L : Yes, in the solar plexus.
Y : We're going to do EFT, don't hesitate to add things yourself if something comes up - emotions, sensations, images, you can add them during the tapping.
Y – L. repeats (KC point): Even though I am very upset about my father.
Even though I want him to leave me alone, the solutions always have to come from him, not from me.

Even though I have trouble managing my irritation with my father and my anger that has been there for a very long time,
> this irritation
> my father
> this tension in my solar plexus

(Y: Notice, she doesn't care, she looks up, part of her doesn't want to get rid of this problem...)
> all my anger and irritation, my father doesn't listen to me
> he never listens to me.

> he's the teacher, he advises me but he doesn't listen to me

> you see charlatans, but he doesn't know anything about them
> It always has to go through him, not me.
> my solar plexus, I'm pissed off by my father
> all my anger, my heart is bleeding, I'm disillusioned
> I don't feel heard, I'm not listened to
> I don't feel respected.
> my solar plexus, I've been angry for years
> (actions from the 9 Gamut procedure)
> I'm disillusioned.

Part 1: The Basics of Clinical EFT

> my father doesn't listen to me.
> my father can't hear me.
> he's never going to change, he's the teacher.
> I have to learn not to want to change him.
> I'm upset about my father.
> It's always what he thinks, never what I think.
> I was in the kitchen: leave me alone
> my solar plexus....

Y : Breathe well, how strong do you feel the anger towards your father when you think about this scene, out of 10?

L : I don't know, there are two sensations: when I have him in front of me or here, here I would say 1 or 2.

Y : It's here and now.

L : 1 or 2, but I tell myself that if I'm in front of him, it's stronger, even with the anxiolytic - it's useless. 1 or 2, I don't care.

> (Y: I notice that this is a futurization. But she says "1 or 2, I don't care"... why? Protection? Or a statement "I need this anger"?)

L : The anxiolytic is useless.

Y : That's a little Psychological Reversal: yes, it could come back because he's not in front of me.

Y – L. repeats (EB point): Even though I think that if I were in front of my father, I would be much more upset.

Even though I think that, in front of him, I would have a much worse reaction.

Even though part of me thinks that if I were in front of him, I would reactivate myself...

> if I were in front of him, it would reactivate everything.
> my neck hurts.
> this pain that is... 8/10, sharp, this pain that pricks
> this irritation could come back if I saw my father
> my body reacting
> all this anger I'm carrying, which I can't get rid of.
> all this anger
> that pain in my neck
> these aches and pains in my body
> all this anger, it would reactivate if I were in front of my father.

    all this belief that I have that it would reactivate if I were in front of my father.
    I feel like it would be reactivated.
    I'm sure it would reactivate itself again.
    it's still not possible for me to get rid of that anger, I've been living with it for so long.
    it's still not possible to heal from all this anger
    there's no way I'm getting rid of this anger, it would be too easy, after all these years
    who would I become if I didn't have all that anger in me anymore, I don't know who I would become
    if I'm in front of my father, it's going to come back
    I don't know what my identity would be if I healed from this anger
    all this anger, it can come back
    I don't know what my life would be like if I didn't have any more anger...

L : I would be fine, that's all, that's what I've been working on for years...
I need to keep some of that anger?
L : Maybe...
I want to keep some of that anger...
L : For me, this anger is a driving force...
so I can't free myself from this anger....
L : Not all the anger....
I would be in danger if I freed myself from all this anger, I would no longer have a driving force...
L : I wouldn't be in danger, but I wouldn't have a driving force anymore...
I'd be safe if I let go of this anger?
L : If I were to free myself a little bit from this anger, yes, a big part, so that I would still have a little bit left....
    all this anger, I'd be safe, but if I keep some of that anger
    what's left of that anger, that little bit of anger I need, I must keep a little bit of it, it's a driving force for me
    all this anger
    all this anger....
Y : How is it going in your neck?
L : It's okay.

Part 1: The Basics of Clinical EFT

Y - L. repeats (EB point): Even though I think I have to keep some of this anger, so that I can live properly.
Even though part of me thinks I must keep some of my anger because it's a driving force for me.
L : I want to cry.
Y : Let it happen....
Y – L. repeats: Even though I want to cry when I say I have to keep some of this anger, even though part of me knows that it may not be good to keep this anger, even a little bit, because it is a kind of poison, but it reassures me because it has always been there, I accept myself with all my beliefs and limitations...

> I can keep some of that anger.
> I want to keep some of my anger.
> I would feel....

Yves noted : We continued working on this without getting to 0 the fact of keeping a little bit of anger. Following this session, this patient no longer showed up, even though she had come several times and we had advanced very well, but that... that was the knot, and the day we touched that knot... she wanted to try other therapies and she disappeared somewhere out there. She was not ready and you shouldn't force it. It's very frustrating for the therapist but you have to respect the patient's rhythm and not force the patient.

On the other hand, the link is not broken, because I regularly receive news and some behaviours have changed significantly. For example, the patient had refused to return to a "resource" country. Later she chose to go back, travel again and start a new life more actively.

XVI. Finding the right target

The effectiveness of EFT depends on the knowledge of the EFT technique but also on a wider therapeutic capacity. A very important ability of the therapist is to identify the thought/event/emotion that is at the centre of the patient's problem.

This is the object of the therapist's training and therefore goes beyond the purpose of the book, but there are many important principles that we will repeat in the second part of this book: the treatment plan naturally derives from the anamnesis - the preliminary inquiry you make about the client's life history in order to determine what type of problem you are facing. If the anamnesis is done correctly, this will help create the therapeutic alliance you will need. It will also help recognize whether you are in a simple or complex configuration. It will also allow you to create the best possible treatment plan to organize the order of the sessions and targets (events, situations, people, beliefs) to be treated first.

All this work is part of the "clinical" recognition, that is, the understanding of the framework hidden by our reactions to events or our way of responding to them, the acknowledgement of everything we have built ourselves upon or survived in order to be who we are here and now. This will be the path, freely chosen, that will lead us from the small "hurts" of life or the simple or complex traumas to our liberation and the happiness which we all aspire!

For the time being, in this first part devoted to the "Clinical foundations of EFT", we limit ourselves to finding the right target in a given session. We consider that we are in a case of simple "EFT sessions" and not of a real therapeutic follow-up that begins with an anamnesis and the establishment of a treatment plan, as we will see in the second part: "Advanced Clinical EFT".

A. The conditioning

By Brigitte H.

1. Introduction

Part 1: The Basics of Clinical EFT

Conditioning is a fundamental aspect to understand in order to find the right target. Remember Pavlov: after having fed the dogs by ringing a bell, he just had to ring it to get the dogs to drool. The bell is the triggering stimulus causing salivation, a conditioned stimulus. Note that the cause-and-effect relationship does not need to be logical, it is enough if it has been chronologically associated with the facts.

Similarly, any stimulus (smell, environmental element, tone of voice, physical appearance element, etc.) occurring in a current event that refers to the same stimulus (acting as a bell) from a previous event will automatically trigger the same overall response. That is to say, all the physiological but also psychological aspects of our feelings of the past are reactivated.

Any event that consciously or unconsciously recalls, in many ways or in one detail, a painful experience from the past, will provoke the same emotional reactions as the original event. This often happens without the awareness of the concerned person, whose reactions will therefore be as irrational as disproportional.

This explains the fact that we find ourselves "like a little child" in front of our boss who reminds us of our father who is too strict.

It is common for the triggering stimulus to remain unconscious. We then find ourselves anxious, depressed or uncomfortable "for no reason", or at least an apparent reason.

A painful experience has two ways of conditioning the emotional brain: either by a single but strong impact (punctual trauma) or by repetition (trauma by toxicity).

As our emotional functioning is eminently conditioned, the event of the past that has conditioned the present is the "fire under the pot" for our current emotions. It is difficult to try to prevent the pot from boiling by acting on it if the fire is still burning underneath. **It is therefore necessary to address the emotional roots of current events.**

2. The logic of conditioning in the search for targets

Let us recall the neuronal logic of the conditioning links:

- any part/aspect of an event that caused stress in the past has become a Pavlov's bell (an element that can, on its own, reactivate the associated physiological state: stress or post-traumatic stress, or disproportionate or incongruous emotion);
- this bell can be: a factual or sensory aspect, a perception of oneself (negative belief), etc.
- an event can only be (permanently) stressful today because it contains a bell. Otherwise, we would react calmly, or we would calm down quickly (as will be the case after the treatment). A common mistake is to forget this and believe what the patient says: that the problem is in the current situation and not in what created the bell;
- we have to find out what this bell is;
- if the bell of the past is deconditioned, no bell of the present can reactivate the conditioned stress reaction.

By this logic, any traumatic event responds to an existing bell.

Example: I am afraid of my boss. Is there an anterior bell that conditions this reaction to my boss?

Ask yourself: "Would anyone be stressed at this (current) event?" If not, there's a bell.

In the case of someone stressing in front of their boss, it is possible to imagine that other people would not be afraid of that boss. So, there's a bell that triggers this fear in the person. This could be his experience with his father, for example.

In fact, we can go back very far: a trauma only forms if there is a fragility of the person to this theme. This means that "the acorn contains the oak": traumatic (traumatogenic) events only traumatise because we are already weakened/traumatised.

All these notions return us to the concept of resilience: why do some people miraculously recover from certain things that would have traumatized others? Because they have no fragility to this theme, while others have it. In epigenetics, we would say that some genes have acquired earlier expression in order to allow us to better defend ourselves if the environment sends us back to a certain type of situation that our ancestors may have experienced. For example, we know that war veterans who have experienced trauma in childhood have a higher risk of developing post-traumatic stress disorder (PTSD) or have a more difficult (complex) PTSD than veterans who have had a safe childhood.

By treating a current event that rings the bell, we will act on the neural network that "resonates" with it (and therefore also on the past, containing the initial bell).

But if this current bell is anecdotal, we will only treat the part of the initial network that vibrates to this bell, and not the entire initial network.

Another bell present during the initial situation could still, if agitated by a current event, trigger disproportionate reactions again.

These different bells are the "aspects" of EFT. In conventional EFT, all current bells that appear to the patient's consciousness are treated as they occur.

With an understanding of the genesis of conditioning, we can lean on the fact that <u>if we can return to (treat) the scene that generated the bells, they will all be present there at the same time.</u> And so, we can treat them all at once, which makes the treatment more efficient and faster.

That is why, when a patient reports a problematic situation, it is important to ask yourself:

- what are the bells? The main bell?
- on what occasions were they created? (past events),
- and then you should process the events related to the creation/conditioning of bells preferentially to those that simply agitate them.

3. How to find the past events

The simplest (but not precise) way to find the events of the past that have created a bell is to look for the emotion felt by the patient and ask if this feeling reminds him of other moments in his life. Preferably target childhood, as it is rare (but possible) for roots to be found in adulthood, except in the case of accidents or traumas that occur in adulthood and that people remember well. This approximate method can give very good results but can also lead to "false roots".

In order to find the event of the past (the bell) that has conditioned the emotional trigger of the present in a more clinical and reliable way, it is necessary to make an **Affect bridge or Regression bridge/Float back**. The affect bridge is detailed below, and the regression bridge is explained in the second part: "Advanced Clinical EFT".

B. Negative beliefs

By Brigitte H.

When you experience a difficult event, you store it in your memory. If similar events occur, they will be stored together with the beliefs that accompany them in specific electromagnetic circuits. These emotional roots, linked to their specific negative beliefs, create and maintain specific problems that can be psychological or spiritual, or can generate physical symptoms that will manifest themselves repeatedly.

The emotional root comes from a unique experience containing unresolved negative emotions (grief, fear, anger) that are accumulated in the subconscious mind. These emotional roots will eventually produce a **belief system**. This belief system, which lies in the person's subconscious mind, determines the timing, duration, intensity, reason, and effect of a specific symptom, behaviour or negative experience.

A problem can be broken down into several problems or aspects, each with its own emotional roots and beliefs. Therefore, they will all have to be treated separately, except in certain cases where several aspects disappear on their own in conjunction with the treatment of one of them.

The identification of Negative Beliefs (NB) in EFT is of great importance, as Psychological Reversals (PRs) are most often generated by these NBs (as shown in the tables of specific PRs). However, it is necessary for the success of the treatment to correct these reversals in the setup and/or during the rounds.

The use of negative beliefs in a structured way is described in the protocols of the second part of the book, the "Advanced Clinical EFT".

Part 1: The Basics of Clinical EFT

C. Focusing on specific facts

By Brigitte H.

Aiming for specific facts is very important. Most of the failures of the technique are based on a lack of precision in the choice of the treated events.

When the emotional root is identified, for example: a patient feels like a little child in front of his boss because of a once overwhelming and downgrading father, it is appropriate to target one of the events that really happened.

The principle is that the dysfunctional origin of emotions was created by specific events and experienced at a specific time, in a specific place, with a specific person ("that time when my father called me a little jerk in the kitchen and I was 6 years old"), and not by general concepts ("my father put me down all the time").

The treatment must target these specific events, not the concepts.

Metaphor of the Tabletop

The general concept (my traumatic memory of when my father beat me) is the visible surface of the tabletop. But what keeps it stable is its legs: the precise events that gave rise to this more general emotion/memory.

To make the tabletop fall – to desensitise the general concept, we act by removing one by one the legs of the table (by desensitising one by one the source memories).

Concept of the Generalisation effect - the Oil stain effect

For example, in the event of a general problem rooted in childhood, which lasted for years with 100 targets, treating 10 to 20 of them will be enough. The other targets will be desensitised by the Generalisation effect/Oil stain effect.

Generally speaking, you treat the strongest targets (with the highest SUD), most often chronologically, if there is a cause-effect relationship between them.

Metaphor of the Trees of the forest

Part 1: The Basics of Clinical EFT

When there are many source memories, treating them one by one does not immediately show a result in the patient's overall concept or current experience.

It's like in a very dark forest, because the density of the trees would not let light through. We're going to cut down a tree, then another one, then another one, and at first, we won't really get the impression that it's brighter.

But after a certain threshold of desensitised targets/cut down trees, suddenly the light passes much better and the patient feels the difference/relief significantly.

XVII. General protocol for deconditioning a simple trauma

A. Distinction between simple trauma and complex trauma

When you discover EFT, you are amazed at its ability to calm the emotions about a painful event in the past. When it is well applied to a well-defined target, you tap and poof! the emotional disturbance is gone, and the patient is liberated from the past. But this is only true in cases where the patient's Self is strong enough to allow this natural healing.

If we metaphorically compare a psychological injury to a cut on our skin, EFT would then be compared to a procedure that stimulates the skin's natural healing capacity. You tap, and it heals and cicatrizes by itself. However, this only works if the body is healthy enough. If the latter is lacking, the cicatrization capacity will be lacking, and healing will not occur.

The same is true for the psyche: if the patient's Self (his psychological strength) is strong enough, it is enough to tap on what causes a problem so that the emotional trace dissipates by itself (see Part Two: "Adaptive Information Processing"). This can be described as an isolated emotional difficulty or a simple trauma.

We will call an emotional difficulty a difficult event that has left a trace of reduced amplitude. A trauma is an event that exceeds the patient's ability to cope with it at the time, to the point where post-traumatic stress phenomena arise. It is not uncommon in the EFT world to use the term trauma for something that is actually just an emotional difficulty.

If the patient is mentally healthy enough, he or she will be able to cope with the reminiscence of an old trauma while tapping, the latter activating their capacity for "psychological healing". This is the magic of EFT for even severe traumas. In this case, it is recommended tapping only on the negative aspect until it disappears. Indeed, the introduction of positive aspects could temporarily mask the remaining negatives.

Part 1: The Basics of Clinical EFT

But if the patient has had too many psychological difficulties (too strong or often repeated in childhood), his capacity for psychological healing by tapping on the negative is reduced or, for some topics, non-existent. This is called **complex trauma**. These traumas or emotional difficulties were either too intense or often repeated, at a too early age when the patient did not yet have all the resources of an adult psyche that is strong enough. His emotional and affective development has been affected down to his very constitution and his ability to build himself properly. In this case, on the contrary, you should avoid tapping on the negative alone. It will be necessary to introduce the positive, or sometimes tap only on the positive or install the so-called **resources** (see Part Two: "Advanced Clinical EFT"). These are intended to strengthen the patient's Self, in general or on a particular theme, before addressing the negative targets.

A patient's treatment can be compared to the repair of a house: if the foundations are solid, regardless of the defective place in the house (a wall to be repaired, a part of the roof, etc.), workers can enter the house and repair it safely. The hole in the wall or the roof represents the isolated emotional difficulty or simple trauma that has left damage.

But if the foundations of the house are unstable (too many problems when building the house structure: complex traumas that occurred in childhood), even if the owner has called the workers to the rescue, they must avoid entering the house that could collapse as they enter, despite their good intentions to repair. Similarly, the therapist should not give in at the request of the patient with a complex trauma to treat his or her heavy emotional targets. The workers must first, from the outside, consolidate the foundations, put in braces, etc. Then, when the house is consolidated enough, they can slowly enter the house and carefully carry out repairs.

Thus, in the event of a **complex trauma**, the therapist must stay out of the painful targets and, above all, avoid shaking the foundations (working on the past). He puts in braces: tapping on the positive only and installing resources. It is only when the patient is strong enough that he or she will eventually go on to treat negative events – eventually, because the establishment of resources sometimes leads to a spontaneous dissolution of traumatic emotions upon contact.

In this first part, "The Basics of Clinical EFT", the proposed methods assume that there is a case of isolated emotional difficulty or simple trauma, and that the most direct method can therefore safely be used: searching for the most intense point of the target, searching for its origin in the past through the affect bridge (float back) and treating the latter by tapping on it. The more we're at the epicentre of the target, the faster the resolution will be.

B. The Affect Bridge: protocol for deconditioning targets from the past for a simple trauma

By Brigitte H. and notes by Yves W.

Here you will find an adaptation of the article on the affect bridge that we wrote for the *Clinical EFT Handbook*. It provides a protocol that you can follow to decondition targets from the present and the past by a basic use of Clinical EFT on a simple trauma (or problematic topic in general). You will find there a repetition of the general information about conditioning.

The order of this work (tapping on past targets and then tapping on present ones) is only valid if you are confronted with a **simple trauma**, because in the case of complex traumas this order is reversed (see Part Two: "Advanced Clinical EFT").

1. Objective of the Affect Bridge technique

The Affect Bridge is originally a hypnotic regression technique (John Watkins, 1971). Its objective is to trace the emotional component of a current experience back to the initial event of the past that has conditioned it. As its name suggests, the technique bridges the gap between the affect of *the present* and the same affect of *the past*. The objective is to return to the initial cause of the problem currently presented by the client, which in the language of EFT would be called the "core issue". The problem can then be solved at the level of the conditioning event of the past, so that it does not happen again in the present.

2. Mode of action: conditioning and deconditioning

Part 1: The Basics of Clinical EFT

The efficiency of the technique is based on the Pavlovian conditioning process and its extinction by deconditioning.

After conditioning the dogs to hear a bell when he gives them food (*the past*), Pavlov only has to ring it (in *the present*) for the dogs to salivate. The bell is now a triggering stimulus that has the power to cause the conditioned response (salivation).

Because it has been associated (conditioned) with the event, any sensory aspect of the initial situation of the past (visual, auditory, olfactory, kinaesthetic) can become a trigger stimulus later in the present.

This means that any aspect of a *present* situation identical to that of a painful experience of the past can constitute a bell reminding the limbic brain of this *past* situation, and trigger the same conditioned reaction (emotional, cognitive and physiological).

A painful experience can condition the emotional brain and lead to the creation of trigger stimuli in two types of cases:

- by a single but strong impact: a punctual trauma that marks the limbic brain all at once, such as a car accident,
- by repetition: trauma by toxicity, marking the limbic brain over time, as in the case of repeated bullying or devaluation.

It is common for the triggering stimulus to remain unconscious. When it is activated, the person becomes anxious, depressed or uncomfortable for no apparent reason.

Things are happening without his knowledge, therefore his reactions seem irrational and disproportionate.

Example 1 - A patient had a serious car accident. Just before the impact, the other driver tried to avoid it by suddenly braking. The noise of the braking, associated with the impact trauma, resulted in the formation of a bell/trigger. Therefore, when the patient, years later, hears a braking noise while walking in the street, he feels an increase in panic, starts to sweat and feels frozen, unable to move and think (conditioned physiological response). The patient does not make the connection between this braking noise and his accident, which he no longer thinks about because it dates back from years ago. He doesn't understand what's happening to him.

Example 2 - A patient feels frightened (conditioned response) by his boss because his tone of voice (bell) unconsciously reminds him of his father's too harsh tone of voice. Not noticing this element that his boss and his father have in common, the person thinks he is frightened by his boss and consults about that. In reality, it is his father he is still afraid of: his limbic brain triggers a reaction of fear to what reminds him of that.

To ensure that the trigger no longer has any effect in the present, it must be disabled in the past. In the example of the boss, if we treat the current emotion only (fear of the boss), the patient will actually see his fear dissolve. But the bell of the past is not deactivated, and another person who reminds him of his father would trigger the same conditioned response (fear).

Hence the invitation in EFT to look for *"core issues"*: in this case, by identifying the fear of the father as the underlying problem, the patient's limbic brain can be allowed to re-educate itself by deconditioning the reaction of fear to the perception of the father's severity in the past.

Thus, no indication of severity will signify danger to the patient, and no severe person in the present will cause fear.

3. The search for fundamental problems

A very simple way to search for underlying problems is:

- identify the patient's feelings in the current problematic situation,
- and then use this feeling as a "breadcrumb trail" to go back to the past.

To do this, the patient is asked if this feeling reminds him of an earlier moment in his life.

Preferably, it is childhood that is targeted, as it is rare for roots to be found in adulthood, except in the case of accidents or traumas that occur in adulthood and that people remember well.

The question asked can therefore be formulated as follows: "When you are connected to this feeling, and you let yourself go back to the past as far as possible, what does that bring you back to?"

Part 1: The Basics of Clinical EFT

This is the principle of the Affect bridge: to regress from the present to the past by following the thread of the emotional reaction.

This invitation to the patient to see "what it reminds him of in the past" leads us to the process used by Freud in psychoanalysis to discover the unconscious origins of his patients' disorders. He knew that it was the patient's unconscious mind, more than his conscious mind, that could lead them to the sources of the problem. This is why, the fundamental rule of psychoanalysis is free association, which consists in "saying everything that comes to mind". This process activates the limbic, emotional brain, rather than the rational mind.

Watkins was a psychoanalyst and had also noted the importance of ensuring that the patient had limbic, not mental, access to his memories. This is why, he developed the technique of the Affect bridge, under hypnosis, where the unconscious mind activated by the trance could take over the control to regress into the past and see "what it reminds it of".

Specifically, the hypnotherapist invites the patient in trance to focus on his emotion (affect) in the current problematic situation. He then leads the unconscious to go back in time to the event where this emotion was first evoked and felt.

4. Regression bridge and Affect bridge

When a triggering stimulus is activated by an experienced situation, the conditioned response that is triggered is constituted by the emotions, physical sensations (physiological response) and thoughts (cognitions) experienced by the patient.

Doing what we call a "Complete Regression Bridge" (or Float back) is to do a regression by associating the patient with the feeling of *all* these elements.

The Affect Bridge technique, on the other hand, only uses the component of *emotion* as a common thread.

The Regression bridge (or Float back; it considers not only emotion but also physical sensations and cognitions) is more reliable than the Affect bridge. It is described in the second part of this book, "Advanced Clinical EFT".

Actually, in hypnosis, even if the hypnotherapist only focuses the patient's attention on the emotion, by the virtue of the trance, the unconscious mind focuses on all the parameters (emotion, sensations, cognitions).

Indeed, it is obvious that if the current emotion is fear, there was not only one event in the past where fear was provoked. The patient was afraid of his father, but he was probably also afraid of the dark, afraid of not looking up, etc. If the unconscious mind goes back to the situation with the father, and not to the first fear of the dark, it is because it goes back up the thread of fear AND other common aspects between the present and the past (especially cognitions).

In hypnosis, making a bridge using only affect is therefore in fact a complete regression bridge, and leads to the correct cause of the problem.

But in EFT, this is not necessarily true, because of the absence of trance, or its lightness (when the person is well associated with the past, when he or she is well "inside", he or she is in a slightly modified state of consciousness - a natural light trance). Therefore, if the patient is not sufficiently associated with the scene, if he is too much in the mind, in the intellectual description of the memory and not in the sensory reliving, the affect bridge can lead to a memory associated with the same emotion, but not located on the causal axis of the present event. In the example cited above, one could end up with a memory of the patient's childhood fear of the dark, which is not at the root of the current fear of the boss.

The Complete Regression Bridge technique (Float back in this book) requires detailed preliminary techniques that were not the subject of this article. We therefore described the Affect Bridge and gave a clinical example - you will find them below. This is followed by another session transcript using the technical elements of the Complete Regression Bridge, as well as other advanced techniques for patients with complex trauma. You will find them, as well as the description of the Complete Affect Bridge, in the second part of this book: "Advanced Clinical EFT".

5. The Affect bridge in EFT

The simplest transposition of the Affect bridge to EFT is to focus on the present emotion and make a regression.

Step 1: Associate the person to the present event. Measure the SUD of the event (the intensity of the emotional distress from 0 to 10).

Step 2: Identify the emotion that is present.

Step 3: Ask "When was the first time you experienced this emotion (quote the emotion) in the past?" or "When you are connected to this emotion (quote the emotion), and you let yourself go back to the past as far as possible, what does that bring you back to?" Measure the SUD of the event.

Step 4: Decondition the event of *the past* by EFT tapping until SUD = 0 (emotion dropped to zero).

Step 5: Check the event of *the present*: is it disabled (SUD = 0: the emotion has disappeared).

We have seen that it is by remaining connected to one's emotional, limbic brain, corresponding to the unconscious mind activated in hypnosis, that the patient will access the right information - otherwise an intellectual response of little value will be provided by the patient's mind. Without the trance in EFT, how can I talk to the limbic brain and not to the patient's mind?

The whole art consists in associating the person well with his or her emotion and asking the questions mentioned above. Let's go back to the detail of each step from the second example above (fear of the boss):

Step 1: Associate the person to the present event.

It is about allowing the person to get back into the situation, as if they were *reliving* it *now*. So, it goes like this: *now* I put myself in the memory of the past as if I *am* there again. I am *now* in the memory of the past. This is called being "associated" with the memory: being in the experience. The reliving is identifiable by the fact that the patient speaks in the present: "I am very afraid" (*now, when I relive the past*).

It is *not* an intellectual memory, often identifiable by the fact that the patient speaks of the past instead of the present: "I was very afraid" (in the past).

You can tell the patient: "*Go back to the moment you are facing your boss, as if you are there now*" (note the intentional use of the present tense*). "Are you there?*" Wait for confirmation and ask for the SUD.

> Step 2: Identify the emotion that is present.

Just ask the patient: "*Now that you are in this moment, in front of your boss, what emotion do you feel?*"

> Step 3: Ask one of the following questions: "When was the first time you felt this fear in the past?" or "When you are connected to this fear, and you let yourself go back to the past as far as possible, what does that bring you back to?"

It is important to avoid asking the question in a way that activates the patient's mind, such as: "When do you *think* you felt this fear before?" It is not a question of thinking or reflecting, *but of letting the emotion take us back.*

In this case, the patient will respond with a scene with his father raising his voice in a severe tone. For example*: "I see myself in the kitchen with my father, he talks to me in a very brittle tone."*

It is important to check that the patient has the same emotion as in the present event (here it is fear). Otherwise, this is not the root - the patient has found an answer with his mind or was not sufficiently associated with the scene. Start over. In case of persistent difficulty, a complete affect bridge is required. Ask for the SUD.

The therapist's art here consists in keeping the patient connected to his emotion while reliving the scene.

> Step 4: Decondition the event of the past by EFT tapping until SUD = 0 (emotion dropped to zero).

Tap on the scene of the past (*in the kitchen with the father*) until it is completely desensitised.

> Step 5: Check the event of the present *(in front of the boss)*: is it disabled (SUD = 0)?

If the affect bridge is well done, this is usually the case. Exceptionally, there may still be a small intensity, which is then brought to zero by tapping. If the SUD of the present event has not decreased or has only slightly decreased, it is because the past event was not the root of the present event, or that there is more than one event (complex trauma, for example).

6. Notes on the patient's connection to the reliving of the scene

By Yves W.

The good knowledge of the patient's history is more than useful (anamnesis). To help the person associate with emotions, you will need to identify whether the person tends to be associated or dissociated from their emotions. Basically, is the person emotional or mental?

Patient dissociated from his emotions

If the person is mental, avoid tapping until you ask them to explain their problem and look for the specific target from which to start. Indeed, with this type of patient, you will try to make the person contact his emotions with as much intensity as possible, since he tends to dissociate from them. You are looking for the opposite, namely to stimulate and trigger the sympathetic nervous system (corresponding to the accelerator pedal in a car) to be sufficiently in the mental field of (connected to) the problem. On the contrary, tapping activates the parasympathetic system (the equivalent of the brake in a car) and calms the nervous system. Basically, you press both the accelerator and the brake (see the book *EFT, Tapping and EP*, by the same authors, Dangles, 2010). It is a good idea to ask the patient for as many details as possible of the scene, to connect him to it. If he has difficulty identifying the emotion, you will help him by offering a range of emotions that seem to best represent the event to be dealt with or that resonate the most with it. Be careful to make only proposals from which or in contrast to which the patient will choose by himself.

It may be necessary, if the patient cannot connect to his or her emotions, to help him or her by resonating with the emotion and validating it yourself: for example, by pointing out how difficult or hard it could be or how sad or frightening it could be for the patient.

Patient too associated with emotions

If, on the other hand, the person tends to be too emotional, it will be necessary to stay in the comfort zone (do not get too emotional) in order to be able to properly target and do the affect bridge.

7. Example of an affect bridge on simple trauma

Martine, during a training course for mental health professionals, offers herself as a guinea pig. She asks me to work on a phobia and a panic fear that takes her over whenever she has to have her annual medical check-up and have a scan (*present*). Just the idea of being locked in the scanning machine, in this tube, and not being able to move triggers a rise in her anxiety. This causes an acceleration of her heart rate and breathing, she starts to panic and wants to get out at all costs, there is sweating, uncontrollable thoughts of immediate danger, etc. (*conditioned response*).

> Step 1: I then ask her to return to the moment when she passed her last scan *(recent past taken as equivalent of the present)* and ask her for the SUD, which is 8/10.
>
> Step 2: I ask her what emotion she feels when she is reliving the scene. It is an anxiety.
>
> Step 3: I ask her to close her eyes and ask the following question: "When you are connected to this anxiety and you let yourself go back to the past as far as possible, what does that bring you back to?"

She suddenly remembers that a year before the onset of the symptoms, she had to decide to make an abortion. However, she had already had several miscarriages and had also lost a child a few months after birth.

She tells me that she has been suffering from agoraphobia since then, in addition to her claustrophobia. For example, if she sees people getting on public transport and coming towards her, she panics and forcibly exits the train or the bus, even elbowing her way out.

I then ask her what her SUD is when she thinks of that tragic moment. It's 9/10.

Step 4: Decondition the event of the past by EFT tapping until SUD = 0 (emotion dropped to zero).

We made several rounds of tapping with the keyword *"the mess"* that Martine chose to illustrate this moment.

After 25 minutes of rounds, the SUD was at 1. I asked her where this SUD was in her body. It was at the level of the heart. The thought associated with this sensation was that it could not be at 0 without being afraid to forget. She could not risk forgetting these children without being disloyal, or without feeling that she was betraying them. We then made a round on the idea that she could integrate these children into the flow of life and allow herself to live happily now as a tribute to this love; she had been carrying all this for a long time, and she could consider depositing it in order to relieve herself, she had the right to do so and she had done the best she could, and she could continue growing them in her heart.

The SUD then fell to zero.

Step 5: Check the event of the present: is it disabled (SUD = 0)?

I asked her to rethink about the scanning machine. The SUD was at zero. She went home by bus and never suffered from agoraphobia or claustrophobia again.

XVIII. The effect of the treatment

The effect of EFT on the subjective feeling related to the target is expressed in different ways. There is of course desensitisation: negative emotions disappear, but often a more constructive and distant way of thinking also appears. Patients frequently describe impressions in the order of: "it's as if the scene is moving away - it's further away now"; "I feel like I'm distanced from the situation, as if I'm an observer rather than being emotionally involved", etc.

This desensitisation is so natural that patients easily lose sight of the fact that ten minutes earlier, they did not feel the current serenity, but negative emotions. This often leads to a form of "revisionism" such as "SUD is low now, but you know, this problem has never really affected me - it hasn't done much to me for a long time, etc.", while earlier in the same session they reported the opposite and a high SUD.

It may be useful to remind them of the intensity of the previous SUD, to give them confidence in the method and allow them to realize the kind of changes they can expect from it.

Frequent comments following the decline of the SUD are: "But it will probably come back!" It is normal for patients to have to experience between sessions that it does not "come back". It is useful to tell them that their doubt is normal, but that the results last over time and that they will be able to see it. The reasons for the reappearance of a high SUD are generally that aspects have remained hidden and have not been addressed. It is then necessary to go back to them and the SUD decreases.

XIX. Avoiding strong abreactions

A. Introduction

An abreaction is a very strong emotional reaction. If the patient can cope with it and go through it, an abreaction has therapeutic effects. On the other hand, if the amplitude of the emotion exceeds the patient's ability to manage it (see the notion of a "window of tolerance" in the second part of the book), the therapeutic effect is lost and the first thing the therapist must do is allow the patient to return to an emotional zone where the treatment of the emotion becomes possible again.

There are three types of techniques:

1. Techniques to avoid abreactions

In this first section on the foundations of Clinical EFT, we will look at the traditional EFT techniques used to avoid abreactions by gently approaching a specific target: **the Tearless Trauma technique** and **the Split Narrative technique**. They are used **before the treatment of a target** when you suspect that the intensity of the vivacious reliving will be too painful. They allow the patient to treat the target by avoiding connecting to emotions that are too intense or unbearable.

2. Techniques to calm down in the presence of an abreaction

These procedures give the patient the timely opportunity to calm down when an abreaction has begun:

- **the Quick REMAP® 4-point procedure**;
- the classic EFT tapping on what's there;
- the **Safe Place and the Box/Container** that we will see in the second part of this book, devoted to advanced clinical techniques.
- The TRE (Trauma Release Exercise)
- The heart coherence

- The compassionate heart coherence (see Self Emotional Balancing model - SEB)

   3. **Basic techniques to calm the nervous system and manage abreactions**

The objective of these procedures is to train the patient once and for all to deal with the abreactions and emotional interferences and to be able to get over them quickly: **the Container and the Basic State.** They require a longer preparation, however, for a patient with a complex case where abreaction is likely or sometimes unavoidable, this preparation is highly recommended and quickly "cost-effective". We will see these in the second part of this book.

B. The Tearless Trauma technique

This technique allows to treat painful events in an ecological way by reducing the emotional impact felt during treatment. The Tearless Trauma treatment technique, summarised by the term "Tearless trauma", avoids the abreaction (traumatic reliving) to events that are too painful.

This technique also makes it easy to handle even a large group of people without knowing the details of the events handled by the participants and without risking too many abreactions. Indeed, there is little or no emotional pain that is experienced and expressed in this gentle treatment.

   1. Define the target

Ask participants to identify a specific traumatic event in their past. Gary recommends requesting that this be an event that is more than three years old, in order to minimize interference with similar targets/situations that are common for an event that has taken place recently.

Advise people to stay with their original problem, as many of them may move on to other problems when they come up in their minds.

   2. Guess the SUD

Part 1: The Basics of Clinical EFT

Ask participants to **guess** what their emotional intensity would be (on a scale of 0 to 10).

Tell them **not to** imagine the event in a vivid way (although some will close their eyes and do it anyway).

Guessing rather than feeling minimises the pain, and this estimate corresponds surprisingly to reality.

Have them write down the result of their estimation and have them each read their own figure out loud.

This gives you a good idea of the intensity for the different participants.

3. Construct the Reminder phrase

Ask the participants to find a phrase to use with the EFT tapping, such as "that emotion when my father hit me".

4. First round

Proceed with a full round of tapping, asking participants to say the reminder phrase **without** imagining the memory in a vivid way.

5. Guess the SUD again

Ask them to guess again what the intensity is and have everyone say their new number out loud.

Usually, they will give significantly lower figures.

6. Next rounds to arrive between 0 and 3

Have them do more complete rounds of EFT (or your favourite tapping procedure). At the end of each round, ask for the new numbers.

Continue until everyone reaches an estimate of 0 to 3. Usually, three or four rounds of tapping are enough.

7. Last round followed by a vivid image

Once everyone has dropped to an acceptable estimate, then repeat one complete round of tapping and **after that round**, ask them to imagine the incident in a vivid way.

Notice that this is the first time you have asked them to do this. All estimates so far have been relatively painless.

Usually, almost everyone gets to zero, and the others to very low numbers. If there are one or two exceptions, then work with them individually to complete the process.

Part 1: The Basics of Clinical EFT

C. The Split Narrative technique

This technique, like the Tearless Trauma technique, is used when the patient experiences too strong negative emotions while talking about the event, or when you suspect that there may be a strong abreaction.

The person is then invited to tell the first few sentences of the scene, stopping as soon as the intensity exceeds a threshold that is tolerable for the patient. This threshold varies according to the case; we can discuss it beforehand (e.g.: "You stop when the intensity exceeds about 6 out of 10, does that sound good to you?").

When the intensity is reached, the patient stops the story and taps on the beginning of the "movie" of the event until that point. When the intensity has dropped to 0, the patient continues his story, stopping again when it becomes too difficult. We then tap on this segment of the film, and so on until the end.

In very difficult cases, we do it one sentence at a time. If the person cannot say the next sentence, tap on their fears/shame/feelings at the thought of saying it. When the blockage is resolved, we continue.

D. The Quick REMAP® 4-Point Emergency Procedure

The points used are:

- LI4

Acupuncture point on the Large Intestine meridian, on the back of the hand between the metacarpals of the thumb and index finger (forbidden during pregnancy).

IMG 1

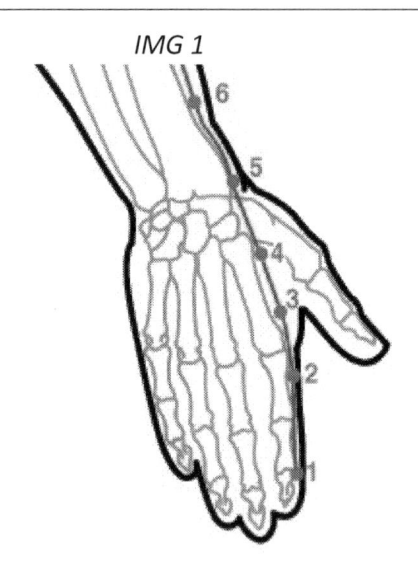

- ST36

Acupuncture point on the Stomach meridian.

To find the location of this point, you need to start from the kneecap. From there, descend just below the bulge (tibial tuberosity) on the top end of the leg bone (tibia). Starting below the bulge, move a quarter of a thumb outward from this bone (laterally from the anterior edge of the tibia); (forbidden during pregnancy).

Part 1: The Basics of Clinical EFT

IMG 2

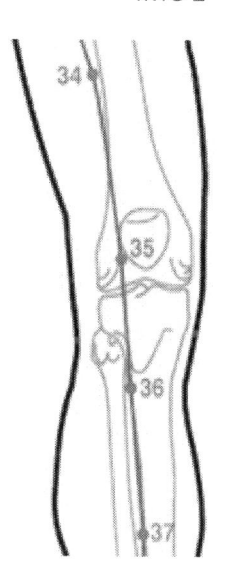

- Extra Point 1

This point is at the root of the nose, on the forehead.

IMG 3

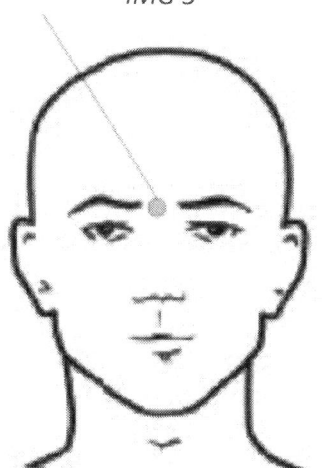

- Relaxation point of the ear

Underneath the front part of the upper edge (the helix) of the earlobe.

IMG 4

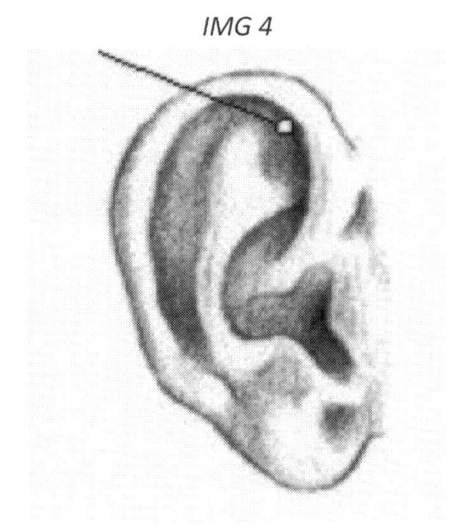

Protocol:
- Hold each point for about one minute or until the intensity stops decreasing ;
- Repeat if necessary.

E. Managing an abreaction by EFT tapping

It is simply a matter of tapping on the symptoms and beliefs that are present, as one would do with a normal target.

Example:

CARINE : I'm sorry (in tears after an exercise where she was in the therapist position and reconnected her patient to a heavy trauma).

YVES : A plastic bag, please.

C: Sorry, I'm sorry.

Y: Breathe in there, breathe, breathe, breathe, just try to breathe, that's it, take a deep breath, hold the air a little bit, breathe out slowly, that's it, breathe in the air, hold the air a little bit, breathe out slowly, that's it, again, again... Great, very good, again... Think about the tree exercise we did here, breathe in some air, hold the air, slowly...

Stimulate slowly, hold the air, exhale slowly, beautiful, that's it.

Part 1: The Basics of Clinical EFT

Please keep looking into my eyes, you are in this room, look around you... (all of this is being said in a warm and kind voice).

Beginning of tapping and reframing to accelerate the stabilisation of the person being helped:

Even though that triggered me, it's normal, it's logical, and even though it triggered me, I accept myself.

Even though I'm ashamed of other people's gaze, we're here in training, this kind of event happens, and when it's not you, it's someone else, and when it's not someone else, it's me, it's normal, take a deep breath, hold it, exhale slowly, very well.

Even though it touched me deeply, it sent me back to my story... in reality, I am no longer the little girl, I am no longer abandoned, I am with the friends here around me, my classmates, my colleagues, my friends and I have the right to let my emotions out.

Even though I am ashamed of having let my emotions out in front of everyone... the reality is that here I am protected; if there is indeed a place where I can let my emotions out, it is here; I am with people who can understand, who can accept me as I am.

Keep breathing slowly, stimulate the knees.

Take a breath, hold it, breathe out slowly, think of a place that feels good for you, that you like.

Even though I felt overwhelmed by my emotions... the reality is that here and now I am safe, I am with my friends.

Take a deep breath... and feel all the relaxation in your body as you exhale through this natural process of relaxation.

Take a breath, hold the air... you can just be present at what's there, feel if it's calming down.

C : I'm shaking.

It's normal, even though I shake... it's normal that I shake, I'm in front of Yves.

Even though I shake... the reality is that it's just the nervous counter-shock, it's my body that reharmonizes, rebalances itself, it's normal, even though I've stepped on the accelerator pedal, now I step on the brake, and my motor brake works fine.

Y : How do you feel?

C : I'm okay....

Y : Shall we continue? And if you feel that it's rising, you call on the team, the bag, etc., and the important thing is the breathing.

Comments:

> If you want to calm an abreaction, it is important to stop the over oxygenation, because these are signs that the body interprets as "I am in a situation of danger, I have to mobilise my muscles", so this only speeds up the process; that's why we use a plastic bag to limit the oxygen, to recover the breathing, and it calms down.
>
> It is important not to leave the person in this state, to make a connection with him, so the look is important, the presence, the humour too... Benevolent humour and provocation can be very important to reduce tension and bring the client back into the comfort zone and the work frame. This work frame tries to keep the client between dissociation and abreaction. In short, our aim is to avoid as much as possible that the client is too active, to the point of cutting himself off from his feelings (dissociation) or being overwhelmed by them (abreaction). Because, in this case, you will have to stabilise the client or reconnect him and this will paralyze the session. I always advise to pay attention to the work frame which oscillates between these two extremes. This is for the comfort of the patient as well as for your own comfort and therapeutic effectiveness.

Part 1: The Basics of Clinical EFT

XX. Counter indications

EFT can be used on people with psychiatric disorders, provided the therapist is trained to intervene in such disorders.

Of course, be sure to evaluate the strength of the patient's Self in advance. In case of fragility, first set up stabilisation tools such as the Safe place, the Safe box, etc. Use the Tearless Trauma technique or the Split Narrative to reduce the SUD as you go along.

It is prudent not to treat with EFT a psychiatric condition that you are not used to treating in other ways (schizophrenia, for example). This is even if the tool could, at the very least, contribute to a better management of anguish or anxiety by simply activating the parasympathetic system which is caused by the stimulation of the acupressure points! If you are outside your usual sphere of work or mastery, consider consulting a supervisor and, if in doubt, preferably refer the patient to a mental health professional such as a psychiatrist or advise them to consult with such. Remember to surround yourself with referees who can help you see more clearly and have a list of referent doctors or other experts.

XXI. Surrogate treatment

Surrogate treatment means treating someone else by tapping on yourself.

We know from new research in physics and biology (Bruce Lipton's book *The Biology of Belief* and his lectures in English on YouTube, or Dawson Church's book *The Genie in Your Genes*) that our energy bodies are like energy fields that surround us - the heart, for example, extends several metres around our physical body. Our energy bodies are therefore "entangled", interconnected, because of our proximity to others.

But they are also connected over a distance, when we project our thought, intention (cf. quantum mechanics), and through the emotional, physical or emotional bond we have with certain people. It is this connection that makes twins or mothers feel at a distance what the other is feeling.

Surrogate treatment is an extension of these concepts of non-localization. EFT is based on TFT (Thought Field Therapy); it is now recognised that our mind, our memory, our thoughts are not located inside our skull, but rather in an information field that constitutes a kind of intelligent energy matrix, containing information networks. A kind of wireless internet.

The surrogate treatment is carried out through this network.

The first thing to do is to set the intention that EFT will be beneficial for this person; you then tap on yourself by directing the treatment to him/her.

This procedure is useful with very young children, animals, people we can't access - in the operating room, for example, or far from you.

Protocol: set your intention and tap in one of the following three ways:

Example: for a little girl, Mary, who can't fall asleep:

- in the 3rd person: "I do this for Mary. Even though Mary can't fall asleep..."

- in the 2nd person: "I do this for you, Mary. Even though you can't fall asleep..."

- in the 1st person: "I am Mary. Even though I can't fall asleep..." and tap on yourself exactly as if you were that person, saying his or her words, imagining his or her situation, feelings, etc.

Part 1: The Basics of Clinical EFT

There is the ethical problem of whether you should have the other person's permission to treat him/her. Gary Craig thinks it's not necessary. However, ask yourself this question in all conscience.

XXII. Borrowing Benefits

The term "Borrowing Benefits" is due to the discovery of a healing link between all witnesses to an EFT session, although each brings a completely different issue to treat.

This backdoor asset offers considerable advantages. It allows you to work in a group, taking turns, dealing with your personal problem in sessions that benefit everyone. Remember that you must target a specific target to be effective.

Conducting a group session with Borrowing Benefits

- Each participant writes down the specific and precise event he or she wants to deal with by just giving it a title. For example, if you want to heal your fear of heights, you will not say: "My fear of heights", but will go into detail by writing down specific facts, such as: "My panic attack while crossing the Alps last summer" or: "My terror in Martine's house at the thought that I was going to jump off her balcony" or: "When Marcel suddenly pushed me in front of the cliff."

- After the title, a number between 0 and 10 should be written down to reflect the degree of emotional intensity of the event.

- While the EFT session takes place in front of them (between the person leading the session and the person directly dealing with his or her problem), everyone in the audience repeats exactly the same words, stimulates the same points, while taking a quick look from time to time at the title of their personal problem.

- Then a reassessment of the level of suffering is carried out for each person at the end of the session, with the frequent surprise of seeing their problem reduced or even completely resolved emotionally.

Part 1: The Basics of Clinical EFT

XXIII. The introduction of the positive statements in EFT

The introduction of the positive statements in EFT can have various benefits:

- unblocks the treatment when the SUD no longer goes down AND we are working on the right target;
- introduces reframing/positive beliefs that help;
- speeds up the process;
- we can use the positive statement alone, in a "boosting" dynamic.

Important rules:

- introducing the positive statement should not be a substitute for finding the right target and eliminating the negative statement;
- introducing the positive statement is not necessary if the patient has sufficient resources to manage the problem. By introducing the positive statement too quickly, we prevent the dissolution of the negative by creating a positive neural path without defusing the negative path;

- introducing the positive statement too early can be a mistake as the patient may feel misunderstood in his still too strong negative belief;
- if the positive statement is introduced with finesse, it will either pass well or create a resistance acceptable to the patient. This resistance (*tail-ender*, "yes, but") must absolutely be worked out directly in the process before continuing with the introduction of the positive;
- if the patient does not have enough resources (positive experiences related to the topic in question), it is advisable to bring positive phrases that will serve as resources. Be careful, however, that the negative statement is gradually deactivated and that there is no "plaster on a wooden leg" effect.

Classified from the subtlest to the most direct, the various methods to introduce the positive statement are:

- the Reframing,
- the "What if" method,
- the Choices method,
- only Positive statements

It is recommended to use them in this order to avoid the rise of oppositions. If oppositions arise nevertheless, the following steps are to be taken:

- erasing unconscious oppositions (*tail-enders*/"yes, but ") by tapping on the resistances and the "yes, but" that appear.

A. Reframing

You can use the phase of the setup and the tapping on the treatment points to introduce reframes.

The power of change of these reframes is enormous; this is one of the great strengths of EFT.

Tapping during reframing makes it easier for the patient to accept it. If these phrases cause resistance, simply tap on them in the next round.

Part 1: The Basics of Clinical EFT

1. "The truth is that..."

E.g.: treatment of a rape. "Even though I feel guilty about what happened, the truth is that he was the adult and I was just a little girl."

2. "I did the best I could"/"He did what he could"

E.g.: emotional lack in relation to a parent. "Even though my mother never gave me physical tenderness, she did the best she could"; "Even though my father was never present, he did the best he could."

3. "I forgive myself"/"I forgive him"

E.g.: "Even though my father devalued me, I forgive him, and I forgive myself for still having these anxieties today."

Use forgiveness with tact: ensure that it is acceptable to the person where he or she is at. Note that this idea of forgiveness will pass much better during EFT tapping, associated in the same sentence with the recognition of harm, than it would pass if "caught unprepared" without tapping.

4. "I want to see things differently"

"Even though I have lacked love throughout my childhood, and I feel like I will always suffer from it, I want to see things differently."

5. "I am open to the possibility"

During the setup or during the tapping itself.

E.g.: "Even though I have always had this problem and it is still with me today, I am open to the possibility that this may change now."

6. Reframing in 5 points (*Yves Wauthier-Freymann - REMAP®*)

   a. Even though I have this specific problem

You name the problem specifically (precise situation with the worst image, emotions, sensations and cognition related to the situation).

> **b. I accept myself (more or less)**

You are opening up the field of the possible.

> **c. And it is natural (or logical) for me to feel... in relation to this problem**

You recognize the activated parts and, as a result, they will normally calm down naturally.

> **d. On the other hand, it is true that... (say something true and real in a positive way about the problem)**

You mention a real and verified element that counterbalances the problem to be addressed. This will install the first counter-conditioning corner.

> **e. and I open myself to the possibility of living things more calmly, keeping a bigger emotional distance, digesting things more easily, finding the right balance.**

The 5th part of the reframing process opens up the possibility of doing things differently. The goal is not to specify how but to let the unconscious do its work. Logically, if point 4 is real and verified, the unconscious will let itself go towards the stated possibility because it has already accepted point 4 as real and, as a result, point 5 becomes quite possible. It is important not to force anything but to let the unconscious do it naturally.

B. The "What if" method by Carol Look

By Dr Carol Look, LCSW DCH, EFT Master

1. Principle

The "**WHAT IF**?" tapping is one of the EFT strategies that open or show other ways out of the problem I am reprocessing.

Part 1: The Basics of Clinical EFT

This opens the door to new options and we will probably feel more and more liberated. This question "What if?" also allows to discover possible hidden blocking beliefs.

So, I'm going to embellish my rounds with "What if?", completing it with various proposals. I can also simply say "What if?" without completing the sentence because the unconscious will complete it by itself. This is one of the ways to "deceive" it and to obtain information that may not have been consciously accessible. In general, I will use this "What if?" after a series of "What if..." that I have completed with the client's beliefs or their opposite. The conscious mind expects to hear a proposal and you let it unconsciously complete the sentence that has started by this "what if". This will often raise interesting awareness.

2. Addictions and compulsive needs

Again, about addictions, no one is suggesting that you stop an ongoing treatment or your 12-step program (AA) if that is effective for you. I suggest that you use EFT to relieve some of your suffering as well as some of your stagnant beliefs about what can be achieved in your life.

Suppose you have had compulsive needs for food, cigarettes or alcohol for years and there seems to be no change in your pattern of substance abuse. Therefore, I suggest that you add the following variation to your daily EFT program:

> (1) Identify the exact sensation you have when you are in the presence of the substance or when you are unable to have or use the substance.
>
> (2) Identify how you would rather feel.
>
> (3) Proceed with the WHAT IF tapping as follows:

WHAT IF I could free myself from these patterns of addiction now, even though I've had these compulsive needs for years, and no method seems to work?
WHAT IF I allow myself to be freed from this pattern, even though I'm tired of the compulsions that control my life?

WHAT IF I could suddenly free myself from the anxiety behind these terrible compulsive needs, even though I can't stop eating/drinking/smoking, no matter how much I try?

Now tap on the points of the sequence: Eyebrow, Side of Eye, Under the Eye, Under the Nose, Chin, Collarbone, Under the Arm, Top of the Head.

WHAT IF I could let go of these so powerful compulsive needs now?
WHAT IF my subconscious was already healing me of this problem?
WHAT IF I no longer need these compulsive needs to hide my emotions?
WHAT IF I could let go of these compulsive needs and finally enjoy my life?
WHAT IF I could feel free from these compulsive needs from now on?
WHAT IF all that tapping had already started to free me from them, deep inside of me?
WHAT IF I could allow myself to feel my emotions without having to eat/drink/smoke too much?
WHAT IF I had definitely neutralized the underlying anxiety (emotions) and could feel completely free now?

Again, you will probably "hear" a few "yes, but" from your belief system about addictions and compulsive needs, and how difficult it is to get rid of them. Identify your most important "yes, but" and introduce them into the following EFT rounds:

Even though I have had these compulsive needs for years, which I don't think will go away, I love and accept myself deeply and completely anyway.
Even though these compulsive needs are just a part of my life and I need to deal with them, I choose to accept and respect myself anyway.
Even though I haven't been able to stop eating/drinking/smoking, despite everything I love and accept myself deeply and completely anyway.

Then tap on the points of the sequence: Eyebrow, Side of Eye, Under the Eye, Under the Nose, Chin, Collarbone, Under the Arm, Top of the Head.

WHAT IF I could let go of these so powerful compulsive needs now?
WHAT IF this tapping liberates me from these compulsive needs?
WHAT IF I no longer need these compulsive needs to calm my emotions?
WHAT IF I could let go of these compulsive needs and finally enjoy my life today?

Part 1: The Basics of Clinical EFT

WHAT IF I could definitely feel free from these compulsive needs?
WHAT IF I free myself from these compulsive needs at the deepest level of my mind and body?
WHAT IF I could feel my emotions and feel safe without having to eat/smoke/drink too much?
WHAT IF I had definitely eliminated my anxiety and felt completely free?

Other "yes, but" may have surfaced again, because of our preconceived ideas about addictions and the "impossibility" of getting rid of them. But WHAT IF...

C. Patricia Carrington's Choices Method

For Patricia Carrington, our unconscious mind has difficulty accepting to say "I am in excellent health" in a meaningful way, when it is not the case. On the other hand, saying "I choose to be in excellent health" seems fairer and offers an opening for change. Preliminary steps:

- Evaluate the intensity of the problem.

- Identify the negative cognition - the negative belief, thought or sensation that the client would like to get rid of.

- Formulate a choice that is the opposite of the negative cognition, like its antidote. For example: "I choose to feel completely comfortable when flying" would be an antidote to "I'm afraid of flying".

- For the Setup, combine the negative statement and the choice: **"Although I am afraid of flying, I choose to feel comfortable there."**

- Then apply the EFT you know by rubbing the Sore spot or tapping on the Karate Chop while repeating the above sentence three times.

1. Treatment steps

Step 1: Make a full round on the negative aspect - "Fear of flying".

Step 2: Make a full round on the choice "I choose to feel comfortable when flying".

Step 3: Alternate the negative and the positive statement, ending on a point with the positive choice.

Reassess the intensity of the problem and repeat the three steps with the choice as described above until the problem disappears.

Over time, you will see that it is not recommended to introduce the positive choice too early. So, sometimes it takes several rounds of tapping on the negative statement, and when the intensity gets low, you install the choice.

2. Important

1. Be specific.

2. Create powerful and attractive choices. Put words in it that induce pleasure, surprise: "surprisingly", "unexpectedly", "I choose to surprise myself by being completely at ease...", "I choose to find a new way of", "I choose to find it easy to...", "I choose to surprise myself by...".

3. Go for the best goal, go for the jackpot, the unconscious is closer to following you than you think.

4. Always establish the choice in a positive wording.

5. Do not choose for others, but only for yourself. You can say: "I choose to feel appreciated by him" rather than: "I choose that he appreciates me."

6. Make choices that are easy to say, to pronounce.

7. As soon as a "yes, but" occurs, tap on what follows that "yes, but" to make you feel 100% comfortable with your choice.

D. Boosting the positive

EFT can be used to amplify positive results. Just tap and say only positive sentences.

They can be formulated simply or according to the "I choose" scheme (see above: the Choices method).

One important rule: first of all, lower enough the negative. Otherwise, the positive statements will be opposed ("yes, but"). They must then be treated before tapping on the positive again.

E. Erasing unconscious oppositions

Part 1: The Basics of Clinical EFT

Each time at the end of a tapping round when the patient reports conscious (explicitly named) or unconscious oppositions (you hear them through what he says even if they are not explicit), it is necessary to erase these oppositions during the next round, as we have seen in the **"What if"** technique.

In English, they are called *tail-enders*, in other words they are often called **"yes, but"**.

They have the following structure (in the case where the introduced phrase was "I am capable of carrying out this project"): "Yes, but I am sure that I will fail at the last moment"; "Yes, but it would be too good for me", etc.

We treat them like a classic target by doing the setup and tapping on the subject:

"Even though I'm sure that at the last moment..." Then tap with the reminder phrase: "I'm going to fail."

If the opposition is minor, it is enough to simply repeat it in the setup as you would do with any Psychological Reversal, then continue tapping on the current topic.

F. Coupling the assertion of the positive statement and the erasing of oppositions

By Sophie Merle

1. First step of the process

Write down what you want. For example, to find the ideal job, to eliminate a harmful habit, to solve a relationship problem, to speak easily in public, to increase your income, etc.

2. Second step of the process

Write this desire down by beginning your sentence with a term that affirms that you already have what you want: I have now, I am now, I feel now, I live since, I do now, I got since then, I have been, I have seen, etc.

3. Third step of the process

Say (if possible, out loud) the sentence confirming the fulfilment of your wish and take note (by writing) of all the contrary thoughts that come to your mind and that constitute the barrier that prevents you from living the desired situation.

4. Fourth step of the process

Now conduct EFT rounds on each of your answers (blockages). If painful memories come back to you, erase their emotional impact immediately. Continue until you can repeat the sentence confirming the fulfilment of your desire in a neutral way, i.e. without further increasing of the frustration, sadness, etc.

5. Fifth step of the process

Now proceed to "the assertion of the positive statement by tapping on the occipital bulge" to give your unconscious mind specific instructions, replacing the limiting beliefs you have just deleted. (The occipital bulge is at the base of the skull, a few centimetres above the neck.)

6. Example of the five steps of the process

1) Express the desire. E.g.: "To live in great financial ease with large, stable and regular income."

2) Affirm the realization of the desire in the present life: "I now live in great financial ease with large, stable and regular income."

3) Fully express your disagreement: "I will never know financial ease... I am doomed to poverty... I would be ashamed to be rich... all my money goes to paying my debts... my life will never be easy...", and so on, without exercising any censorship.

4) Perform EFT: Take each of the negative statements from the previous step and complete as many EFT rounds as necessary to erase their emotional impact. For example:

"I accept myself completely, even though I don't have the ability to earn money." Reminder: "Unable to earn money."

"I accept myself completely, even though I'm ashamed to be rich." Reminder: "This shame of being rich."

"I accept myself completely, even though I feel condemned to always be poor." Reminder: "I am condemned to poverty."

5) Assertion of the positive by tapping on the occipital bulge, which is done by repeating the chosen statements three times in a row. For example:

- I found a very lucrative job.
- Money comes to me from all sides very easily.
- My income is much higher than my expenses.
- I am able to save as much money as I want.
- I always have the money I need to satisfy my desires.
- I benefit from an extraordinary financial renewal, etc.

XXIV.   EFT and the physical sensations

It is essential, before addressing physical problems, to check and advise the client to consult a doctor. It is important to make them aware that this does not replace medical advice or medical treatment.

EFT will focus on the emotional aspects of these physical problems. By the same token, it will help to reduce stress, as a result of which the immune system will be able to function better (see the impact of stress on the sympathetic system, cortisol levels and DHEA).

Studies on pain networks

Pain leaves memory traces in the nerve cells (neurons) and the brain remembers the pain. Removing these traces could help control chronic pain, whether it is caused by arthritic joints, nerve damage or disease such as fibromyalgia.

Terence Coderre of McGill University and his colleagues discovered a mechanism based on this memory that reduces the pain when suppressed.

"Perhaps the best example of a memory trace of pain is the phantom limb," explains the researcher. If a limb is painful before an amputation, the pain may persist after the procedure."

Any pain that lasts for more than a few minutes leaves a trace in the nerve cells. This memory is crucial for the development of chronic pain.

Recent research has shown that *Protein kinase M zeta* plays an essential role in building and maintaining the memory, by strengthening the connections between the nerve cells involved in the pain. The new study shows that this protein is also the key to understanding how the memory of pain is stored in neurons. After painful stimulation, the protein level increases persistently in the central nervous system (which includes the spinal cord and the brain).

By blocking the protein activity in the nerve cells, the hypersensitivity to pain developed by the nerve cells was reversed. Removing this memory trace reduced persistent pain and hypersensitivity.

A. Dealing with physical problems

Part 1: The Basics of Clinical EFT

First you have to specify the nature of the pain or discomfort, as you would do in NLP: size, colour, texture, details of the sensation, location.

Tap by focusing on these aspects: they can be cited successively at each tapping point.

As always, for the following rounds, focus on the remaining aspects.

If you suspect an emotional cause of the physical problem, include it in the setup or reminder phrases.

If this problem evokes emotions, tap on them too.

Tap on all the aspects that appear. You want to be able to observe a movement in the system: decrease or increase in the intensity, that the pain has moved and changes its location, that emotions appear, etc. You continue treating the pain as it progresses by tapping on the successive aspects.

Be careful, be prudent: always check that the patient has made sure that there is no serious physical problem (appendicitis, pain that hides a serious physical symptom), especially when the intensity does not go down to zero. If you suspect a medical problem that needs to be treated, always advise the client to see their doctor to rule out a case of pain that would indicate a serious medical problem. The same applies to the treatment of babies or young children who cannot express themselves: a pain can be an alarm signal; you must make sure that what gives the alarm is taken into account. On a legal level, never promise a cure.

B. The treatment of pain

If you deal with a case of physical problems in particular, here is an example of a treatment plan.

By Caroline Dubois

People usually go to their doctor when they feel pain. This is an excellent thing to do and I strongly recommend it. When doctors have been able to identify what it is about but remain powerless in relation to the pain, then I recommend EFT as an additional work.

1. Intensity, localisation and duration

When I am consulted for pain, I ask questions about the intensity of the pain, its nature and duration. Having all the answers, I can already start working. While working on the description of the pain, in general there are already some changes that appear. If it is not in the intensity, it will be in the nature of the pain. I always ask before tapping about the intensity they have at the moment when they are talking to me and not about the intensity of the pain in general.

2. Description

What is very useful is to describe with precise words what the pain is like. What often happens in this process is that the intensity does not change, but the quality of the pain changes. You will begin with "Even though I have this pain, I accept myself completely and deeply. Even though I have this pain which is like a point that sinks into my shoulder blade... Even though this pain pulses and is boiling", using reminder phrases on all tapping points alternately: "this point that sinks in, this boiling pain that pulses". The person would then tell me that the pain is in the other shoulder, that it tingles and that it's always hot. So, I take the person's words again. "Even though it's in the other shoulder, it tingles and it's always hot..."

During a session with a friend about his knee pain, we did two rounds on the very precise description of the pain. When the second round ended, he said to me, "I feel like crying." Then we took a look at the desire to cry. In his case, I preferred not to ask why he wanted to cry because it seemed to me that we were going too far and too fast into his intimacy. So we just tapped on his desire to cry.

3. Emotions behind the pain and about the pain

After exploring and chasing away the pain by tapping, I then enter the realm of emotions. Depending on the person in front of you, be tactful. Many people do not necessarily associate their pain with their emotions.

Question to ask: if there was an emotion behind this pain, what would it be? Sadness, fear, annoyance, anger, frustration...? You tap according to the answer.

Part 1: The Basics of Clinical EFT

Sometimes, a good place to start is to tap on the emotions related to pain: " If the pain is chronic, describe how you feel about that pain or the part of your body that hurts you." I remember a lady who had chronic tendonitis in her elbow. And she loved playing tennis. We worked hard on her anger against her elbow that stopped her from playing tennis. Her frustration with having this problem. She had not played for two years because of this tendonitis. In addition, tendonitis prevented her from ironing and other activities. We spent two full sessions on the anger against her elbow, against her body, against herself. Then I would make her tap with phrases like "Thank you, my body, for all the matches you've allowed me to play; thank you, my elbow, for always being there; thank you for all the service you've done so far." She wasn't used to thanking her elbow. We solved his tendonitis problem in six sessions. All sessions were not only about the elbow, but also about the poor self-image and the hatred of her thighs. Since then, she has been playing tennis again every week without any problems. But she has learned to be careful with her elbow and to stop playing three times a week but once or twice.

4. Message

I recently worked with a lady who had a carpal tunnel problem. She had previously consulted a homeopath, an osteopath, and an acupuncturist. We worked on the description and then on the emotions. There was anger against the father's cancer not diagnosed early enough, anger against her mother, then sadness. The sadness of the loss of her father, the loss of her freedom as a woman because a child was born at the same time, the pain of her own father.

Every time we tapped, the tears would flow and not stop. This father had remained silent about his pain, and his daughter, a young mother, remained silent about all her pains (sadness, loss of freedom, etc.). All this pain and sadness were contained in her hands. She told me at a subsequent session that when she would listen to the CD of the tapping recorded during the first session on her pain, the tears would still flow. For me, her physical pain is really symbolic of her psychological pain (anger, sadness) and the lack of its expression.

Often, the pains in our body express a message that we are not aware of and with the help of EFT, we can find the meaning - and often the pain disappears.

In all cases, it decreases. For it to decrease completely, all parts of us must agree, which is not always the case. For this lady and her carpal tunnel syndrome, we are starting a whole process.

Here are some useful phrases:

Even though I have this pain... (indicate the place of the pain) and I don't know what causes it, I accept myself. Even though I have this pain for a reason and I don't know what it is... Even though this shoulder pain has information for me, I choose to recognise it and hear it on a certain level, consciously or unconsciously...

Even though this pain has a message for me and a part of me is afraid of this message, I choose to hear it little by little... Even though I have needed this pain in the past, I accept myself completely...

Even though a part of me may still need this pain to express something, I forgive that part of me. I choose to be aware of the message of this pain.

5. The Colour of the Pain technique

This is another way to proceed, especially with people who find it difficult to accept that their pain may come from a negative emotion.

This exercise helps people to get to the cause of their problem by elegantly filtering out conscious beliefs. To help these clients put their conscious minds aside, ask them the following questions. Take note of the answers so you can come back to them later. Then, if needed, tap on all the remaining emotions. Speak in a low voice and ask calmly and slowly, adjusting your breath to theirs. Ask them to close their eyes and move their consciousness to the area where they feel physical discomfort:

    1. If this area had a colour, what would it be?
    2. Is it smaller or bigger than your hand?
    3. Is it moving or is it motionless?
    4. Is it opaque or transparent?
    5. Is it solid or liquid?

Part 1: The Basics of Clinical EFT

6. What noise would it be?
7. If it had a feeling or an emotion... What would it be?...
Just guess... The first thing that comes to mind.
8. And when you think about this emotion, what is it about more specifically?
9. And does that remind you of something?

And then you tap, making sure that each round involves this **"EFT in 3 elements"**:

Each round MUST include the following elements :
One: an emotion - for example, anger, sadness, fear.
Two: a specific reason for the emotion - for example: "He let me down."
Three: intensity on a scale of 0 to 10.

Write down these numbers to see the changes after a round of tapping. Notice the changes. In some cases, and by using "EFT in 3", the client changes his or her emotional aspect by remaining aware of these changes. This makes it possible to check before each tapping round if the specific emotion and reason for the emotion are still the same.

The emotion can still be the same, sadness for example, but the reason could be different. This could be a similar event that happened earlier in life.

After all emotions have been released, ask your client to close their eyes and move their consciousness to this area and repeat questions 1 to 7. Often you will notice changes in colour or movement and you continue with the tapping. Until the pain disappears.

Advantages

What I found quite remarkable was the way a person "prefers" to have physical pain rather than psychological pain. I myself have suffered from colitis for thirty years. For the last seven years they have been rare or even totally absent. But as soon as they stopped for good, I realized that I had been afraid to face my psychic pain. My sadness was well buried in my belly. I didn't want to "know anything" about my emotional pain from the past and the present. In addition, I had serious secondary benefits from my pain. The first one that appeared to me during my therapy at 37 years of age was that if I got sick, I would be better cared for. As children, the only moments of tenderness received from our mother were during illnesses when she had to take care of us.

Even though I have this pain, I accept myself completely and deeply. Even though I have needed these pains in the past... Even though I am afraid to feel my emotions and especially this sadness... Even though this pain has served me in many ways, I am now ready to let it go.

Even though there was an advantage to keeping this pain, I choose to know this consciously and unconsciously. Even though I have this stupid pain, I am open to the possibility of forgiving anyone who has contributed to this pain, including myself...

Reminder phrases:

This pain - It tells me something - The information in my belly - This pain has served me well - I don't know what it is yet - I don't need to know what it is - It's not OK to know what it is - Maybe it's OK to know what it is - All the information in my belly - I'm ready to let go of it – It has done its time - And now I can move on - I don't need to keep it in my body - I agree to face this pain and its message - Everything that is in my belly - Everything it symbolizes - Everything it means - I thank this pain - I honour it and I release it.

Secondary benefits

I also always ask the question about the interest you may have in keeping the pain. Some people look at me, confused, and others answer me directly. Another way to ask the question is: "What does this pain allow you?" And then I get the answers faster.

At the end of the first session with this lady, the pain in her hands rises and I ask her: what is the benefit of this pain? The pain gives her freedom. When she is in pain, she has someone to help her raise her children. So, we worked from the next session on her lack of freedom.

This lack of freedom has been recurrent since the birth of her children. This lack of freedom is concomitant with the pain of losing her father.

She calls me by phone shortly after to tell me that the pain has returned, I ask her what happened. She told me that one of her children was sick during the night and she said to herself "here it comes again" and, from that moment, the pain came back. For me, her "again" was a lack of freedom again with her sick young child. I advised her to tap by herself on this moment when she says to herself "again".

At the beginning of her third session, she told me that sometimes it is easier to have this pain than to face the sadness and lack of freedom. We worked hard on her impatience to heal and the difficulty of accepting her emotions. She was like her father; she kept her emotions silent and "transformed" them into pain. So, the work we began in the third session was almost exclusively dedicated to emotions. I have to see her again soon.

C. Physical sensation associated with a target

When processing a target, it is not uncommon that after a few rounds there is only a physical sensation left, accompanied or not by an emotion.

We then tap, linking the event, the emotion and the sensation in this way:

"This sadness in my throat" - "the rest of this event in my throat", etc.

D. Body Scan

The Body Scan is used at the end of the process to check if the SUD is really at zero.

If your patient tells you "I'm at zero" but you have a doubt or you non-verbally calibrate that something is wrong, have the Body Scan done:

- with the problem in mind;

- the patient scans his/her body from head to toe, slowly moving his/her attention down;

- the scan must be done without any difficulties.

If a part of the body manifests itself, hurts or simply holds the attention, it is a sign that something unconscious is not resolved.

Tap on it as in the article above "Physical sensation associated with a target".

XXV. Treatment algorithms and shortcuts

Gathered by Yves W.

A. Searching for the points by Muscle Testing (MT)

The muscle testing can be used to find the specific points to tap on.

B. Treatment algorithms (TFT - R. Callaghan and F. Gallo - G. Nicosia - D. Gruder)

Source: The Energy Psychology Desktop Companion © 2000, 2002 Dr. David Gruder, pages 54 to 58.

A set of algorithms taken from TFT, TEST® and other tools.

An algorithm can help you speed up a process or find a fast track. That being said, we still advise you to target well if you have to deal with a simple or complex situation. Because, in case of complexity, you will have to check in advance for the presence of other elements necessary for the proper functioning of the therapeutic work (the Self, therapeutic alliance, resources, present triggers, etc.).

1. General notes

You can add a tapping at the beginning of any algorithm to increase its effectiveness:

- Under the Nose (Governing Vessel) for any fear of the future;
- or Chin (Central Vessel) for any guilt/shame,

If you decide to use both points, start with UN, continue with CH and then include the chosen algorithm (Nicosia & Gallo).

Note: all these algorithms are traditionally followed by the nine steps of the 9 Gamut procedure (9G - Gamut) and again by the repetition of the algorithm.

2. The Short version points

Part 1: The Basics of Clinical EFT

KC karate chop / SH side of the hand   SI3 and HT8 - vulnerability, compulsion, obsession, sadness.

NLR neurolymphatic reflex point/sore spot - it is not on a meridian; against reversals.

EB   eyebrows   BL2 - trauma, frustration, fear, impatience, agitation.

SE   side of the eye   GB1 - rage, power, blockage, fury, wrath.

UE   under the eye   ST1 - fear, anxiety, phobia, hunger, deprivation, bitterness, disappointment.

UN   under the nose   GV26 - embarrassment, helplessness, despair.

CH   chin   CV24 - shame, indignity, defect, uselessness.

CB   collarbones   KI27 - fear, indecision, cowardice, deficient libido, self-confidence.

UA   under the arms   SP21 – anxiety for the future, worry, addiction.

UB   under breasts   LV14 - excessive, generalized anger, lack of joy, resentment.

3.   The Long version points

KC karate chop / SH side of hand   SI3 and HT8 - vulnerability, compulsion, obsession, sadness.

RNL neurolymphatic reflex point / Sore Spot - it is not on a meridian; against reversals.

EB   eyebrows   BL2 - trauma, frustration, fear, impatience, agitation.

SE   side of the eye   GB1 - rage, power, blockage, fury, wrath.

UE   under the eye   ST1 - fear, anxiety, phobia, hunger, deprivation, bitterness, disappointment.

UN   under the nose   GV26 - embarrassment, helplessness, despair.

CH	chin	CV24 - shame, indignity, defect, uselessness.
CB	collarbones	KI27 - fear, indecision, cowardice, deficient libido, self-confidence.
UA	under the arms	SP21 – anxiety for the future, worry, addiction.
UB	under breasts	LV14 - excessive, generalized anger, lack of joy, resentment.
Th	thumb	LU11 - grief, sadness, intolerance, contempt, prejudice, disdain.
IF	index finger	LI1 - guilt, relationship/contact problem.
MF	middle finger	PC9 - jealousy, regret, sexual tension, stubbornness.
LF	little finger	HT9 - anger (specific).
9G	Gamut point	TH3 - depression, physical pain, despair, grief, despondency.

4. Algorithms

a. Specific Phobias (TFT)

1. Phobias, except those below: **UN, UE, UA, CB**.
2. Trapped: UN, UE, CB, UA.
3. Spiders, claustrophobia, turbulence in aircraft: **UN, UA, UE, CB**.

b. Anticipated anxiety / Lack of confidence (TFT)

1. Anticipated anxiety: UN, UE, UA, CB.
2. Lack of confidence and assertiveness: UN, UE, UA, CB.

Complex anxiety / panic attack / agoraphobia (TFT)

Notes:

a) The first panic attack often causes post-traumatic stress - hence, you should also treat the original panic attack as a classic trauma.

b) Treat agoraphobia as a set of specific phobias and panic (one at a time).

Part 1: The Basics of Clinical EFT

c) Work on the different triggers one at a time (for example: leaving home, moving away from home, going to the store, etc.).

c. Phobias

UE, UA, EB, CB.
UA, UE, EB, CB.
EB, UA, UE.
UE, EB, UA.
CB, EB, UA.

d. General Anxiety / Addiction (TFT)

Ask for SUD after tapping UA - if SUD increases, remove UA from the algorithm (if it is not a reversal); try variants 3 to 6 if 1 and 2 do not work.

1. UN, CH, UE, UA, CB (pure form).
2. UN, CH, UE, UA, CB, LF, CB (anger and addiction).
3. UN, CH, UE, CB, UE.
4. UN, CH, UE, CB, UA.
5. UN, CH, UE, CB, UA, CB, UE.
6. UN, CH, UE, UA, CB, UA, UE, CB (Greg Nicosia's favourite).
7. UN, CH, CB, UE, UA, CB.

e. Post-traumatic stress disorder / Lovesickness (TFT)

Note:

Grief is treated as a trauma.

"Mega-algorithm": 1) Trauma; 2) Anger/Rage; 3) Guilt; 4) Sexuality.

Frustration = PR + trauma.

1. Pure trauma: UN, CH, EB, CB (traumatic memory - simple trauma).
2. Trauma + Phobia-Panic: UN, CH, EB, UE, UA, CB (the most frequent trauma algorithm - complex trauma).
3. Trauma + Phobia + Anger: UN, CH, EB, UE, UA, CB, LF, CB (complex trauma with anger).
4. Trauma + Phobia + Anger + Guilt: UN, CH, EB, UE, UA, CB, LF, CB, LF, CB (complex trauma with anger and guilt - Greg Nicosia's favourite)
5. Trauma and sexual disruption: MF, UN, UA.

6. Trauma Rape/Fear: MF, UN, UE, CB, UA.
7. Trauma + sexual problems: UE, UE, UA, CB, MF, UN, (UE, CB), UA.

f. Obsession: OCD Obsessive Compulsive Disorder (TFT)

OCDs generally require corrections:

1. Obsession: CB, UE, CB.
2. Another version: UE, CB, UE, CB.
3. Compulsion: KC (SH), UA, CB.
4. Combination: UE, CB, UE, KC, UA, CB.

Since traumas are often present at the roots of OCD, trauma treatment will generally be required.

g. Depression / Loneliness or Grief (TFT)

They will often require correction of a Psychological Reversal.

1. G (40-50 times) (while focusing on your depression), CB (if the SUD does not decrease to at least 2/10 in less than a minute, change to one of the algorithms below).
2. EB, SE, UE, UA, CB, LF, LF (ask for SUD here), CB, G (40-50 times), CB.
3. EB, UE, UA, CB, LF, SE, G (40-50 times), CB.

It may also be necessary to include the treatment of trauma, guilt, anger and rage.

If treatment occurs while the patient is taking antidepressants, it may be useful to re-administer it after stopping the medication.

These algorithms can also be helpful for people who stop taking antidepressants.

h. Frustration / Impatience / Loss of sleep (Gallo)

1. EB, CB.
2. EB, UE, UA, CB, LF, CB.

i. Anger (TFT)

Part 1: The Basics of Clinical EFT

1. LF, CB.
2. At LF point (Little Finger), say 3 times (X = myself, the other, Life, the Universe, God):

"I forgive X, I know that I/she/he can't help it"

OR "I know I am/she is/he is doing my/her/his best"

OR "There is forgiveness in my heart".

j. Rage (TFT)

1. SE, CB.
2. At point SE (side of the eye), make a statement of your anger or "I surrender it all with forgiveness and love".

k. Guilt / Shame / Embarrassment (TFT, Gallo)

1. Guilt: IF, CB (at the Index Finger point say 3 times: "I forgive myself because there is nothing I can do about it.") (TFT).
2. Shame: CH, IF, CB.

(At the IF point say 3 times: "I forgive myself because I / anyone / God can't do anything about it." (TFT).

3. Shame: CH, CB (Gallo).
4. Shame: CH, UA, CB (Gallo).
5. Embarrassment: UN, CB (Gallo).
6. Embarrassment : UN, UA, CB (Gallo).
7. Shame + Embarrassment : UN, CB, CH, CB (Gallo).

l. Sexuality related problems (Gallo)

1. MF, UN, UA.
2. MF, UN, UE, CB, UA.

Frequently associated with trauma - consult algorithms related to sexual trauma.

m. Negativity

Correct any eventual PRs.

n. Self-hatred (Gruder)

EB, UE, UA, CB, LF, SE, G (40-50 times), CB.

idem.

    o. Intolerance, Disloyalty, Arrogance, Prejudice (Gallo)

Th, CB.

    p. Regret, Jealousy, Stubbornness (Gallo)

1. MF, CB.
2. MF, UA, CB

    q. Eating disorders

Their aspects often include trauma, sexuality, images and body distortion (SUD = To what extent, from 0 to 10, do you think you are fat?), addiction and anxiety.

    r. Awkwardness / Feeling uncomfortable

Correct the non-polarisation (Cook's Hook Up).

    s. Physical pain

This probably requires starting with non-polarisation treatments: Cook's Hook Up, Gallo, Energy routine, etc.

Also check the PRs.

If you want to help someone reconnect less intensely to an area of discomfort or pain, you can speed up the treatment by applying the following algorithm:

1. G* (40-50 times) (while focusing on your pain), CB.

EB, SE, UE, UA, CB, LF, CB, IF (ask for SUD again here), CB, G* (40-50 times), CB.

*If you use this algorithm to treat carpal tunnel syndrome, use GV2 or the side of the EB (eyebrow) instead of G.

You may also need to deal with associated traumas: guilt, anger, rage, anxiety, etc.

Part 1: The Basics of Clinical EFT

Alternative treatment: place one hand on the head and the other on the place of greatest suffering; hold for 15 seconds or more (Nicosia).

(Editor's note: This is a pose that recalls the positions of some Reiki treatments and therefore is more of an energy type of work.)

t. Headaches

1. Rub the valley between your thumb and index finger.

u. Toothache

Start by correcting any PRs that may be present.

Hold a finger on the painful tooth during treatment.

1. Clenched teeth (remember not to lock up your jaws), UE*, mouth open, UE*.

Tap the UE point on the side of the face where the toothache is located.

v. Pain reduction

er, 9G, er.

(er = eye roll)

w. Fatigue (Gallo)

1. UE, CB, EB, CB.

x. Insomnia (tired and exhausted)

Correct the over-energetic NDs.

y. Jet lag

If you're going East:

UE, CB or UE, UA, CB

To the West:

EB, CB or UA, UE, CB.

z. Allergies / Blocked nose / Congestion

1. Respiratory allergies: MF, UA, CB (same algorithm as jealousy).
2. Blocked nose/Congestion: UN (40-50 times), CB.

3. Allergies/ Choking: UN (40-50 times), MF, CB, UA, CB.

aa. Nausea / Feeling sick

1. Rub the Wrist point (2.5 cm below the hand on one side and on the other side of the wrist - front and back).

bb. Morning nausea

1. UE, UA, CB.

cc. Visualisation (TFT)

1. UA.
2. UA, EB.

dd. Increase your performance level (PEAK PERFORMANCE)

PRs: UN ("I accept myself totally and completely even though I never excel in...").

Ask the person to imagine doing something they would like to do (or do better) that they have been unable to do (you can also visualize solving a problem that has not been completely dissolved in TFT). Measure the ability to imagine the success from 1 to 10: the treatment will be complete when the person can visualize himself at 9 or 10.

1. UA (30 seconds, while you are imagining), EB (30sec, while you are imagining) > 9G (30sec) > and start again > er (eye roll).
2. UA (30sec, while you are imagining) -> 9G > UA (while you are imagining) (start again & er optional).

C. Integrated algorithms [NICOSIA, GALLO, CRAIG]

1. Accidental treatment when nothing else works

"When you doubt it, bet it!"

1. EB, SE, UE, UN, CH, CB, UA (check the SUD here - if it decreases, do the 9G; if it does not decrease, continue with this and then do the 9G), KC, SH, IF, MF, LF, TH (Head) (Craig - EFT).

2. EB, CB, SE, CB, UE, CB, UN, CB, CH, CB, UA, CB (check the SUD here - if it decreases, do the 9G; if it does not decrease, continue with this and then do the 9G), KC, SH, CB, IF, CB, MF, CB, TH, CB.
3. TH, IF, UE, UA, LF, TH, EB, CB, MF, G, SE, r (Nicosia: chronological biorhythm-based) LF.

2. Persisting problems

1. Check for chemical sensitivities (brain allergies), energy toxins (use Muscle Testing), structural problems (such as brain damage) or subtle forms of ND.
2. Refer the person to someone else if you cannot diagnose and treat them yourself.

UN ("I deeply and completely accept and respect myself even though I haven't had more success at...").

D. Energy emergency care

1. Extreme nervousness, excessive febrility:

EB, UE, UA, CB.

2. In case of a long list of things to do and when you feel overwhelmed by events:

CB, IF, 9G.

3. If you are very concerned about a future situation:

UE, EB, IF.

4. If you are obsessed with a situation (person or situation):

UE, CB, UA.

5. Frustration, strong feelings of lack:

EB, SE, UE, CB.

6. Anger, hatred, rage:

UB, SE, UE, CB, 9G, LF.

7. Feelings of guilt:

LF, IF, Th, CB

8. Emotional rupture - abandonment:

EB, UE, UA, IF, CB, 9G, Th

9. Dramatic memories:

EB, CB, 9G.

You can simply apply a gentle stimulation on a single point. This can help you quickly regain your composure. Try the Gamut point, or Under the Eye point, or the one on the side of the Index Finger. You can also let your intuition work, at your own pace.

10. Stress reduction protocol: "Touching the points and breathing" (Touch and breathe, based on the work of John Diepold Ph. D.)

This method is particularly effective in order to quickly relieve stress and remains very discreet in public.
Touch the EFT points, one after the other, by stimulating each point and pressing it slightly. Then take a deep breath and exhale slowly and just as deeply. Repeat the operation on each of the 14 EFT points.
(Inspired by Sophie Merle in her *Collection of Energy Protocols* that I warmly recommend!)

XXVI. The Palace of Possibilities

The Palace of Possibilities is one of Gary Craig's foundational ideas. The general idea is that we live in a house with many rooms. The problem is that we have become accustomed to only visiting some of these rooms. We no longer even ask ourselves the question of their decoration. It is part of the furniture we are used to. We no longer even look at them, but we think they are necessarily part of our environment, of ourselves, of our inner museum. These writings on our walls become our beliefs. We do not even question them because we are convinced that they are within us, that they are us!

While a little introspection would probably show us that these are thoughts expressed by others, inscriptions heard so often that we have taken their colour, meaning, identification! However, we are not obliged to keep them as they are, without contesting them and examining them in our thoughts and daily lives... A good re-examination criterion could be the strictly factual analysis if these writings push us towards happiness, joy, serenity or rather towards their opposite?

A. The writings on our walls

We live in a Palace of Possibilities.

It is up to us to rediscover it or discover it and let go in order to explore all its parts or build them rather than always make the same journey, sometimes simply by habit, lack of perspective or conditioned by our environment.

B. My consistent thoughts become my reality

If we cultivate the slightest doubt about our abilities, we unintentionally sow seeds that will sooner or later hinder us. It is interesting to spot these kinds of thoughts in order to free ourselves from them and return to the present moment... Reconnecting to our Self - this inner space spontaneously and naturally serene and compassionate - will help us remain emotionally balanced, at peace and connected to that inner happiness that we all possess from before birth.

C. Affirmations are the sleepers

It is clear, that our thoughts create our reality and that they thus become sleepers that can unconsciously influence us, limit us in our personal realisation or, on the contrary, boost us and bring us more or less onto our life path. Practicing meditation in full consciousness can allow us to separate limiting or polluting thoughts from our positive and constructive thoughts of a serene, compassionate, empathic present.

Part 1: The Basics of Clinical EFT

XXVII. The Volcano technique

A technique based on Gestalt: imagine asking your client to sit in front of himself or a person with whom he has a conflict, a relationship difficulty. Then ask him, while tapping on the points one after the other, to allow himself to say out loud and firmly, with all accessible emotions and as powerfully as possible, everything that comes to his mind about the situation and the person he has chosen. Round after round, you should observe that the emotional intensity decreases and that other aspects of the problem appear spontaneously. You will desensitise these aspects one after the other in order to bring the SUD to 0.

XXVIII. The treatment of conflict

A. The Opposites technique or Polarisation technique

Think of a situation that bothers you and balance it with exactly the opposite cognition/belief. For example: I have value vs I suck; I am unable vs I am capable; I will not succeed vs I will succeed.

I remind you to explore the most common Psychological Reversals. By Psychological Reversal, I mean blocking, limiting, self-sabotaging beliefs, all the negative thoughts or unpleasant sensations that arise when I think of a positive or current situation, or simply a memory.

The purpose of this exercise is to become conscious of all those forms of resistance or unconscious opposition that we might have towards the resolution of this inner conflict or feeling about an event, an inner state, a difficult emotion, heavy sensations, etc.

The principle will be to alternate these oppositions, both positive and negative beliefs, round after round, and de-sensitise what is presented in order to free us from them.

This technique can allow us to deblock a treatment where the SUD would not move at all. Be careful about dissociation, which can be a defence mechanism installed by the unconscious mind to avoid being brought into contact with sensitive memories.

B. Carol Look's Conflict Technique

By Carol Look, EFT Master

This technique, proposed by my friend Carol Look, also makes it possible to seize the unconscious resistance by alternating the negative and positive from one point to another, or from one side of the body to the other.

First version

For example, I start with the setup phrase "Even though I have this specific problem, I accept myself... (Karate Chop point).

Corner of the left eyebrow: no.

Corner of the right eyebrow: yes.

Corner of the left eye: no.

Corner of the right eye: yes.

And you continue like that for a few rounds, integrating all the elements that would appear during this round of tapping. You continue to stimulate the points until the SUD is extinguished.

Second version

For example, I start with the setup phrase "Even though I have this specific problem, I accept myself..." (Karate Chop point).

Point on the corner of the left (or right) eyebrow: no.

Point on the corner of the right (or left) eyebrow: yes.

Corner of the left (or right) eye: no.

Point under the right (or left) eye: yes.

And you continue this stimulation for a few rounds until the SUD is extinguished.

PAIN CONTROL

We can also approach the "emotional conflicts".

I remind you that it is also important to ask our unconscious mind to keep only what it needs from our pain to prevent us from further injury or to let us know that we need to keep some of this pain to protect ourselves physically. It is therefore more than important, when addressing physiological aspects or psychosomatic assumptions, that you recommend and check that the client has actually seen a doctor.

The Conflict technique can be added to these other techniques.

Side of the hand: "Even though I don't think I can get rid of this kind of pain, I choose to accept my body as it is, more or less. And sometimes it's a little more or a little less, or the other way around.

Even though I don't expect to free myself from these symptoms, I love and accept myself anyway.

Even though I don't expect this pain to necessarily disappear, I love and accept myself anyway as I am, or not!"

Eyebrows: I can't heal from these symptoms

Corner of the eye: Yes, why not.

Under the eye: I don't deserve to heal from these symptoms.

Under the nose: Yes, I deserve it.

Chin: No, I would not be loyal to my story or family.

Collarbone: I do not expect to recover from these symptoms.

Under the arm: Maybe I could open myself to the possibility of preparing to free myself from it.

Top of the head: I am ready to free myself from these symptoms, or not!

Side of the hand: "Even though this disease is incurable, or probably too advanced, I choose to accept my body anyway and I am a good person anyway.

Even though I'm afraid of being stuck with this pain for life, I love and accept who I am, more or less.
Even though this disease exists in my whole family, I choose to love and accept my body..."

Part 1: The Basics of Clinical EFT

XXIX. EFT and children

A. EFT and children - some tips

1.The environment: the first thing to do is to be in connection with the child.
You must check whether the child has come by their own free will or by the will of their parents. Often the parents will be the ones who initiate the child's presence. This means that depending on their age, you will have to spend time establishing this link, this connection, this therapeutic alliance. You must therefore adapt to the child's vocabulary and especially to their imagination.
Know their favourite heroes, their habits, what they like, what they don't like, what they love and what they are afraid of.
All this will allow you to strengthen this bond and open a dialogue that will lead to the reprocessing of what brings this child into your office.
Think about illustrating the child's story; make them draw it; re-tell it to them, adapt it to them, to their age, fears, imagination, games, parents.

2. Tapping can be done in several ways. The most important thing is that it respects the child's rhythm or what the child likes or prefers.

For example, you can: have the parents/the accompanying person tap on the child; ask the child to tap, rub or touch the points themselves... tap on yourself while they are tapping on themselves. Tap with them on yourself and also tap on any point you have decided with them on yourself in order to show that adults or people they love or who love them are doing the same thing.

3. Is there an ideal time to do EFT?

Personally, I prefer the evening sessions when they are young, or after-school sessions where I would ask them how their day went, what they did or learned, what they liked or didn't like, etc. I add as much tapping as possible and I try to teach them to do it as soon as they feel embarrassed or bored, or when unpleasant sensations or negative emotions/cognitions arise, as well as when they have self-devaluating beliefs.

4. The duration of the EFT sessions will be directly related to the child's age. The younger they are, the shorter the session or slices of sessions will be, and they will probably have to be supplemented by games and emotional education, for example. Whether or not the child has requested the therapy will also make the session more voluntary and natural or more effective. We can't force a child to come, talk, act or anything, but we can, on the other hand, use our own stimulation to try to help them, or move from left to right and right to left of our whole body in order to do bilateral stimulation while tapping on ourselves. We can recognize that it may seem ridiculous to tap on ourselves while having fun ourselves, because this will create or strengthen the link and desensitise the unconscious oppositions.

The bond and the therapeutic alliance are very important with children. Even more than with adults!

5. it is also important to explain to both the child and the parents that what happens in the sessions remains between us and the child, in order to let the child feel free to talk about everything, without any reservations and at their own pace.

Conclusion: the imagination is in power here and remember that "chatting = tapping" (we keep on tapping while talking).

B. EFT and children: the Daily Serenity procedure

The basic idea is simple. Every night, when the children are in bed, the parents can ask them:

"Can you tell me about your good and bad thoughts, as well as the good and bad things that have happened to you today?"

Then, as the child recounts the events (letting them tell both the good and the bad), parents should lightly and lovingly stimulate the EFT points by tapping or even simply by gently caressing them.

Expected results

The experienced practitioner can immediately extract useful information from this practice. Parents, if they play the game with their children, will also benefit from better management of daily life and will be able to better

Part 1: The Basics of Clinical EFT

support their children in all the small life challenges that our children encounter in their evolution and learning path.

Thus, the listening and the simultaneous stimulation of EFT points are likely to solve or, at the very least, alleviate the emotional impact on the child.

Children build their inner world and their representation of it on the basis of what they observe and experience and this museum of beliefs, these maps of interpretation of the world can accompany them for a long time if we do not help them to sort it out.

Some examples of "bad" cognitions that children can unconsciously put in place are: "Good dad told me I was a bad weed"; "My daddy scared me when he yelled at me"; "I was afraid Daddy would hit me when he turned all red; he told me I was just a shitty kid!"; "I saw a bad guy kill people on TV"; "My teacher doesn't think I'm very smart or told me I was stupid"; "She's more beautiful than me"; "The religion teacher said: I have to be nice or I'll go to hell".

All these examples that can populate our children's daily lives could be reduced or even eliminated if we thought about tapping at the end of the day or teaching our sweeties to tap as soon as they realize that something hurts them or makes them sad. Empowering parents to support this can save them years of therapy. This is really a mental hygiene that should be taught to everyone from an early age.

The whole process is also useful at the pre-verbal stage of development of infants. Even if babies are not able to tell you what bothers them, the fact that there is crying, for example, or the discomfort felt by parents indicates that this discomfort must be resolved.

The very fact of being activated shows that EFT can be usefully applied with children to calm or desensitise the triggers.

Should we start with the setup phrase when working with children? - It must be adapted to the children's age and their understanding of what bothers them.

For example: "Even though I have this _____, I am still a good boy or a beautiful princess."

C. Working with children and pain

By Caroline Dubois

When you work with children, it's very simple. And they even prefer it when you use metaphors. Sometimes, in cases of pain, I use basic EFT with a metaphor instead of the pain. I often use metaphors in cases of pain with adults too, because metaphors prevent the conscious mind from getting too involved in what is happening.

I'll tell you this little story. Sacha is a 9-year-old boy who is part of my stepfamily. He had been sick the previous night. He had a small intestinal flu and no fever. His body overflowed from everywhere. The evening after the difficult night, he didn't eat and had a stomach ache and headache. I ask him if I can make some tapping. He answers "if you wish", which sounds as "yes".

So, I stand next to him and ask him how bad his headache is, showing him that the maximum pain is equivalent to my two arms apart and the minimum is when my hands are against each other. He's halfway there for his stomach and a little less for his head. Since I don't think there are emotional causes - but you never know - I decide to play the metaphor. I asked him: "If there were an animal in your stomach, what would it be?" He answered: "A German shepherd." I correct my question because I know he likes dachshunds (he has one). You really have to be very specific with the question. "If that stomach ache were an animal, what would it be?" A lion. "And if that headache were an animal, what would it be?" An elephant. "And what would you like instead?" For the belly, a German shepherd, and for the head, a cat. So, I start tapping on him, because he's lying on the couch, looking a little pale.

Even though there's a lion in my belly, I'm a good boy. Even though I have an elephant in my head, Mom and Dad love me. Even though I have these animals in my body, I'm OK.

And we tapped the whole sequence, as well as the finger and Gamut points, while I repeat "elephant in my head, lion in my belly".

I ask him how he is and he shows me that his hands have come closer for his stomach and head.

We start exactly the same round again. In the end, the hands are still getting closer. The headache is almost gone. I asked him what the lion looks like in his belly. He tells me he looks angry, and the elephant doesn't look that angry. And we continue by including "angry lion in my belly", "not so angry elephant in my head" in the setup phrases and on each point, while making a complete round.

And the two hands were joined at the end of the third round. It took us five minutes and he was smiling again. Thanks to EFT and its effectiveness. He slept very well during the night that followed.

XXX. Seven other therapeutic approaches

A. Narrative Meridian Therapy

Sometimes a problem is too personal to share with someone. This is a good time to stimulate the acupressure points yourself by saying out loud what you are concerned about - you can also do it mentally.

Say a new sentence at each point and continue tapping until you are satisfied with the result.

B. Two-handed tapping

You can tap with one or two hands. John Diamond reports that tapping with both hands simultaneously brings greater determination.

You can also tap bilaterally, especially in case of a short version in order to keep some of the benefits of 9G stimulation (see EMDR). I recommend this kind of tapping to be done as soon as you can.

C. Mental tapping

Use your imagination while thinking about the problem and then do your sequence but touch each meridian point by focusing your attention on it.

D. The body knows

The body knows that every tension, discomfort, etc., indicates a negative emotion and gives you a message and a doorway to reprocess what bothers you. Pay more and more attention to the signs that the Unconscious addresses to you through the body.

E. Touch and breathe

Created by John Diepold: instead of tapping, you gently rub the meridian points and take a slow, deep breath by holding a pose on each meridian point. Repeat this at each step.

This technique is particularly helpful for people suffering from osteoarthritis, arthritis.

Part 1: The Basics of Clinical EFT

F. Daily work

Tap every day to remove any negative emotions (see Children's section).

G. Increase the result by using a short version

Feel free to use a short version or algorithms to amplify your results, and try to identify the emotions present in order to target the acupressure points that are most affected by the problem.

Part 2: Advanced Clinical EFT

This part of the book is a transcription of the courses I created for Therapeutia trainings: "Conceptualisation and Treatment Plan"; "Stabilisation" and "Resources" courses.

My gratitude goes to all the clinicians who have contributed to the complex topic of building an appropriate treatment plan: Francine Shapiro, founder of EMDR - the therapeutic approach that has instructed me the most on this subject. Andrew Leeds and Ludwig Cornil, who have made significant contributions to the protocol structure; Kathie O'Shea, Guy Sautai, Onno Van de Hart and many others have also contributed significantly to my understanding of this subject.

Part 2: Advanced Clinical EFT

I. Introduction

The results of a treatment do not only depend on the applied tool or model and its effectiveness. They also depend on good case conceptualisation and an appropriate treatment plan.

Inappropriate conceptualisation can lead to relative ineffectiveness of the treatment, but also to more or less severe complications.

These can be: a treatment that stagnates or goes in circles, leading to the patient abandoning the therapy; a displacement of symptoms; decompensations following the excessive fragility of the patient, etc.

A. Need for case conceptualisation

The conceptualization of the case establishes the patient's problem, put into perspective in the broader context given by the anamnesis. It allows you to select a specific treatment plan.

You need to identify:

1. If the problem is mainly current and does not require going back to previous periods in the patient's life in order to be treated.

Or

If the current problem has its roots and finds its causes in the past, then work on these causes is needed to solve the current problem.

As we will see in the formation of memory networks, and given the deeply conditioned nature of our brains, all the current difficulties of people in therapy are in fact caused by the conditioning due to their history and mainly by the beliefs that have resulted from it.

However, the need to take the past into account when dealing with present difficulties may be more or less unavoidable.

2. If the person's problem is limited to the specific topic suggested by the patient

Or

If, on the other hand, **the person's problem is the tip of the iceberg or a symptom of a much larger problem.**

For example, the anamnesis may lead to considering the phobia a well-targeted and autonomous disorder if the person does not have another anxiety disorder and has not had a context of insecurity in childhood; the treatment plan will then be that of treating a phobia.

The same phobia, correlated with an anamnesis of generalized anxiety and other anxious traits, childhood maltreatment and many factors of child insecurity, will lead to a case conceptualisation of the "complex trauma" type, where working on basic safety will be the first treatment objective. The phobia protocol will not be used at the beginning of the treatment, and the phobia may disappear as the background treatment progresses, without being specifically worked on.

B. Need for treatment plan

A treatment plan aims to define the steps of the treatment in such a way that it is as effective as possible.

It defines the order of succession of the different steps, the targets to work on, and often the order in which they are processed.

In the example of phobia, it will be more effective to work on the triggering event if it exists, then on the strongest phobic crisis, etc. These are the criteria that, when gathered and organized, constitute the plan for treating phobia.

An inappropriate or non-existent treatment plan can lead to greater or lesser ineffectiveness and treatment that is longer than necessary.

Part 2: Advanced Clinical EFT

II. Prerequisites and preparation

A. Memory Networks

1. Content of Memory Networks

When we experience an event, it is stored in our memory with its different aspects. When we evoke it in our memory, these different aspects may have already evolved, as our memory is not fixed or objective.

These different aspects of the memory in the present are:

- **The perceptions** of the event: **VAKO - Visual, Auditory, Kinaesthetic, Olfactory**. For example: the sound of the car accident, the vision of the front car that crashed into the car in front of it, the feeling of the foot jumping on the brake. Among these visual perceptions, particular importance will be given to the image of the worst moment, because of its particular connection to the emotional impact of the event: it is the visual element of the sensory memory connected to the event.
- At the auditory level, we could also add the category of the **thoughts** (Shapiro, 2001), which refer to memories of things we have said to ourselves, such as: "What a bitch!", "He's going to kill me", "Oh, my God!". Shapiro classifies them separately from beliefs, which refer to ideas that we always have about ourselves. In the case of the accident, it could be: "That's it, I'm going to die."
- At the physical level, there are also the **physical sensations** that primary affects translate into. The latter are generally identified exclusively through their perceived location.
- The memory is also accompanied by the **emotions** that appear in the present moment when it is recalled. These emotions can be the emotions felt at the time of the event, and still present today; they can also be current emotions that were not present at the time. Example: A humiliation as a child gave rise to a sense of shame at the time. Today, when remembering the event, the patient can report a feeling of shame, or a feeling of anger (current but not present at the time).

- **Beliefs** are ideas that the person has about himself, about life or about others in relation to the event. **Particular importance is given to the strongest negative belief about oneself generated by the event. It easily becomes widespread in the person's life and is a powerful trigger for discomfort and disproportionate reactions**

IMG 5

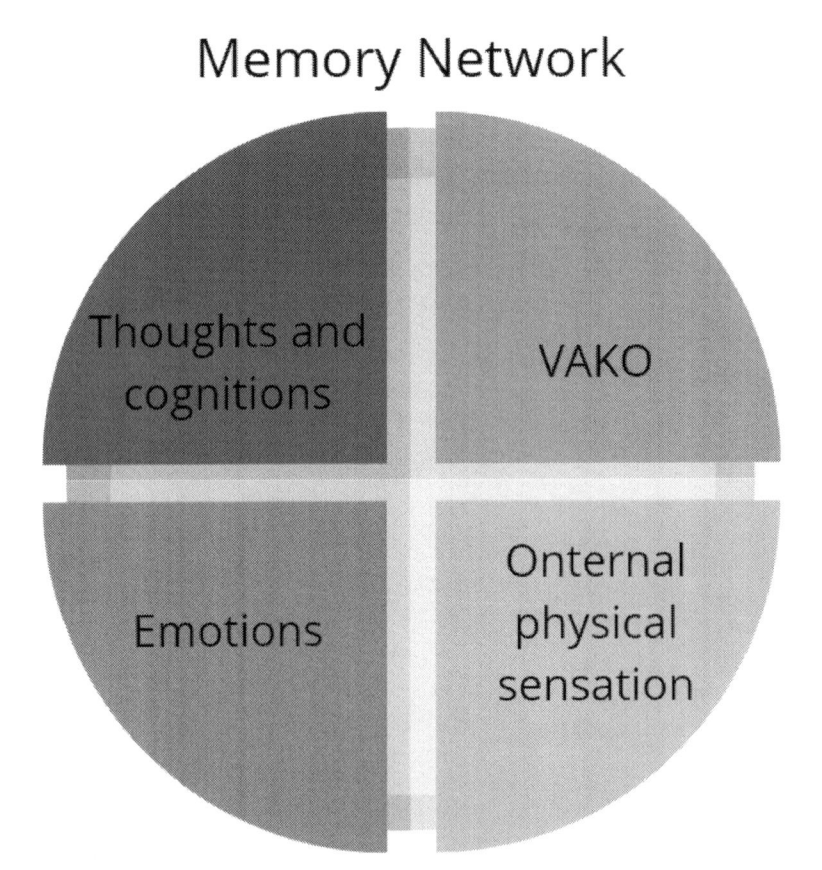

Memory Network

- Thoughts and cognitions
- VAKO
- Emotions
- Onternal physical sensation

2. Hierarchy and connection of the Memory Networks

Memories are collected in the memory storage and connected to each other according to a logic: birds of a feather flock together. Any aspect, even partial or approximate of a memory, can lead to a connection to another memory if they both share it.

Part 2: Advanced Clinical EFT

IMG 6

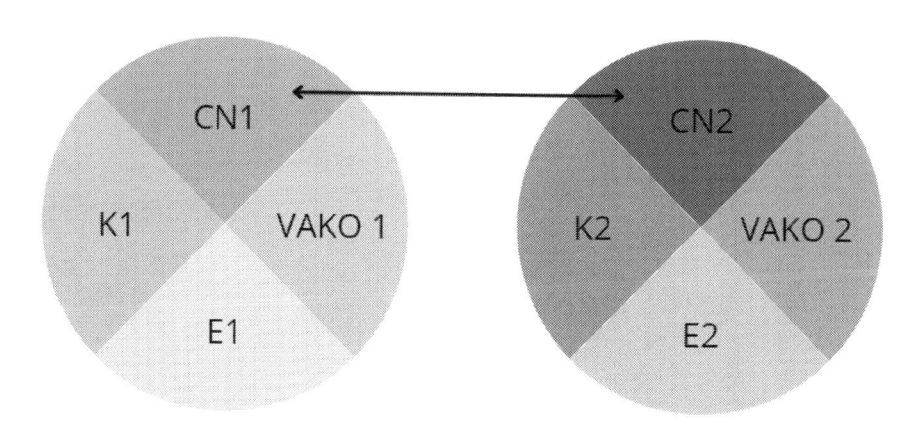

Thus, the different memories form "clusters", networks of memories linked by the same theme or by other common aspects.

Networks are particularly formed on the base of common Emotions (E) or Negative Cognitions (NCs).

For example: all the memories with NC "I am in danger" (in a car accident, when someone yells at me) will join the same network. These events can be activated at the same time in another situation where I feel in danger.

For example: all memories of humiliations; all memories related to a place, etc.

Small networks formed by specific common aspects bind together to form larger networks connected by more general aspects: a small network containing memories of humiliation experiences at school is connected with another small network related to humiliation memories at home, and with that of the professional environment. All this forms the bigger network of memories related to humiliation.

IMG 7

HUMILIATION

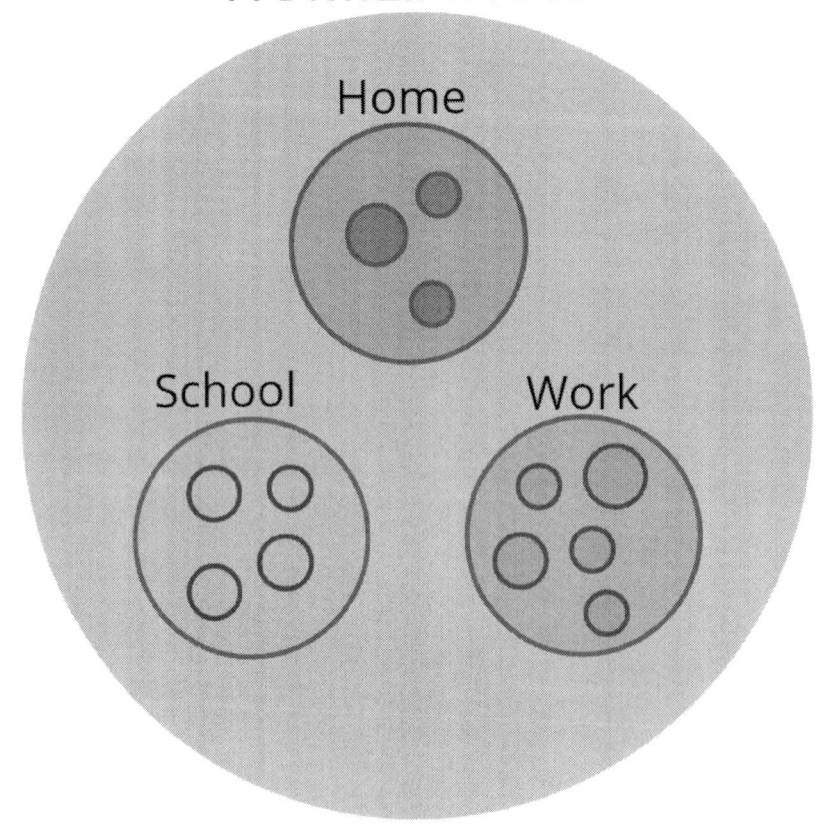

B. The Adaptive Information Processing (AIP) model

1. Principles

This model was proposed by Francine Shapiro, who developed EMDR (1995, 2001).

Francine Shapiro proposed three principles that form the core of the AIP model.

1. There is an intrinsic information processing system that has evolved to allow humans to reorganise their responses to disruptive life

events. This is what allows us, after the first emotional reactions to an event, to calm down and see things with more distance.

In the same way that we have the ability to heal by ourselves when we injure ourselves (cicatrisation, etc.), we also have the ability to recover from our psychological wounds.

AIP is our neurological system for self-healing.

2. A traumatic event or persistent stress during a developmental stage can disrupt the information processing system.
3. It is possible to restore the balance of the adaptive information system through the use of adapted protocols, applied together with methods acting on the limbic brain. This restarts the blocked processing of the information, which can then progress until it reaches an adaptive resolution for the patient.

According to the metaphor of healing a physical injury, while a surgeon can remove blockages to healing, such as a tumour or infection, no surgeon can heal a wound: you must "let nature do its work".

In the same way, when we as therapists do a technical intervention, it is to remove the grain of sand that blocks the machine from our self-healing capacity. We do not have the power to heal someone, but to allow them to be in the conditions where their psyche heals on its own.

2. How it works

In psychologically healthy adults

<u>Negative network:</u> when a psychologically healthy adult is exposed to a stressful event, such as a friend getting angry and suddenly screaming at us, we usually have a first stress reaction made up of agitation, fear, shame or anger. Physiological stress markers such as heart rate, blood pressure and stress hormones suddenly rise, and irrational and impulsive thoughts such as self-criticism arise, as well as the impulse to save ourselves or to attack, or to suffer without saying anything.

All our perceptions, thoughts, sensations, emotions and beliefs constitute the negative information network initiated by the stressful situation: **our system is out of balance.**

<u>Adaptive network</u>: as healthy adults, we also have a good self-esteem and the memory of experiences where we have acted correctly, and where others have respected us. These memories are accompanied by beliefs such as "I usually do things right", "I'm okay", etc.

All the perceptions, thoughts, sensations, emotions and beliefs related to these resource memories constitute the Adaptive information network.

<u>AIP</u>: After talking to friends or ourselves about this, possibly sleeping and dreaming, we come out of our emotional disturbance and learn from it.

Our emotional state returns to balance and our cognitive perspective (our thoughts) becomes adaptive. Instead of thinking "I did something wrong", we realise that "he is a little on the edge at the moment because of his wife's illness; he reacts badly to all the annoyances for the moment"; "I haven't done anything wrong."

Not only do emotions, physiology and thoughts return to normal, but we have also put in place a pattern of recognition so that, if a similar situation comes up again, we can react differently. For example, we can say "I understand that you are going through a difficult time, but I would appreciate it if you could talk to me more calmly."

All our perceptions, thoughts, sensations, emotions and beliefs then return to balance and form an adaptive information network.

Functioning: AIP acts on the memory networks - **it connects the network of negative memories** (the belief that "I did something wrong" and all other aspects of this network) **with the adaptive network** ("I am okay" and all other aspects of this network). By simply connecting the two networks, the negative aspects are erased by the information of the adaptive network, **to form a new network that would be adaptive as well.**

Part 2: Advanced Clinical EFT

IMG 8

STRESS NETWORK ADAPTIVE NETWORK

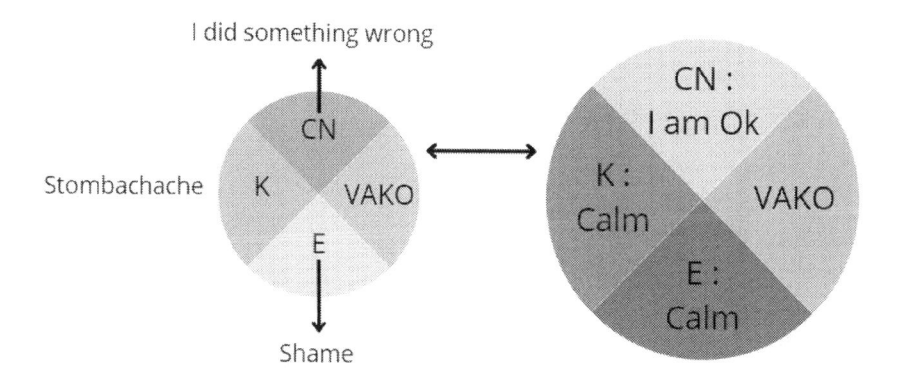

I did something wrong

Stombachache K CN VAKO E

Shame

CN : I am Ok
K : Calm VAKO
E : Calm

3. AIP and the treatment plan

a. How to treat a dysfunctional memory network?

There are several ways to treat a dysfunctional memory network.

Some therapeutic methods do not work well when trying to treat the entire network. On the other hand, they become very effective as soon as the worst or strongest memory of the network is targeted, or better still, the "hot spot" of the **worst** memory. This is the situation with the EFT and REMAP methods of Energy Psychology (for information: EMDR also). In this case, a certain (or total) generalisation is made, achieving the **oil stain effect**, so the rest of the network is also partially (or totally) treated.

Other methods are very successful in directly addressing the **entire network** (a set of memories and events). This is the case with TAT and hypnosis. But they can also, when necessary, focus more on a specific target in the network.

IMG 9

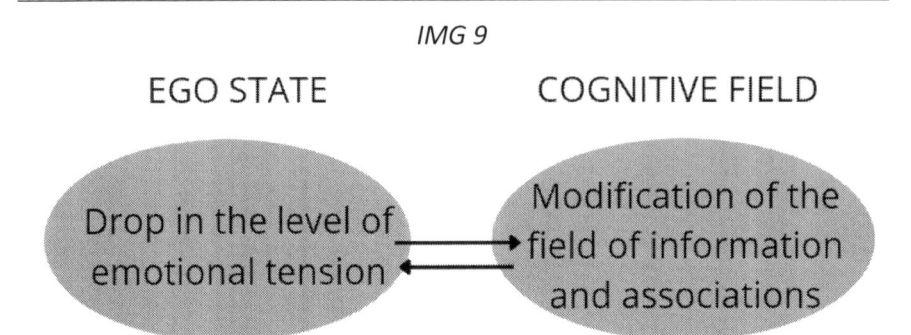

EGO STATE   COGNITIVE FIELD

Drop in the level of emotional tension ⟷ Modification of the field of information and associations

During the treatment, the memory stops being associated with the previous emotional content until finally it relates to an ego state of well-being. The traumatic representation is no longer associated with the same ego state.

b. The chronological logic of the conditioning process

Under conditioning, any current event sharing a common element with a dysfunctional network of the past will trigger the information (sensations, physiological reactions, beliefs, etc.) stored in this network.

As a result, our current response will also be dysfunctional.

This is why **it is important to first address the dysfunctional networks of the past that are reactivated by the current problem.**

Once the dysfunctional network of the past is transformed into an adaptive network, nothing prevents us from being adaptive in the present.

The standard protocol is therefore a protocol that respects the following succession for targets: working consecutively on the past, then the present, and finally the future.

c. AIP action

The Adaptive Information Processing system reacts differently depending on whether the person has enough stability and therefore resources, or not.

(1) AIP's action on the memory networks of a balanced adult

Part 2: Advanced Clinical EFT

- **In a situation that is not too disruptive**

AIP will **automatically** do its job and things will return to normal over time (self-healing): negative networks will be modified, relieved of their emotional load and accompanied by cognitive change (the scenario changes, as well as the associated beliefs).

- **When the situation is too disruptive**

AIP may not be able to do its job. It is then necessary to do an **unblocking intervention** (therapeutic technique) to allow it to continue its action afterwards: remove the grain of sand so that once again the adaptive network can modify the encoding of the negative network through their interaction (see above: Francine Shapiro's principle 3).

(2)   AIP's action in the event of a lack of resources in a specific area

To say that the patient (child or adult) lacks resources means that the adaptive networks that AIP would need – in order to connect them to dysfunctional networks of the same theme - are missing because the person has not had (or observed) enough positive experiences to feed them. Thus, dysfunctional networks cannot dissolve and remain as they are. Therefore, healing cannot occur.

In the case considered here, this phenomenon is limited to an isolated theme. The reactivation of AIP will then require additional procedures such as the installation of **resources** on this theme.

For example, if the person has not had enough positive experiences in terms of their intellectual abilities, each time the person lives or will live an experience in this field, they strengthen their negative network. For AIP to be reactivated, it is necessary to strengthen the positive network, by setting up resources in the theme of intellectual capacities, which then become positive experiences in the person's life.

These resources will **strengthen the adaptive network**: they make it grow, amplifying its positive feelings, and give it the power to influence the negative network when they are connected.

(3) AIP's action in the event of a lack of resources in a broad area of the identity construction.

When a person has not been able to have enough positive experiences or has had too many (or too strong) negative experiences in important areas of identity construction - such as security and self-esteem - then they do not have sufficiently strong adaptive networks. **This is referred to as a patient with complex trauma.**

In this case, the very functioning of AIP may not be blocked, but may be affected from a developmental point of view: **it may not have been able to establish itself sufficiently.**

This will require not only the establishment of **resources** (creating or strengthening adaptive networks), but also **stabilisation** and the use of a **reverse protocol** (future/present/past).

Indeed, since AIP does not function normally, and the infantile parts are provided with so few resources, it may be too destabilising to work on the past as a priority.

It is therefore necessary to stabilize the patient, give him/her resources and work first on lighter targets (see the "Complex traumas" section).

C. Reminder of the measurement scales

1/ The SUD

SUD = Subjective Units of Disturbance.
It is a scale measuring the negative disturbance between 0 and 10.
0 = no disturbance (neutral or positive).
10 = the strongest disturbance imaginable for this event.

2/ The VOC

VOC: Validity of Cognition.
It is a scale measuring how much, between 0 and 10, a belief (positive or negative) resonates as true.
0 = completely false.
10 = absolutely true.

D. The stabilisation

Stabilisation is in itself a very important part of the treatment, not only for severely traumatised patients. This is why stabilisation is the subject of a separate course in the therapist training. As the name suggests, it is about helping the patient to be more "stable", as opposed to being "destabilised " in a momentary or lasting way by his or her negative experiences. The more the patient develops neural networks associated with positive experiences or resources, the more easily his psyche will be able to "heal" from the traces of painful events (cicatrisation). Although I have been trained for years in trauma through EMDR, I have only fully recognised the importance of stabilisation gradually over the years, through the growing confrontation with patients for whom targeting the negative was not enough. Due to their positive and inspiring effect, the stabilisation and the installation of resources are among the patients' favourite moments, and often also the therapist's as well! If this is not part of your approach yet, I really invite you to start practicing these methods which are wonderful companions for EFT.

1. The Window of Tolerance

The Window of Tolerance is the zone in which the patient must be located in order to be treated. He must neither be overwhelmed by his emotions (abreaction, too much emotional activation), nor cut off from his emotions (dissociation, not enough contact with emotions, vegetative reflex response).

Let us represent the patient's emotional excitement about a stressful event (or his memory during a therapy session) as an electroencephalogram-like pattern between two horizontal lines. The bottom line is the minimum level of excitement for the patient to be able to integrate the treatment. If he drops below this line, he's in hypo-excitation. The top line is the maximum excitement line so that the patient's limbic brain is available to treat emotions.

We say that we get out of the patient's window of tolerance if his emotional arousal is too strong (hyper-excitation, emotional overload) or too weak (hypo-excitation, numbness, drowsiness). In this case, integrative cognitive capacity, i.e. the ability to deal with memory in an adaptive and constructive way, is replaced by a reflex response where treatment is not possible.

When treating patients with a heavy history, or with whom we approach a major trauma, it is not uncommon for the patient to have a tendency to fall asleep "just as" we approach the sensitive emotional zone (hypo-activation). And it is even more common that when severely traumatised patients (victims of abuse, for example) connect with the memory of the abuse, they cannot control their emotions. They are then overwhelmed by emotion and the priority becomes to relieve them of enough distress so that they can again be accessible to therapeutic treatment. This is called " stabilising " them.

It is only when the patient is within the window of tolerance that the therapy can work, regardless of the method used. It is therefore essential to know how to bring the patient back to this area, using the techniques described below.

Stabilisation is preventive (before working on destabilising targets) or curative (when the patient is destabilised by a target).

When to stabilise the patient?

- before starting curative treatment of targets for all patients, as a preventive measure;
- before starting the session if the patient is not stable (very disturbed before even starting
  to work) or if a target seems very heavy;
- during the session if the patient activates too much (or is in hypo-activation);
- at the end of the session if the patient is still activated.

2. The different stabilisation tools

The **Safe Place, the Safe box**, the **"Container-Basic State" couple** and the **CIPOS** are psychotherapeutic techniques used in trauma care, where it is crucial to help patients cope with overwhelming emotions.

The **Safe Place** and **the Safe box** are used **after the incomplete treatment** of a target to soothe patients at the end of the session if the SUD has not decreased sufficiently. These techniques allow the patient to return to a state of calmness sufficient to return home and avoid "rebound" effects between two sessions.

The **Container** and the **Basic State** are intended to teach the brain to leave various concerns aside, so that it can feel safe and relaxed when it is safe, like in the therapist's office. These are basic techniques to allow the nervous system to calm down in a sustainable and daily way, and especially during a session.

The Container generally makes it possible to "set aside" disruptions or to soothe the parts that arise and prevent the proper progress of the therapeutic task. Indeed, for patients with complex traumas, there is frequently some "interference", disturbances or resistance, given the number of targets or parts of the Self, connected to a given subject.

Having a tool to manage these interferences makes it possible to complete the work on the target designated by the treatment plan rather than getting lost in the labyrinth of the interferences that arise. The Container and the Basic State are therefore valuable tools for the therapist who accompanies patients with a heavy history.

The **4-point Quick REMAP® emergency procedure** is used to ease the nervous system in the event of an abreaction. It can be used without prior preparation, especially if the therapist had not anticipated the occurrence of the abreaction.

The pendulation or **CIPOS** is a tool derived from traumatology. It leads the patient in and out of the reminiscence of the trauma in a matter of seconds. This gives the patient the feeling of being able to control traumatic emotions, which is extremely relieving for patients who have to deal with very painful memories in which they are afraid of being "swept away".

Resources are also considered as stabilisation technique, since they allow the patient to approach destabilising targets without being overwhelmed by them. They consist of strengthening positive neural networks associated with a particular theme before addressing targets related to that theme. Through this preliminary work of the positive aspects, the negative experience of the targets is considerably reduced even before the therapist approaches them.

N.B. You will find videos illustrating these methods, as well as other techniques, on the IEPRA website: https://www.iepra.com/, "e-learning" tab (for more information on the available videos: info@iepra.com).

Important: When a session is difficult, always keep an eye on the time and **keep 5 to 10 minutes for stabilisation** (Safe box and/or Safe Place, Container, the first 4 points of the REMAP® points).

3. The Safe Place

In order to be used, this technique must be done before treating a difficult target, and if the patient has a heavy history, even before starting any work on the negative material (to be determined via the anamnesis).

a. Establishing the Safe Place

1. Ask the patient to choose and mentally evoke a place associated with an atmosphere of peace, well-being, serenity and security.

> *"I would like you to imagine a place where you feel good, a place where the atmosphere is peaceful, a place that evokes well-being, serenity and security. It may be a place you have been to, such as a vacation spot, or a familiar place - some people choose their bathroom or their garden. It can also be a totally imaginary place, but one in which you would like to be."*

2. Ask the patient to specify in **all sensory modalities** what he likes and feels in this place: visual, auditory, kinaesthetic aspects.

3. Then ask him **to imagine himself** there, focusing on his breathing and closing his eyes to relax. Meanwhile, we are talking to him about all the sensory elements he has described to us, to associate him with his sensations.

> *E.g.: "Imagine that you are really on this beach. You can feel the wind on your face, the warmth of the sun. You can hear the sound of the waves, and the children playing further away. You can feel the sand under your feet. And you are standing there doing nothing*

special, thinking about nothing special, just enjoying the atmosphere of peace and security of this place."

4. For more effect, and after asking the patient's permission, you can do **alternating** and **very slow** tapping at the same time (about one tap every two seconds) on the outside of the knees (point GB34 - EMDR technique using REMAP® points). If you do not know the point GB34, simply gently tap on the outside of the patient's knee with the flat of your hand, pushing it slightly towards the other knee, then alternate (tap the other knee with your other hand, pushing it towards the first knee), thus producing a "pendulum" movement. This can be done twice for greater efficiency.

5. You can also associate an **anchor word**: it can be the place (for example: Beach) or the pleasant feeling (for example: Relaxation).

6. Take notes of all the information given to you by the patient (sensory data, description of the place in the form of keywords, etc.) so that you can easily immerse him in it when you need it (see below).

N.B. You will find a free video demonstrating the creation of the Safe Place on Iepra website: https://www.iepra.com/, "e-learning" tab.

Notes:

- To avoid possible subsequent negative activations: neither another person nor a pet is generally accepted in this place.

- If the patient finds a real place where there is automatically another person: "Imagine that person going away to do something else... and then you are alone..."

- We can include animals, symbols, etc.

- This place can be modified over time.

- This place can be strengthened: tell the person to think about it when he is experiencing a time when he feels good, safe.

b. Use at the end of the session

After a difficult session, if the SUD is high (and/if the patient wishes), we propose to put things in the Safe box if necessary, then to go back to the Safe Place again, by closing the eyes.

To help the patient connect to it, **it is essential to talk to him again about the sensory elements** (see above), in order to connect him well to the Safe Place, because it is necessary to divert him from the negative sensations of the traumatic target.

c. *Example of the creation of a Safe Place*

Transcript of a session performed by Brigitte Hansoul on a student during the therapist training.

BRIGITTE: If you think of a place where you feel safe, a place that is soothing, relaxing, of which place do you think?

STUDENT: A house in Tuscany, on a high place in the hills.

B: What do you like about this place, what do you like seeing? (Visual)

S: It's isolated, there's a great view in the distance and there's a very beautiful evening light, there are crickets (Auditory), the smell of lemon (Olfactory), and I also have a swimming pool in front of it; then the kitchen is something very important, it's well furnished and it looks upon the pool, you can see in the far distance. (Visual)

B: If you have to choose the place in this house where you will feel really good, it is in the kitchen, where you can see the pool and in the far distance? (The therapists must be able to put themselves in the patient's place.)

S: Yes, it is the most important place.

B: You told me about the crickets, is there anything else you like hearing? (Auditory)

S: The general atmosphere, the crickets, the wind, the windows are open, there is some heat, it is soothing. (Kinaesthetic.)

B: You mention the heat, the kinaesthetic, what can you feel in your body, how do you feel in this place?

S: I'm standing, I'm doing many things...

B: Okay, you go about your business in the kitchen....

S: That's right.

Part 2: Advanced Clinical EFT

B: Okay, so if you close your eyes, put yourself in this kitchen and see the open view, the pool, there's the sound of crickets, the wind, the smell of lemon, what do you feel in your body, how do you feel your body is reacting to the atmosphere of this place? (Repeat all sensory elements)

S: I feel it's very soothing... the wind comes in and out through the windows, it's a warm wind, there are the crickets and there are also smells: rosemary, basil, lemon....

B: In your body, when you're there like that in this place, how do you know that your body feels good, that it is good? Do you feel more relaxed? How do you know that you feel good?

S: Just like that, I can breathe, relax.

B (tapping): So you do nothing but that, just stay in connection with this place, and I'm going to do a little tapping on your knees, while you stay connected to this view of the pool, this clear view, you're in the kitchen, with the view, the light, these smells, the lemon, the rosemary, the basil, the wind, the heat... and you feel that you can relax...

B (without tapping): And this place, if I have to tell you about it next time, how would you call it, what word could indicate this place?

For example: Tuscany, cooking, which word would you choose?

S: It is still the house in Tuscany, but I would say more precisely...

B: A word that is associated with this place for you, with the sensations you have there... it can also be a word about how you feel...

S: Breathing and relaxing...

B: The word most associated with this place for you?

S: "Breathing".

B (tapping): We're going to do the same thing again, close your eyes... You're there in the kitchen, you're connected to what you see, the pool, the view in the distance, you can smell the wind, the smells... (repeat all the sensory elements) and you occasionally repeat the word "breathing" inside your head...

When you want to connect to this place, you think about what you can see, hear, feel, sense and say the word to yourself.

4. The Safe Box

Ideally, you should explain it to the patient before treating overly strong targets, but it can also be used urgently (without preparation) after a difficult session.

<u>Creation at the beginning of the work</u>: build the mental image of the Safe box with the patient, preferably before starting any therapeutic work.

<u>Use at the end of the session</u>: put the remaining disturbing issues in the Safe box. Then, connect the patient to his or her Safe Place to allow him or her to leave the session in a stable and soothed emotional state.

Construct the mental image of the Safe box with the patient, for example, as follows:

"Close your eyes and imagine a solid Safe box. Take a good look at it and see its size, colour and thickness of the walls. Now look at the mechanism for opening and closing the door: do you need a key, is it a code or something else? Operate the mechanism, open the door. Now, put all your negative feelings, all the difficult memories, all the things that are bothering you and that you want to get rid of by the next session, put all that in the box. Your mind can do this as it pleases: in the form of symbols, images, photos... Make sure you have put everything that weighed you in the box. Now close the door and lock it with the key or code. Look at the box, everything's locked in there now. If you want, you can put this box somewhere, or leave it there. You can bury it, put it away, or send it to orbit around the Earth; whatever you want. Let me know when it's done."

After that, you can eventually connect the patient to his or her Safe Place.

During the next session, it is not necessary to open the Safe box. We simply take the target indicated by the sequence of the treatment plan and tell the patient: now we will go back to....

N.B. You will find a free video demonstrating the creation of the Safe box, as well as other methods, on IEPRA website: https://www.iepra.com/, "e-learning" tab (for more information on the videos available: *info@iepra.com*).

5. The Container-Basic State couple

Based on the work of Kathie O'Shea ("Reconstruction of Foundations, Reconnection to the Self" - EMDR Conference, Istanbul 2006)

Thanks to Gaetana Vastamente, past Director of Therapeutia's Therapist Training Cycle, for her review and reorganisation of the notes in this part of the course.

a. General information

The "Container-Basic State" is intended to re-educate the brain to leave various concerns aside, so that it can feel safe and relaxed when it is safe. It is a basic technique to allow the nervous system to calm down in a sustainable and daily way, as well as when necessary during a session. The Container generally makes it possible to "set aside" disruptions or to soothe the parts that arise and prevent the smooth running of the ongoing therapeutic work.

It could look like the Safe box since we also "put things in" it, but it's different, because we put not only what's active at the end of the session but everything that still disrupts the psyche, all the origins, all the imprints of it, in order to connect to the Basic State (identical to the state of the foetus when it's not disrupted by the outside world). We put in the container ALL that is to be worked on, everything that has always been active.

It is an extraordinarily useful tool for patients with a heavy history or suffering from the so called complex traumas.

The "Parts of the Self" correspond to neural networks presenting a certain pattern of reactions, attitudes, beliefs, memories, events; it is a kind of "sub-personality" (which is not pathological) which has a structural stability, even if it appears (is activated) only intermittently, sometimes without the knowledge of the consciousness.

For example, the patient's feeling of "This will never work. I'll never feel well. It will not work on me", if it corresponds to a recurring pattern, can be related to "a part" of him/her. Actually, at that moment, a particular neural network is activated in the brain. This network is similarly activated in the situations that trigger it. It is possible to help the patient "slip" into the Container everything that has nourished the emotional or cognitive state of this part, so that the patient can connect to the Basic State.

Reminder

The Container is used:

- as a background technique to allow the nervous system to soothe itself in a sustainable and daily way, providing the patient with a tool that he can use himself when he needs it;
- when necessary during a session, to put aside disruptions or calm the parts that arise and prevent the session from running smoothly;
- at the end of a session, if the patient is still too active;
- as a therapist (after having created it for yourself with a colleague, or during the training of your students), when you feel activated during the session, or between two patients.

To install the "Container-Basic State", the procedure consists of:

- **installing the Container, and then**
- **installing the Basic State, and finally**
- **consolidating the Container-Basic State assembly.**

b. The Container

(1) Installation

Use the following scripts to explain to your patient what the Container is for:

The Computer metaphor:

"When our brains are stressed, our worries are like so many open pop-up windows on our computer desktop. All these worries or imprints of past events are active, and they clutter our minds, preventing us from being available in the present moment for what we want to devote ourselves to. Using the Container is like running a program that automatically closes all pop-ups, leaving the desktop free and clear. No need to look at what the pop-ups contain or to know how the program works..."

Part 2: Advanced Clinical EFT

What the brain does:

*"Your right brain is used to putting things aside easily and naturally, especially when you move on to an activity, forgetting the previous one. It is not your left brain, the analytical, voluntary one, that operates this. It is your right brain, your unconscious, that does it <u>without you having to do anything</u>. When you use an antivirus program, you just click on "go" **and you don't have to look for which files to clean or make an effort to clean them**. Similarly, to close pop-ups, you don't need to ask yourself which ones, just intend to launch the program. That is, by simply putting your attention on your Container and effortlessly sliding in everything that gets in your way, you instruct the anti-pop-up program to clear your desk."*

Trust the amygdala:

"Sometimes we stay on guard, even if we are safe. Our amygdala is on duty 24 hours a day, whether we are asleep or awake, looking at all aspects of our environment inside and outside. It can respond in half a millisecond; thus, we have no need to be consciously vigilant. Staying alert exhausts us and prevents us from being able to respond to danger when it exists. Our amygdala protects us effectively and unconsciously. Our conscious vigilance is very ineffective compared to that of our amygdala. We will learn to put aside conscious vigilance to let our amygdala be vigilant for us.

You will teach your brain to let go of conscious vigilance and trust your amygdala again. This way, <u>you can feel safe when you are safe</u>. Your amygdala will notify you immediately if there is any danger. To feel safe when you are safe, you need to close the pop-ups that say "danger", which are no longer relevant now that you are safe. So, all you have to do is let everything that needs to be treated (memories that are just memories and not dangers of the here and now) slip into the Container."

Define the Container (Katie O'Shea):

"We know there are many things that need to be emotionally soothed. For that, we need a way to put them aside, until we can deal with them piece by piece. Our right hemisphere stores experiences, knowledge and information until we can give them all the attention and learn all we need to learn from them. We can help our right hemisphere to put aside the

things we are not working on, by using the mental image of a container (or place) where we can put them.

What comes to you mind when you think of a container where you can put aside everything that needs to be soothed until you have the opportunity to give it your full attention? It can be an image in your mind or the memory of a container you know. This container must be solid, safe, large enough to contain anything disturbing or upsetting and it must close tightly.

(Pause)

What is your container?"

Take the time to make it perfect for the person; let the person modify it until he/she is satisfied.

Take note of what the container is for your patient so that you can connect him/her more easily when necessary.

Remarks

    1. The Container should not be something that people frequently see in their daily lives, otherwise it could function as a trigger.

If, despite everything, the patient wants to choose an object that really exists, tell him that it is not really this object that he takes, that it looks the same, but it's another one... so that he is not activated when seeing the real object.

    2. The Container must have a door or a lock, a cap or other means of holding the contents inside.

    3. Preferably not a garbage bin, because it is a matter of putting aside what will be worked on later and not of "throwing away".

Let it slip into the Container:

Guide the patient with the following text. Note that it is a matter of "letting it slip" into the Container and not "putting it in" because the Container is governed by the Unconscious, it is "passive", it is not "doing anything".

"Now, put your attention on your (Container) and let everything that still needs to be worked on slip into it, whatever those things are and whatever their shape is. Maybe you are aware of some of the things you put in it, but

Part 2: Advanced Clinical EFT

there may also be things you don't know. In fact, you don't need to know what goes in there. Let all these things slip into the container... knowing that they will be available later, when you are ready to manage them effectively... Let them slip... Don't try anything. It's just like watching a channel on TV, a special channel that "contains" things. Just watch, simply and effortlessly. Your brain knows how to do it, let it do what it can do on its own. Take all the time you need... Tell me when everything is there, and if everything went well." (Wait until the person indicates that everything is in the container.)

If all goes well, go to the Basic State.

(2) In case of blockages during the installation

A. If the patient reports a particular difficulty

"Put your attention on your Container and let all the memories, all the imprints, everything that has led to (this problem) slip into it."

Here is an example.

Patient: It's not okay. Every time I put everything in the Container, it makes me anxious.

Therapist: Your brain is so used to the stress that it stresses out when it doesn't feel stressed. That's normal. Put your attention on your (Container) and imagine that everything that has led to your brain being stressed all the time, all the events, all the imprints and traces of it, everything slips into the Container.

B. If an urgent item shows up and refuses to go in the Container

"Something important is really ready to be worked on. We will take care of it, but the first thing is to be well prepared to do it. I suggest that you let it slide temporarily into the container while you make room on the desk, while your brain can calm down and be in the ideal state to treat this. Be sure that we will process this thing as soon as you are ready and we decide to do it. Is that all right for you?"

We can also set up an "appointment" to accompany what is blocking: "Be sure that we will work well on this. We can do it next time. Would it be okay for you to do it next time, and today we finish learning how to use the Container?"

C. If you notice that the blockage is due to the appearance of a part of the Self:

Take care of this part: be reassuring.

You can use the Container method: identify (for yourself and the patient) the part of the Self, its need, its fears.

Then say: "Put your attention on your Container and let all the events, all the imprints, everything that has led to this part feeling (...), being afraid that (...) and needing (...) slip into it. You don't need to know them."

Let's look at a new example.

Patient: I'm not going to make it, I feel bad, I tell myself I'm not doing the right thing.

Therapist: There is this part of you that worries and feels anxious because it is afraid that you will not succeed and that it is your fault, because you are not doing the right thing (identification of the part). This part of you has certainly experienced things that make it fear that. Put your attention on your Container and let all the memories, all the imprints, everything that has led to this part of you fearing that you won't make it and that it's your fault, slip into it.

Remarks
1. It is also possible to offer the patient's part a personalised Safe Place and ask her if she agrees to rest there, while the therapist and the patient install the Container - Basic State so that the patient can find the peace and strength necessary to take care of her.
2. You can also do a TAT or EFT surrogate session for her, where the therapist and the other parts of the patient's Self do the TAT for that part. See EFT and TAT courses from the therapist training.

D. If the blockages persist:

"Imagine what it would be like if this problem (name it) was solved."

Part 2: Advanced Clinical EFT

Example: If the person has a physical sensation in his chest that does not leave: "Imagine what it would be like if that sensation had disappeared and you felt your chest free and clear."

Example: if a part is triggered and the patient cannot continue:

"Imagine that it's solved, that the part isn't triggered anymore, and put everything in the Container..."

(3) The Basic State

A. Installation

When the patient confirms that everything is in the Container, he does not feel the Basic State yet. We have to get him there.

1. "Your body and mind already know what to do, let's trust them. Just note, simply and effortlessly, with curiosity, <u>what your body feels</u>. I will do some left/right stimulation to speed up the process and we will just see what happens. Can I do the tapping on the side of your knees? Just observe what happens to your physical sensations."

2. Continue tapping (to the rhythm of a slow heartbeat) until the person reaches a state of relaxed consciousness, the state in which you find yourself when there is no danger.

3. "As you let your attention focus on how you feel now, what is or are the words that come to your mind? I would like you to have a way to quickly bring back this feeling you have now, by associating this/these words with it... I continue tapping. Just think of that/those words."

4. Tap for 30 seconds, then ask:

"Are this/these words still the same or have they changed?"

5. If they have changed, continue until the word(s) and the state have stabilised.

6. When the word(s) no longer change, and the physical sensations are stable, ask the patient to mentally repeat the word(s) while continuing with the bilateral tapping.

7. Give your patient instructions for the daily practice of the Container-Basic State (see below).

B. If it blocks and the patient can't connect to the Basic State:

A. If some distress arises: "Let it slip into your Container for now. We will come back to this later."

B. If the patient still cannot access a relaxed state: it may be a dissociative state (a part of the Self). Proceed as with the Container.

(4) *Consolidate the Container-Basic State assembly*

To consolidate the assembly and thus completely install the Container-Basic State, you must check that the assembly no longer has any blockages.

- "Put your attention on your Container (name specifically what this container is), and let everything that activates you, everything that clutters you, everything that causes it and all the imprints of it, let all of that slip into your Container (name it specifically) and while you do that, at the rhythm of your breathing, repeat mentally your Basic State word (name specifically the word chosen by the patient when the Basic State was set up) again... and again... until you can feel the sensations you had when we set up the Basic State."
- Check that nothing is blocking anymore.
- If something is blocking: let it slip into the Container and start again.

If nothing is blocking, give daily practice instructions.

Note: Installing a Container can take from a few minutes to several sessions in the rare cases where the person is hyper-vigilant and several blockages occur. Stay consistent, trust yourself, stay centred (use your own Container if part of you is activated). The more difficult it is to install the Container, the more likely it is that this patient needs it.

Indeed, if the patient cannot manage to install his Container at this stage of his personal development, it is the sign of a zone of instability/insecurity which requires a particular attention from the therapist in regards to its stabilisation. Set up a Safe Place and ask the patient to reinforce it (use it outside of sessions) as often as possible. And when he is more secure, try again to install the Container.

(5) *Instructions for the daily practice of the Container-Basic State*

Give your patient the following instructions:

Part 2: Advanced Clinical EFT

"Your amygdale can be unconsciously vigilant for you, 24 hours a day. You no longer need to be consciously vigilant.

It takes about two weeks of practice for your body and brain to get out of the habit of being in a constantly vigilant mode and to develop a healthy, natural and relaxed mode.

I ask you to practice the Container-Basic State during these fifteen days (or until the next session). You do this simply by putting your attention on your (Container) and letting everything that... slip in, while telling yourself (the Basic State word). You don't need the tapping. If your Container changes or evolves, that's fine.

Do it when you get up, go to bed, and when you change activities. A maximum of times during the day.

At first, train yourself without being activated, you can also do it simply when you are calm for a moment to feel even better.

Then, after a few days, or even faster if you have done it as many times as possible in the previous days, you can do it when you are disturbed by something light.

Be sure to do this only when you are objectively safe (no real danger in the room), even if you do not feel subjectively safe.

After this installation period, you can use the Container-Basic State when you are overwhelmed by emotion or you fear being overwhelmed, after a nightmare, during a period of insomnia, when you have ruminating thoughts, irresistible cravings... and we can use it together in the sessions whenever it would be useful for you."

(6) Follow up

At the next session, check if the patient has practiced his Container and ask how it went for him.

If he has not done it, look together for what prevented him from doing so; unblock that and ask the patient again to do it for the next session.

Sometimes it may be useful to give some details about the daily practice instructions and/or to redo part of the installation together.

Often, the blockage comes from the fact that the patient does not "let it slip" but tries to voluntarily "put things" into the Container. Make sure to check with him that he doesn't "try" to do anything, but just puts his attention on the Container knowing that his brain knows how to slip everything in it without any effort.

(7) Usefulness

It is extremely helpful and reassuring for beginning therapists to be able to use the Container-Basic State with a patient during the session if he is overwhelmed by emotions, or if "parasitic" memories interfere with those being treated. It is also an invaluable tool for working with patients with a heavy history, as we have often said above.

During the therapist training at Therapeutia, as our students train on each other targeting real memories, all students must have their Containers installed. This ensures that the exercises are conducted in complete safety. All students must also be able, at all times during the training, to install and connect another student with whom they would work in EFT (or other) to his/her Container. Actually, aspiring therapists often have a rather burdened past (the desire to be a therapist is not without significance), and benefit from these methods for themselves before offering them to their patients.

(8) Examples

These various examples are transcriptions of demonstrations during the therapist trainings at Therapeutia and IEPRA. We would like to thank the students, now therapists, who transcribed them or gave their consent to use them! These examples show an increasing degree of complexity, due to basic insecurity or the manifestation of more parts of the Self in the student who lends himself to the exercise.

A. Example 1: Simple case

This first example illustrates a Container-Basic Condition that is easy to install.

BRIGITTE: While I was telling you about the Container, did you have any idea what could this Container be for you? So as to let everything that could be treated slip in it...

Part 2: Advanced Clinical EFT

STUDENT: A drawer.

B: Is it part of something?

S: A desk drawer unit.

B: Okay. When you see this drawer, does it give you the impression that it's going to be good to put everything that needs to be treated in it?

S: Yes.

B: Okay... close your eyes... it's here...

Put your attention on your drawer and just let everything that needs to be treated slip in it, you don't need to know what it is, you just let everything that needs to be treated and that you don't need to take care of now, slip in it. And then you just tell me how it goes...

S: I feel calmed down.

B: Great, now observe what you can feel, I'll tap, and you just observe your physical sensations.

(Bilateral tapping.)

B: Tell me, what word fits with what you're feeling?

S: Loosening.

B: Loosening, okay, we continue (tapping). Is that still the word loosening?

S: Relaxation.

B: Okay, relaxation, we keep going... just let yourself feel.

Is it still the word relaxation or is it something else?

S: Well-being.

B: Well-being... (tapping) Okay, what now?

S: Relaxation.

B: We do it again to see what suits you, don't think about that word, just stay with your feelings.

S: Relaxation.

B: Okay, we're just going to do the same thing and this time you repeat a few times "Relaxation" inside of you. Are you all right?

S: Very good.

Consolidation

Daily practice instructions

B. Example 2: Case with blockages, the Container-Basic state well installed at the end

This second example presents some difficulties; it should be noted that from the outset the student says that it seems difficult to her to calm down in order to reach the Basic State, which is a sign of basic insecurity. It is therefore a very good demonstration of how the establishment of the Container allows the patient's reflex vigilance to calm down, despite the appearance of several insecure parts of the Self. For one of these parts in particular, the student explains that this part is activated during each therapy session. This clearly shows the interest of using the Container-Basic State which allows this part which is "activated in the background" to calm down during the session.

Finding the right Container

BRIGITTE: You remember the idea of the Container, the fact that we have all these pop-ups open. The idea is that you can teach your brain to close all these pop-ups, to put them aside, so when you are here with us, you feel good without a part of your brain telling you "boo-hoo, I have to be alert."

Do you think that's a good idea, to be able to be here and feel good about being here?

STUDENT: It seems quite impossible to me, but yes, I'm willing to try.

B: In any case, the idea of getting there....

S: Yes, I like the idea.

Part 2: Advanced Clinical EFT

B: Just let an image come to your mind, something which might be appropriate as a Container, take what comes to you and tell me if something comes to mind.

S: I am searching, yes, I have an idea but that doesn't suit me.

B: Okay, talk to me, tell me....

S: I thought of a shoe box, but it doesn't suit me because there's a hole in the box, some kind of a little circle on the side, and it disturbs me!

B: The hole disturbs you. What could you do to your box to make sure there's no more holes? You can do whatever you want, you can take the same one without a hole or close the hole.

S: Yes, I can take another box.

B: Okay, does this box look good to you when you look at it?

S: It's okay.

B: Is there anything you could do for this box to make it look even better, to make it more secure, to make it better for you?

S: Again, it bothers me, and yes, I could change that... it's a cardboard box, so it's not strong: you can break it, it can absorb water... I would like to put it in the sand, actually...

B: Yes, it's not very appropriate, a cardboard box. What could you do to make it better to put it in the sand? It could be anything, you can take your box and it could be...

S: I have a little coffin in my head, it's not very romantic, but I like it.

B: A little coffin? Okay, and you like it? When you tell me it's not very romantic, you want to...

S: The image is not very pleasant, but it's fine. I'll just choose a rectangular shape for it so that it has the advantages... That's it, it's a box, but it is made of a kind of wood and it's metalized inside.

B: That's good?

S: Yes, it's solid!

Overcoming the blockages

B: Great! What I invite you to do, you know that it is your right brain that will do it; you, you have nothing to do, only focus your attention on the box now, and let it go inside, all by itself, everything that needs to be treated, everything that simply prevents you from being well with us here and now.

S: Do I have to think about this thing?

B: No, actually, you put your attention on your box and let the thing slip in, you don't need to know what it is, we gave the instruction to your Unconscious, so everything that clutters you goes in, and really let it go, send everything that prevents you from feeling relaxed now in there.

How is it going?

S: I feel more tense, but it's okay, I felt some tension, when you said "everything that clutters you", I liked the sentence, I imagined everything that cluttered me, but there was a little tension that came up.

B: Did it go up and down or did it go up and stay?

S: It went up and stayed, and it's still there.

B: It's there, and you'd say it's some tension....

S: A kind of burning sensation that comes from the belly and that has risen, and a kind of tightness in the fingers, some tension.

B: This tension is caused by a part of you who has been worried about something, something that is not well identified. Anxiety signals to your body that this part is worried.

Can you now just put your attention on your box? We will let slip into the box all the experiences, everything in your life that has made this part experience this physical reaction, this anguish; everything that has created this, all the origins of this, all of it slips into the box.

S: I feel it's really decreasing... yes, it's calming down.

B: It's calming down, okay; so how are you feeling right now?

S: Good!

B (connection to the Basic State): Okay, here's what I propose, now I'm going to tap on the side of your knees, and you're just going to be attentive to what's going on in your body now that you're fine, and you don't have

Part 2: Advanced Clinical EFT

to do anything else. You're not doing anything at all, just feeling how it's going....

S: It's getting a little tight again.

B: Okay, is it the same tension again?

S: It's in my back, it tingles, a little nervousness coming up, some tension.

B: Put your attention on your box and let go inside everything that is responsible for this tension, you don't need to know what it is. Everything that causes this tension, everything slips into the box.

S: Okay.

B: Let's go back to tapping... you just pay attention to the positive impression you have on body level... and you tell me...

S: Well, it's moving around, I feel it's going well but underneath it's more nervous. I often react to the tapping, it stimulates me down in the legs, but it's not negative, it's more of a tension that circulates.

B: Would it help you if I did it on your hands?

S: Maybe, yes.

B: I do it on LI4 (the hand - see Quick REMAP points), put your attention back on your Container and let go in there everything that causes you to have tensions in your legs when it circulates, you let all that go there... and now just be careful about what happens in your body. (Tapping on hands.)

S: In the body, things are going well, and I have small electrical currents in my elbows.

B: Do you think it's due to the tapping?

S: Yes, I think so.

B: What do you think is going on? Does it stress a part of you when I touch you?

S: Yes, I feel like it, yes, every time I've had to do this kind of technique, it goes up a bit.

B: Does it have to do with touch? Is there a part of you that doesn't like the touch in a certain way?

S: Yes.

B: Pay attention to your box and let slip in all the experiences you've had in your life that make that <u>part of you</u> stressed by touch, so then it triggers all this; all these experiences, let them slip there into your box.

S: I did, but it's shaking a little inside, I have tremors everywhere.

B: What do you think about that, about what it might show?

S: It often happens to me, this kind of tremor that triggers something I don't really understand; the triggers are sometimes very different, it comes out all of a sudden, and it's true that it's something I don't really understand because I'm a fairly tactile person in life, I don't have a problem with contact, but in certain situations, such as when I'm in therapy, when it's about freeing myself from my problems, then that can activate me.

B: So, <u>a part of you</u> can be activated - and especially in therapy - by the idea that we will free you from your problems?

S: Yes, I think so.

B: So, it triggers that part, it worries her and you feel these tremors?

S: That's it.

B: Could you see, for this part, if it would be okay if we told her that obviously there is something she is demonstrating and that she needs help with that? And that we're going to take care of her later, but first of all, we want you to be in a state where we can take care of her?

S: Okay.

B: And so, we understood that she needed help, that she gave us this message; we're just going to let you put it away until we get the Basic State done, and then we can take care of her. Would she be okay with that?

S: Yes, I think so.

B: Put your attention on your box and let slip in all the experiences/imprints/origins of the fact that this part is activated when you talk about getting rid of your problems; let it slip in the box, without having to know what it is.

S: Okay.

Part 2: Advanced Clinical EFT

B: I can tap here, just let yourself feel what body sensations are present...

S: I'm fine.

B: You're fine? And <u>what word</u> would you say to me, how do you feel that you're fine?

S: I'm fine, I'm more relieved...

B: You're more relieved, and physically, how do you feel that?

S: It circulates better.

B: It circulates better, put your attention on that feeling and see what word would be the most appropriate for it, for the description of that feeling, the word that comes to you...

S: Soothed, I think (The patient should not repeat the word mentally yet because it can change during the next tapping.)

B: Soothed... Is that still the word? Soothed resonates with it? (If the word changes, repeat tapping until the word no longer changes, and then ask the person to repeat that last word mentally.)

S: Okay.

Consolidation

Brigitte: In the next 15 days, I suggest that you use this tool, all you have to do is in the evening, in the morning, and when you change activities, and when you simply think about it during the day, you put your attention on your box, you instruct your Unconscious to let go inside everything that prevents you from being well now; everything that needs to be treated goes into the box and you repeat the word "soothed" a couple of times, this word is associated to that relaxing state.

If you do that in the morning and in the evening, that's ideal, you can also do it if during the day you're not busy and you think: ah, I could do that.

Do it even if you are not particularly activated by something, you put your attention on your box, you let it slip in and say "soothed..., soothed..., soothed..., soothed..." and you will see that you will connect quite quickly with this feeling.

Do it when you feel good, to make you feel even better.

You can also use it if there is something that has upset you, when you have returned to an environment that is safe but you feel you are restless; you can do it - think about your box, let everything slip in, including what is restless right now, let everything slip in while repeating "soothed..., soothed..., soothed...".

C. Example 3: Complex case: the Container-Basic State could not be installed at one time

In this example, we can see that the work of installing the Container-Basic State is in itself a therapeutic work in its own right. The student who lends herself to the demonstration presents a big picture of complex traumas, and many parts of the Self manifest themselves at the thought of calming down. As mentioned above, for a person accustomed to being in a significant state of activation, the idea of relaxing and accessing the Basic State can be stressful in itself, and time must be taken to tame the concerned parts of the Self. The student was invited to continue installing her Container in her personal therapy in order to use it for further training.

BRIGITTE: We're going to install your container... do you have any ideas?

STUDENT: I have a hard time finding something.

B: What if you close your eyes and let come whatever comes next? I invite you to let something come to you, a box, a basket...

S: What is difficult is that I feel that I am panicking, at the physical and emotional level there is... I have a lot of trouble with...

B: How do you feel physically when you panic?

S: I have a ball in my throat, the tears that are there, quite close, it's moving very, very strongly, I want to run away... it's shaking.

B: At what level?

S: In my arms, my stomach... I am oppressed.

B: What if you try to find a simple enough container in which you can let all your feelings slip? I suggest you close your eyes....

S: The image that comes to me may seem strange; I see a boat in space.

Part 2: Advanced Clinical EFT

B: Leave your eyes closed if it's possible for you... You imagine it as your container... the shaking, the ball, the tears, do you think that all that, you could make it slip towards this boat? What's your boat like?

S: It's big.

B: And are there windows, is there a door?

S: I can see mostly the sails.

B: And can you see a particular place in the boat where you could let slip everything that embarrasses you, everything that physically obstructs you?

S: I have difficulty seeing, I can only see from afar...

B: How do you feel right now?

S: I see... physically, I feel it's in my head, a bit like I feel a kind of paralysis and I want to shake myself...

B: Anything that caused these symptoms, let it slip in.

S: I feel something in my neck that stiffens.

B: Pain, discomfort?

S: A strong discomfort, I want to free myself from that.

B: You're going to be able to get rid of that, everything that caused that discomfort in your neck, you're going to let it slip in your boat, at the place where you want to put it, anything that prevents you from being here as relaxed as possible... when you get there, tell me.

S: I'm trying, but it seems like everything is getting away from me, I'm having a hard time visualising the boat and putting something in it.

B: Do you see a particular place in the boat where you could let everything that hurts you slip?

S: Yes, at the bottom of the boat.

B: In the hold?

S: Yes.

B: Is there a hole, an entrance through which you can get things in?

S: Yes.

B: Can you see this entrance?

S: Yes, there is a ladder.

B: Can you put your attention on your boat and let everything that causes this discomfort in your neck slip down through the ladder to the bottom of the hold... breathe deeply....

What are you feeling right now?

S (crying): I don't dare, I can't do it.

B: It's okay... let it happen by itself... can you still feel these neck pains? Is there anything else? Tell me a little bit, what's there, when you say I can't do it, and it makes you feel something, what's there?

S: Tears...

B: You are frustrated because you can't....

S: Yes... there is also something else, it's like it's still hanging on to me, I can't get away.

B : Okay, that means that in all the experiences you've had in your story, you've experienced very heavy things, which, because they're heavy, stick like that, and you can't get away with it because they're very heavy, it's a big package... yes... that's why you feel it's not fine, because in your story there are all these things you've been through... yes.... what we're going to do is... put your attention on the hold of the boat and we're going to ask your Unconscious to let slip in everything that makes it cling, everything that makes it heavy, everything that contributes to its clinging; we're also going to let all this slip into the hold, you can just put your attention on the hold, you have nothing to do, your Unconscious knows how to find everything that makes it cling and it's going to let it slip into the container too, yes, can you do that?

S: Okay.

B: You do nothing but put your attention on the hold, you don't have to do anything, you just let everything that makes it cling slip in,... tell me how it works.

S: I feel something else; I feel like something is running down my body like I'm in the shower, it's flowing down.

Part 2: Advanced Clinical EFT

B: And that's good?

S: Yes.

B: Great, let your Unconscious continue doing that, making everything flow down, and it lets slip in the hold everything that needs to be treated, it knows that's good for you, it allows you to be in a state where you can install this Basic State and then you can treat all these things that are in the hold... and in the meantime, you just let it all flow there... and you don't do anything... you just put your attention on the hold and let this happen... it flows, it flows, it flows, until... everything has flowed down... you tell me how it works.

S: It flows a little like a stream into a big hole, and I also feel my breath soothing.

B: Great.

S: There is also some movement, I feel it is flowing.

B: Great, keep doing nothing, let that happen....

How are you doing now?

S: I still feel tremors, but less strong, in my arms, in my shoulders.

B: All these tremors that remain in your shoulders, in your arms, it's still the trace of experiences, of things that have happened; put your attention on the hold, do nothing, while your Unconscious lets all the experiences, everything that is at the origin of these remaining tremors slip in; all of that goes in the hold.

How is it now?

S: I feel... it's calming down but there's still something restless, I feel tossed, unstable.

B: There is a part of you that feels tossed and unstable because all this goes into the hold; there are reasons why you feel this tossing, and your Unconscious Mind will let slip into the hold everything that you've experienced and that still makes it like that, everything that led to this tossing, that it's not yet stable, all of this goes into the hold...

S: I feel something else, something that crushes my shoulders; it flows, it's better than before, but I feel it more in my shoulders, and still in the neck....

B: There are all these things happening inside you that just prevent everything from going easily into the hold and you feeling relaxed; all the experiences you've had, everything that prevents things from going easily, that prevents you from feeling safe, all the reasons that weigh on your shoulders, on your neck, all that, it slips into the hold... everything that prevents you from feeling good, everything slips into the hold.

S: I can still feel my neck quite tense and at the same time, I don't know if it vibrates everywhere... I can't put words on what I feel, there are movements... I imagine something sticky that is sticking to me, it's.... it's...

B: There are still all these things out there, these are parts of you that need help... but now we're going to have to stop... (Time is up and we have to help the person suspend the process until the next time.)

We're going to give them a message, that we heard them well, that you observed that there was all of this inside yourself and you should to fix it again, and you can tell them that there will certainly be other times when you'll work on this container and that you'll take care of it with them... How do you feel about the idea that we'll stop now?

S: I'm more relaxed than I was before....

B: You've already done a big job with the container; you managed to let things slip in...

S: I feel like I'm a little stunned...

B: It's normal, it's because it's not just words, it really happens, when you let it slip into the container, there are really things you put aside in your mind and so it balances and moves emotionally and energetically, so it's normal for you to be stunned....

D. Example 4: Working with the parts of the Self

In this demonstration, we also see many parts of the Self appear. It is important to realize that all these parts are generally silent, but nevertheless present in the background during "traditional" therapy sessions. Taking the time to get to know them, tame them and install the

Container will then ensure that, during each therapy session, the person can have a "free field" to treat with EFT what is chosen rather than being constantly infested by those parts of the patient's chronic condition, which are easily activated and make the treatment of the targets interminable or even impossible. Most patients with complex trauma are aware of the parts that are activated "in the background" during therapy sessions, but they do not mention them to the therapist. Installing the Container-Basic State therefore makes it possible to start a real background therapy, before treating the targets required by the EFT treatment plan.

This demonstration is long, and there are several moments when we could have been satisfied with the result. However, given the didactic context of demonstration and teaching, I continued the session and let all the present parts come to light in order to give many examples of how to speak to parts of the Self and get them to collaborate in case of blockage.

Searching for the right container

BRIGITTE: In regards to the nature of your container, you said you had found something that suited you when I suggested you to think about it?

STUDENT: Yes, an empty detergent container where there is a little product left that would not be likely to damage what I could put in it.

B: So that's fine with you. When you think about that container, does it fit you?

S: Yes, but on the other hand, there is a part of me that would like something even more neutral, that there is no detergent, and also something bigger.

B: Okay, can you do that? Imagine it's just bigger?

S: Yes.

B: And more neutral, what could you do to ensure that it keeps all the qualities you like about what it is while meeting the wishes of that part?

S: There is not much that comes to me, except the same container without product.

B: Without product. And when you test a little, how do you feel about the same container without product?

S: I'm missing something, because it's too light, it should be able to stay on the ground.

B: Yes, all right, it's too light. What could you do to make it heavier?

S: The first thing that comes to mind is to put water in it.

B: That's one way. If it's okay with you... Try it.

S: Yes.

B: When you imagine that it is bigger, that there is water in it and you look at it, you feel that it is good, that it would suit you to let everything to be reprocessed slip inside. Would that be right?

S: Yes.

B: Now, we're going to do the exercise of letting all the things that are to be put in there, slip inside. All you have to do is put your attention on your container. Is it around here?

S: It's right behind me.

B: It's right behind you, that's it. Put your attention on your container, and now you let everything that needs to be treated slip inside. You don't need to know what it is, but everything that needs to be treated, all the conscious and unconscious dysfunctional networks... all this slips into this container, and then you tell me when it is done and how it works.

S: Yes, I have the feeling that there are things that settle down and at the same time, I would like to be able to see when... I have the feeling that there are things that are leaving me and are settling in the container but at the same time, I would like to see to make sure that everything is properly settled... that it is settled to the end... as if I could not be sure that everything is settled there. Maybe I am afraid that it takes too long.

B: What takes too long?

S: Letting things settle.

B: Okay. You mean that not everything is there yet and you have the feeling that it should last longer, and you're afraid it takes too long?

S: Yes.

B: Okay, and at the same time, do you need to check it out?

S: Yes.

B: So, in any case, you feel that not everything is there yet because you tell me that you are afraid it takes too long?

S: Yes.

B: How do you know it's not all there yet? How do you feel that?

S: Because I feel the way it settles is like layers of onion and it gets slower and slower to come off.

B: Okay. So, when things go in your container, you feel it and you feel that the more the layers are in the centre, the longer they take?

S: Yes.

B: Okay, so if it takes longer, while sometimes it can be very fast, even very old things that can really slip very easily into the container, there is a reason for that. It must be that there is something going on inside you that makes it take longer when it is more at the centre. So, all these experiences, all the things that make it now take time when it's the layers of the center that have to slip, could you just let slip inside everything that has led to it taking so long, everything that has led to it being slow? All these experiences, you let them slip into your container. You don't need to know what has led to this, but you just let them slip in. Can you do that?

S: Yes.

B: Then tell me when it's done.

S: There is the area around the heart that is very tense and I have the impression that it is dangerous to... it could be deposited and at the same time I can't let it go otherwise I will...

B: Okay. Do you have the feeling that if you let go of what's tense around your heart, it could be dangerous?

S: Yes.

B: Okay. Can you put your attention on the container and let slip inside all the experiences you have had that make it seem dangerous to you today if this tension in your heart is no longer there? Just let slip inside all the experiences, all the things that you've been through and that are doing this, that are responsible for this... and tell me when it's done.

S: It subsides, but there is still something left.

B: What's left, what are you still feeling?

S: Still something like protections around the heart, and feelings of oppression in the throat.

Working with the parts of the Self

BRIGITTE: Okay, so those parts of you that have experiences that make one of them keep that pressure a little bit longer and another one manifest something around your throat, they've experienced things and they're now showing their concern or thoughts, let's say that about what's happening now. They speak through it. So what we want to tell them is that we hear they have fears and things to say about that; put your attention on your container now and let slip inside everything that has led to these parts having these fears or these considerations that prevent them from simply letting all this go into the container so that you can just feel good when you are safe... everything that they have experienced and that gives them these fears, all of this slips into the container. Tell me how it works.

Letting it slip

STUDENT: It subsides, but I realise that I tend to push things into the container.

B: It subsides, but you see that you tend to push things. All right. You're telling me this, so you know you could just let them slip?

S: Yes.

B: Yes, so, as I explained, it's like a TV channel. You put your attention there, on your container, and then you just wait with the intention. The intention that all this be done by itself is like the "go" button that closes all the windows that are still open, that puts all these experiences on the side. Just by the fact that you say to yourself "Now I'm letting everything slip inside," and then it just happens. Do you want to do it again, put your attention on the container and just... like that... by not doing anything in particular, you let it happen, you just let it slip inside... everything that still needs to be reprocessed, all the experiences that have led to all this. It all goes in there.

S: It is evolving. I'm a little dizzy.

B: You're a little dizzy. This may be normal and due to the process because we are relieving tensions a little.

S: I was talking earlier about pushing into the container and I realize that I have trouble really staying focused on the container and seeing what happens. I tend to imagine everything that's going on.

B: Okay. You tell me "I have a hard time letting it happen and I imagine what's going on". In fact, you don't even need to imagine anything.

S: In fact, rather than putting my attention on the container, I see the container far away and try to see the movement. I have trouble staying focused only on the container and seeing what's going on.

B: Okay. When I say, "tell me what's going on", I'm not talking about what's going on in the container. When I ask you how it went, you just tell me how you feel, if it went well or if there is something wrong. But you don't have to put a particular intention on what's changing there. It's just that you think about your container and, by the very fact of thinking about it, your unconscious lets everything slip in. You don't have to identify anything by that, just put your attention on it. Is that possible?

S: Yes, it is possible.

B: And so, you tell me you have the feeling of accompanying something at the level of movement?

S: Yes.

B: It may be, if that's your psychic way of letting go, why not.

S: I realise that by just staying focused on the container, it's much freer.

B: All right, okay, do that then. Let it slip inside without having to do anything but let it slip. Your unconscious knows how to do it, it does that many times every day, several times a day. Let everything go into the container.

S: There's really not much left.

(We could have stopped there, because it is already a success with this student with a complex trauma profile, but the remaining "little something" shows the presence of parts in the background.

B: There's really not much left, okay. You mean that it's okay, or there's a little bit left, or does it look okay?

S: I have the impression that this will take time.

B: Okay.

S: But it's already tremendous.

B: There is a little something left and you have the impression that it would take time for that little something?

S: Yes.

B: And why would it take time?

S: I don't know.

B: Put your attention on the container and let slip inside everything that led to the idea that it will take time and also everything that led, all the experiences that led to this little something left... All this, you let it slip inside, it slips by itself.

S: I have the impression that it moves between the front side of my throat and a more specific place in my heart. It's like something that wants to stay inside.

B: Okay, something that wants to stay inside, so it moves when you put your attention there, on the container. It's moving. Can you ask this thing, this part of you, why it wants to stay inside, what is important to it?

S: At the same time, she wants to go unnoticed. She just doesn't want to be taken care of.

B: She doesn't want to be taken care of, okay. And for her, going into the container is disturbing... not that she is going inside, not the part herself, but letting go of all the experiences that led to her feeling everything she feels. Would it be disturbing for her if we explain to her that it is because we want to install something for you, this Basic State that will help you take care of all parts of yourself more easily, including her. Do you think you

Part 2: Advanced Clinical EFT

could ask her if she would agree to let go of all the experiences, she's had that make it move, rather than go into the container?

S: I think she is afraid of losing her importance.

B: Okay, she wants to go unnoticed, but she needs you to notice her and not put her there, just on the side. Is that it?

S: In any case, she wants whatever is problematic for her to be recognized, not be left out.

B: Okay, so we really want to explain to this part of you that here we're not saying, "Come on, all this, we're putting all this on the side, we're going to do important things and we're putting unimportant things on the side to do this," you just need to be able to clear the ground to do some basic work and soothe this Basic State, and then you can take care of her. She's not going to be put on the side forever, not at all. Ask her if she would agree, during this little time, just now, during this session where I do the Basic State with you, to leave on the side those experiences that make her afraid that she will lose her importance, if she would agree for just that amount of time.

S: Yes, I think it's okay.

B: So, put your attention on the container and let go inside all the experiences, everything that led to this part having this fear of losing her importance and this desire to stay there. All this can temporarily slip into the container.

S: It's moving, but my head is really spinning.

B: Your head is spinning. This can really be normal because these are things that are always there in you and here, we move them a little bit, we move them a little bit and it can lead to a kind of change, a balance inside there.

Do you think it's that or do you think it could be a part that expresses something by spinning your head?

S: I don't really feel a conflict.

B: Okay, apart from the spinning head, does it seem to you that there is still something that should go in the container, or does it seem okay to you now?

S: There is still a little bit more, actually.

B: Okay. How is that compared to before, what can you tell me about what's left?

S: It is two to three times less intense. This continues to be discreet. The sensations are more soothed, I have this impression that there are many things that have settled.

B: And that part of you that's afraid of losing her importance, where is that fear? Is it still there?

S: No, I don't know very well....

B: It's something else. It's not really that same feeling anymore, the fear of losing importance and wanting to stay there. That's not really how you feel anymore.

S: Yes.

B: Is it physical? What word would you use for how you feel?

S: Yes, it is as if part of my heart remains contracted.

B: Okay.

S: A feeling of dizziness. When I try to connect with this part, there is still a connection.

B: Okay. So, something special must have really happened with this part for there to be something that remains like that, that lasts, that really clings to that particular place in your heart. So, put your attention on the container and let slip inside, without you needing to know what it is, the most important trauma or the most important event so that now it clings like that and makes you dizzy when you put your attention on it. Everything that this part has experienced and that leads to this, all this can slip into the container... Tell me.

S: Yes, there is still something left, and I can't help observe what I feel in my body as I see my container. And when I observe my sensations at the same time as I try to observe my container, I feel that it creates something that prevents the process, but I have this need to look at what I feel in my body.

Part 2: Advanced Clinical EFT

B: While having your attention on the container, you need to look at what you feel in your body and feel that it prevents the process?

S: Yes.

B: Okay. So, put your attention on the container and we'll let everything that makes you need to keep your attention on your feelings, everything that has led to this state of affairs, everything that you experienced that has led to this, the imprints, the experiences... all this slips into the container. How is it going?

S: A lot of heat coming up. I want to say that I am satisfied like that.

B: Are you satisfied like that because you have had enough? How is it going there for the part?

S: She would not mind continuing.

B: Are you satisfied because you feel it's okay? How is that going?

S: I still feel a little something, but it doesn't impact me. There's a little restraint, though.

B: And what has changed from before?

S: I no longer need to control and observe, or at least much less.

B: Okay, now that you no longer need this control, we could do it again... Put your attention on the container and everything that has led to that little thing still remaining there, everything that has led to its existence and the fact that it is still there, all that slips into the container.

S: There is always something blocking, something that tells me that this can't go away without emotions coming out at the same time.

B: Okay. So, there is a part of you that says, "if it goes away, there will be emotions that will come out" and that poses a problem for her, is that right?

S: Yes.

B: What is she afraid of if emotions come out?

S: Already of this.

B: Outgoing emotions, yes.

S: That maybe the emotion will be violent, and I will be struck by it, maybe it will be really painful.

B: Yes, okay. And can you ask her why she thinks that if it goes away and you're just there with everything that went into the container, it's going to be accompanied by violent emotions?

S: Because she can't let go of that without expressing emotions.

B: Okay.

S: I don't know, that's what's coming to me anyway.

B: Would she be the one who would express these emotions if she let go of that?

S: Yes.

B: Okay. I would need to understand... You're telling me you're not sure why she couldn't let go without expressing emotions.

S: That's because she's not often heard.

B: Okay. This little restriction is that part, and if she really let go of that, then she would dare to be heard, right? And she'd let go of the emotions?

S: It is as if she absolutely must take the opportunity to be heard. She refuses to let go of what is causing her problems because she already has the opportunity to be heard, which is unusual. I think she's afraid we won't go back to what's important to her.

B: Okay, I understand that. And what could we tell her about that? Could you commit yourself to focus your attention on her after the session, or tomorrow, or in therapy? What could help?

S: Yes, indeed, I could commit myself to taking care of her in therapy knowing that there are new things at that level...

B: Tell her that inside of you. Tell her you understand that she is afraid that if she gives up, she will no longer have a chance to be heard, and that you are committed to seeing how she is doing and giving her a voice in therapy. She would agree then that we can let things go into the container temporarily, while we do this Basic State, to help you and her?

S: ...

B: We're just going to do it, and we'll see if it can be done now. So put your attention on the container and now that she knows she can drop this because you will give her the word again, you can let go into the container everything that led her to experience this, that she is afraid not to be heard, that she needs to express herself... all this goes into the container... just for the time that we do what we will do.

S: ...

B: Just let yourself feel how you feel now. Is that okay with you?

S: Overall, yes, except that I have this dizziness.

B: Put your attention on the container, we will let go in the container everything that leads to this spinning which appeared at one point, and we will let go in the container everything that has led to it. How are you doing?

S: This is decreasing sharply and in parallel with the other part.

B: Do you feel that there is still a clash, a resistance?

S: I don't feel it's a resistance, just the impression that it would take time and there's a part of me that doesn't want it to take time.

B: Okay. Put your attention on your container and you can let slip inside everything in your life that has made that now you feel uncomfortable because it takes time. You let all this slip, as well as everything that leads to you having this belief that it must take time and everything that leads to it really taking time. Anything that prevents it from happening quickly, goes into the container.

S: There's something growing, I want to burp, but it doesn't come up. There you go.

B: Okay. Put your attention on the container and let everything that has led to that feeling you have slip inside. How is it now?

S: It's comfortable.

B: Okay, what word would you use for that comfortable? What sensations do you have that make you say it's comfortable?

S: Relaxation.

(Installation of the Basic State)

B: You could, while I'm tapping, just feel these sensations in your body. That's all, you're just observing.

Tell me how does that feel in your body?

S: A lot of heat circulating. I feel that some muscles are tired. I feel tension at the bottom of my throat.

B: Put your attention on your container and let slip inside everything that has led to this weight and tension in here (shows the throat). Tell me.

S: There is a part of me that begins to activate the mind and says "no, it's okay, that's enough".

B: Okay, there's a part that says "it's okay, that's enough" and where is it now? Is it okay or...?

S: No, it's stronger.

B: Okay. Do you know what that says?

S: No... It's a feeling of mine... that I find mysterious and that I have since...?

B: Okay, so already you can put your attention on your container and let slip inside everything that has led to this part of you saying "come on, it's okay, that's enough", everything that has led her to say that. And then I would like you to tell me what we could imagine about that part of you that has been manifesting herself in your life these days and that is manifesting herself here now... it is a part that expresses something and we don't know what she wants to express, but it is clear that if she appears now and these other times, she has something to say and she wants to manifest herself. So, here, we are in the process of installing the Basic State. If that part shows up, what would she want? What could we do to help her just stay on the side for a while, while we do the Basic State? Does she agree with that? We can already simply ask her that. You tell her that we have seen and understood that she was coming regularly these days, that she has something to say and that you are aware of it, but that here and now, since we don't know what she wants to say, we don't know how to take care of her. But, again, what we're doing with the Basic State, it will help you be able to communicate with her afterward, and move forward with your therapy, and pay her attention. Ask her if she would agree, during the exercise, to stand right here, near us, she can stay and just leave the ground clear, so we can do the Basic State. Would she agree with that?

S: Yes.

B: We're going to ask your part to stand here, on the side, and you can put your attention on the container and just let slip inside everything that prevents you from being in the state that allows you to do the Basic State free from all that, knowing that this part will have your full attention afterwards. Let everything that prevents you, including feelings, slip inside so that you can be free of all this to now do the Basic State.

S: It's halfway there.

B: Okay, I think that this part needs to be reassured about something on order to accept that everything goes to the side. Do you have any idea what that is?

S: Need to defend.

B: Need to defend.

S: I don't even know.

B: Here, it is a case where we should take care of this part in particular because she tells us "I need to be reassured of this first in order to continue with the container". For the sake of the demonstration, we're going to stop here, but it's really important that you can give a listening to this part and the other part that showed up earlier, which have manifested themselves to you, even only by checking where they are when you go back to therapy. Is there anything you need now?

S: No, I feel much better. I'm quite happy that this part was able to feel safe enough to calm down. It's something I find very positive, knowing that I will take care of her afterwards.

6. The 4-Point Quick REMAP® Emergency Procedure: Advanced Method

This procedure allows the nervous system to be quickly calmed down.

a. Basic method

See the first part of this book for a complete description and diagram of the points used.

Protocol:

- The patient stimulates (rubs or presses without hurting himself) each point for about one minute or until the intensity stops decreasing;

- Repeat if necessary.

b. Adaptive method

Stimulate a point for at least 15 seconds to see if the point is having an effect. Then ask, "Does it help?"

If so, continue the stimulation as long as the internal tension (emotion, physical sensation) decreases. Tell the patient: "Keep going until it doesn't get any better" (one minute maximum). Then change the point.

If this does not help or if the tension increases, change the point.

The order of the points is not important.

c. Method including standard reframing phrase

1. Even though I have this specific problem,
2. .... I love and accept myself completely and deeply as I am (or I open myself to this possibility) ...
3. .... and it is normal (or logical/natural) that I feel this problem...
4. .... but from another point of view (or in reality/another reality is that):

d. here and now, it's over... It's all in the past, I'm safe now...

5. ..... and on the other hand, I am open to the possibility

   - To have now the right to be at peace with all this,

- because I learned from this experience... or I open myself to the possibility of living things differently now and find the right balance.

7. The pendulation – CIPOS

Constant Installation of Present Orientation and Safety (Jim Knipe)

Adapted to EFT and Energy Psychology techniques by Marco Di Tomasso and Brigitte Hansoul for Therapeutia

CIPOS is a technique that aims to help patients keep the control when they come into contact with their trauma. Many patients are afraid of being completely invaded when they think of the trauma. Thanks to the CIPOS technique, they learn to decide for themselves how long they will focus their attention on their trauma in order to be able to detach themselves from it again. They are often extremely relieved and grateful.

We can use this technique when we fear that the patient will be overwhelmed when establishing contact with the trauma. It is recommended to consider it for patients with chronic trauma when the SUD is greater than 8.

With CIPOS, the trauma does not have to be described in all its details. It is enough for the patient to be able to tell us what the topic is (safety/survival, distress/abandonment, shame/guilt or self-esteem). Then we let him estimate the degree of disturbance on the SUD scale.

a. 1st passage

(1) Confrontation with the trauma

Question to the patient: "When you think about it, what is the topic of the disturbing situation? If you wish, you can describe what it is about. However, you are not required to provide all the details. Just give a title to the memory; for example, is the topic related to safety/survival, distress/abandonment, shame/guilt or self-esteem? Now, on a scale of 0 to 10, how much does the memory disturb you, if 0 is neutral and 10 is the worst you can imagine?"

SUD =

Let the patient decide how long, between 3 and 7 seconds, he agrees to think about his trauma. After that, you will ask him to get in contact with the trauma and you will count the seconds aloud to give a reference on the duration of the contact. You indicate the end with a stop signal. It is wise to count out loud and backwards.

Formulation of the question to the patient: *"How long between 3 and 7 seconds do you want to think about the trauma?", "I'm going to count out loud and when I get to 0, I'm going to ask you to take a deep breath and erase."*

"Now think of the trauma!"

Count out loud and count backwards (5 - 4 - 3 - 2 - 1 - 0), then tell the patient: *"Take a deep breath and erase!"*

(2)   Reorientation in the present

The patient is not always able to detach himself immediately from his trauma. This can be demonstrated visually, by asking the patient to hold his hand next to his head. The hand at the height of his neck indicates that he is still fully involved in his trauma. The hand in front of the forehead shows that he has completely detached himself from it. The intermediate stages indicate the degree of contact with the trauma.

During the pause, we want to achieve complete detachment from the trauma. If there is still a contact, then we apply techniques to stop it, respectively to dissolve the dissociation. The recommended exercises for this purpose are varied: calculating backwards (1000 minus 7, minus 7, minus 7, minus 7, etc.), throwing balls or other objects, getting up and moving around the room, naming objects in the room (e. g., 5 objects that are yellow), etc.

Repeat these exercises alternately until the patient is at least 95% present and ask the question directly ("How many percent present are you now?").

(3)   Strengthening the present

As soon as the patient is fully oriented again in the present, you ask him to focus on his perception and what he feels. Then you reinforce this perception by (you choose):

Part 2: Advanced Clinical EFT

- EFT: Triple Heater (**Back of the Hand**) or Governing Vessel 27 (**Under the Nose**).
- REMAP: Stomach 36 (Outside the Knee).
- TAT: Installation.

(In the rest of this protocol, we will take the example of EFT stimulations. You can continue with the ones you have chosen: EFT, REMAP, TAT, etc.)

Ask the patient how much he or she is "in the present". As soon as he is 95-100% "there", tell the patient: "Be aware of how you feel now and stimulate:

E.g.: EFT: Triple Heater (**Back of the Hand**) or Goveringr Vessel 27 (**Under the Nose**).

Take a deep breath. What is happening now?"

Under the effect of stimulation, no return to trauma should occur. On the contrary, only the perception of the present should remain, accompanied by a pleasant feeling. If you have difficulty getting the patient back into the present, do stabilisation and complete the CIPOS.

This corresponds to the first passage. In total, three passages are usually made.

b. 2nd passage

(1) Confrontation with the trauma

You now ask the patient if he or she is ready to think about the trauma again within the same defined time frame, and then count down and out loud again.

Say: "Now think again about the trauma for x seconds. (e. g.: 5 - 4 - 3 - 2 - 1 - 0). Take a deep breath and erase. What's there now?"

(2) Reorientation

During the second passage, patients are generally less disturbed by the contact with the trauma and detach themselves from it more quickly. But often support is also needed to ensure complete detachment from the trauma. To this aim, you do exercises again to stop the dissociation (countdown, ball throwing, etc.).

(3) Strengthening the present

When the patient is fully oriented in the present, you repeat the stimulations to reinforce the perception of the present:

E.g.: EFT: Triple Heater **(Back of the Hand)** or Governing Vessel 27 **(Under the Nose)**.

You say again: "Perceive once again how you feel now and stimulate:

E.g.: EFT: Triple Heater **(Back of the Hand)** or Governing Vessel 27 **(Under the Nose)**.

Take a deep breath. What is the situation now?"

The second passage is then completed.

c. 3rd passage

(1) Confrontation with the trauma

Ask the patient for the third and final time to think about the trauma; again, for the same amount of time.

Say: "Now think again about the trauma while I count out loud and then come back here with all your attention." Count e. g. 5 - 4 - 3 - 2 - 1 - 0.

"Take a deep breath and relax. What's there now?" Then ask: "On the scale of 0 to 10, how much does the memory disturb you now if 0 is neutral and 10 is the maximum disturbance you can imagine?"

SUD =

(2) Reorientation or strengthening of the present

At the third passage, the disturbance has usually decreased, and it is no longer necessary to stop the dissociation. You can then **create a connection with a resource that must come from the same thematic circle as the trauma**, but this time with a totally positive connotation (e. g. paralyzed - mobile, distressed - competent, at the mercy of others - able to protect themselves, etc.).

"Think of a positive idea or an image that represents for you a positive pole opposite to the treated theme."

(It is easier to do this if you have installed a resource beforehand.)

Stimulate: e. g.: EFT: Triple Heater **(Back of the Hand)** or Governing Vessel 27 **(Under the Nose)**.

"What is there now?"

d. End of the session

It is surprising to note how significant the decrease in the SUD of the targets to be treated can be, thanks to the CIPOS, and despite the fact that no work on trauma has yet been undertaken. What appears so clearly here is probably related to the experience of no longer being exposed to the trauma without assistance, but, on the contrary, of being able to decide for oneself how long the contact with the trauma will last.

If the SUD of the trauma has decreased sufficiently, we can then, within an hour, work on the remaining disturbance during a normal treatment session. In case this disturbance is still quite high, it is possible to repeat the CIPOS again.

8. The Resources

The methods for initial stabilisation are the establishment of the Safe Place, the Safe box, the Container (= Container + Basic State). This is a prerequisite for any support work.

Making Resources is also stabilisation in itself. Given the importance of working with resources for both complex trauma patients and others, we devote an entire chapter to this topic below, transcribed from my "Resources" course in Therapeutia training.

E. The Resources

1. Stabilisation by General Resources on a theme

Making resources is stabilisation in itself.

However, unlike the initial stabilisation which stabilises in a general way, **a resource is always related to a particular theme**, for example the lack of self-confidence or the security. The resource amplifies the positive neural network related to this theme.

When working with a fragile person whose problem has been identified (e.g. self-esteem), you should set up resources before starting to work on the targets, on the negative events.

Important: strengthening resources does not treat the negative aspect in any way, the person can get better but remains fragile and it will be necessary, when possible, to treat the negative - sometimes alternating with strengthening of the resources and the positive aspect. As we have seen, the processing of the negative will be much easier when a resource installation has been done previously.

2. Stabilisation by Specific Resources for a given target

When the patient is sufficiently stable, either at the outset or as a result of working with the general resources, it is then possible to treat targets.

It is possible to make resources specifically focused on the ability to reprocess a given target. This is what we will call a "specific resource" (to a target).

Example of a resource for a target: a specific resource to deal with an interview with the boss (future target) that generates anxiety and the negative belief "I feel very small".

In addition to resources focused on dealing with a target from the past or the future, it is also possible, from a "brief therapy" perspective, to make resources in relation to triggers of the present, for example: I would like to remain calm towards my husband.

3. Types of Resources

Resources are networks of memories or positive experiences.

They can be:
- from direct memories (experiences);
- taken in the evocation of a model (relational resources);
- from symbols or other imaginary figures.

Part 2: Advanced Clinical EFT

    4.   **Protocol for the installation of Specific Resources**

Adapted from Korn and Leeds (2002) for EFT and Energy Psychology.
Select at each step the questions or instructions that suit the patient best.

(1) Identifying the resources needed for a current problem

- Think of a situation that is weighing heavily on you right now in your life. You may think of a difficult event. You can also think of a particular person with whom you have difficulties.
- When you think about this situation, what is your degree of disturbance between 0 and 10? (SUD)
- When you think about this situation, what qualities, resources or strengths would you need?
- What would you like to think of yourself in this situation? (PC)
- How would you like to feel? (emotions/sensations)
- What would you like to be able to do? (behaviour)

Examples of answers:

I would like to feel stronger.

I would like to feel more connected.

I would like to feel more anchored in the ground.

I would like to have more self-confidence.

I would like to feel more courageous.

I would like to feel more determined.

I would like to feel more flexible.

I want to increase my confidence in the healing process.

I want to be able to calm down. I want to be able to manage my emotions.

I want to be able to establish my limits better.

I want to feel loved.

I want to be able to say what I need.

(2) Identifying the types of available resources

A. *Experiences of success*

Choose the questions asked to the person from the following:

- **Remember a time when you felt...** (e. g. strong, safe, calm, etc.).
- **Remember a time when you were able to behave...** (being more confident, brave or flexible).
- **In which experiences can you find this desired quality or feeling?**
- **Think about these experiences or states that you have had that could help you now** (for example: your inner wisdom, your professional Self, your fighting Self).
- **Can you see an image of yourself in the future with the qualities you want to have?**

B. *Relational resources (models and reference figures)*

Choose from these questions:

- **Think of people in your current or past life who have or represent these qualities: think of your friends, family members, teachers, therapists.**
- **Think of people, wherever they are in the world, who possess or represent this quality, and who serve, or can serve, as models** (for example: famous characters, characters from books, television, films or cartoons).
- **Think of the person you would like to have close to you who would encourage, guide and help you feel...** (for example: stronger, more supported, more confident).
- **Think of people who have had a supportive role. Do you have a spiritual guide, something or someone who gives you hope on your life path?**
- **Are there any domestic or wild animals that you associate with these positive feelings or qualities?**

C. *Metaphors and symbolic resources*

- **Think of other images or metaphors that can help you feel...** (calmer, loved, protected, etc.).

Part 2: Advanced Clinical EFT

- **Think of all the possible positive images or symbols you have used in your dreams, drawings, works of art, reveries, or guided imagery** (for example, a strong but flexible tree).

(3) Feeling the resources

Work with one resource at a time.

- **When you think about...** (for example: experience, person, symbol, etc.**), what do you see? What do you hear? What do you feel? What do you notice about your body? What feelings do you have when you focus on this image or memory?**

Note down the person's words literally to continue to use them throughout the process.

The most important thing is the feeling (physical, emotional). The resources have the nature of a lived, felt experience.

Note: In the case of a relational resource, it may happen that the person being cared for (the patient) has, in contrast, a negative feeling about the resource that has the desired quality.

Example: the person being helped feels weak and wants a resource of strength. He chooses a model, "a particular actor". When asked: "Think about this actor, how do you feel? ", he says: "He is strong, but I am not like him."

Explain to him then that the idea is not so much to see how he feels about the actor, but rather that he lets himself be immersed in the energy of power that this model emanates, and that he notes his perception of this energy. How does he perceive that his body feels this energy of power that emanates from the actor? A bit like when you are facing the image of a tiger, you feel its energy. The idea is not to compare yourself, but to feel the energy that comes from the model.

You can also explain the following:

When you look at an obscure painting, you feel bad; however, when you look at a luminous painting, you feel good, full of joy, full of hope... it is not that you become luminous, but you feel the positive effect of what the painting emanates.

Facing a model, you are not the model but you connect to what you feel in the energy emanated by the model.

It's not trying to be in each other's shoes, it's just looking at a beautiful painting: oh, how nice it is...

Part 2: Advanced Clinical EFT

(3 Bis) (optional) Checking the resource (in case of doubt)

Verify that the chosen resource is effective.

- **When you focus on...** (repeat the description of the image) **and...** (repeat the description of sounds, smells, sensations and feelings, etc.), **how do you feel now?**

Verify that the selected resource can help the person deal with the problem situation (target) by asking:

- **When you focus on...** (the problematic situation), **how much do you now think is true or supportive** (repeat descriptions of the image and feelings) **on a scale from 0 to 10 where 0 is completely false and 10 is completely true or useful?**

(4) Installing the resource

- **While you now continue focusing on...** (repeat the client's descriptive words for the image, emotions or associated sensations), **tap on EFT points or stimulate a REMAP point, or take the TAT pose; do this for a fairly short time: 10 seconds.**

N.B.: in REMAP, not all points give the same effect: some can be relatively neutral and others very positive amplifiers. If one point has no impact, change and try another.

Make several passages of stimulation, and ask after each one:

- **What do you feel and what do you notice now?**

Continue as long as the person being cared for reports an increase in the positive or additional positive aspects.

IMPORTANT: do not continue the poses if the person reports associations or interferences of negative effects. Negative material must be separated in an imaginary way, in the Safe box or the Container, before continuing. It is also possible to have a dialogue of the parts and see if this solves the problem. Otherwise, the process must be restarted with another resource.

(5) *Strengthening the resource with verbal (PC) or sensory (K) anchors*

For an experiential resource:

- **When you get back into this (resource) experience, what are the most positive words you could find to describe yourself now?** (PC)
- **Observe where you feel this in your body.** (K)

Ask the person to stimulate (tapping, TAT...) and tell him: **Repeat to yourself...... (PC), feeling the effect of this in your body.** (K)

After each stimulation, ask: **How much does it (PC) sound true? With 0 if it sounds completely false and 10 completely true** (VOC)?

If VOC < 10 (less than 10), repeat the stimulation until VOC = 10 (equals 10).

For a relational resource:

- **Imagine that this person is next to you and gives you what you need. Imagine that he/she knows exactly what he/she has to tell you, exactly what you need, or imagine merging with that person or entering his/her body.**
- **Observe where you feel this in your body.** (K)
- **What are the most positive words you could find to describe yourself now?** (PC)

Ask the patient to stimulate (tapping...) and tell him: **Repeat to yourself... (PC), feeling the effect of this in your body** (K).

After each stimulation, ask: **How much does it (PC) sound true? With 0 if it sounds completely false and 10 completely true** (VOC)?

If VOC < 10, repeat the stimulation until VOC = 10.

For a metaphorical or symbolic resource:

- **Imagine holding the resource. Imagine being surrounded by this image or feeling. Breathe in that feeling.**
- **Observe where you feel this positive quality in your body.** (K)
- **What are the most positive words you could find to describe yourself now?** (PC)

Ask the person to stimulate (tapping...) and tell him: **Repeat to yourself... (PC), feeling the effect of this in your body.** (K)

After each stimulation, ask: **How much does it (PC) sound true? With 0 if it sounds completely false and 10 completely true** (VOC)?

If VOC < 10, repeat the stimulation until VOC = 10.

If the VOC no longer rises, ask: **"What prevents it from reaching 10?"** or **"What prevents it from being higher?"** Depending on the answer, treat this as a part that you welcome (and then get her agreement to stand on the side), or use the Container to let slip inside all the negative experiences she has had that led to the fears she expresses.

Then, resume the protocol until VOC = 10.

(6) Projecting the resource into the future

Choose one of the following sentences according to the context.

- **Imagine having this resource in the future, at a time when you are facing...** (describe the problematic situation that has been identified before). **Imagine having...** (for example: courage, tenacity, calm, etc.) **to deal effectively with the situation**.
- **Imagine feeling...** (for example: confident, serene, anchored) **in this scene.**
- **Imagine feeling connected to...** (for example, name of the support figure or relational resource) **when you are confronted with this problematic situation. Observe how this would be for you. Listen to how this person who is your resource tells you exactly what you need.**
- **Feel your resource** (for example, for metaphorical or symbolic resources) **exactly as you would like to feel it.**
- **Tell yourself the words that express how you feel.**
- **Become aware of your resource, exactly in the way you need it.**

Continue with the stimulations or the short TAT poses, as long as it has a positive effect.

(7) Checking the SUD

Check the SUD of the problematic situation (how much it has decreased thanks to the resource).

Ask:

- **Now, when you focus on** (the problematic situation), **how supportive do you estimate** (repeat the description of the image and feelings)**, and how much on a scale from 0 to 10 do you still feel a disturbance, where 0 is not at all and 10 is very strong?** (SUD)

The alternative is to ask if the installation and the future projection of the selected resource helps the person in his impression that he can face the situation better:

Now, when you focus on (the problematic situation)**, how much do you think is true or supportive** (repeat the description of the image and feelings) **on a scale from 0 to 10, where 0 is completely false or unhelpful and 10 is completely true or supportive?** (VOC)

This process can be repeated for each of the qualities that the person wants to reinforce.

e. Use and maintain the resources

Once a resource is installed, it may be a good idea to suggest to the person being helped to use it between sessions:

- **I suggest, at times that seem appropriate to you, that you take some time to reconnect to this resource. Visualise (the resource), tell it to yourself (PC) and let yourself feel it (K), and if it's helpful, accompany all that by stimulations, tapping, or the TAT pose.**
- **If you feel it's difficult for you, stop and we'll do it again together.**

f. Resource Gallery

Parallel to the resource installation, it is possible to propose to the person being helped to imagine a "gallery", a bit like an art gallery, where he or she will be able to "expose" his or her various resources, in the form of paintings (of the image of the resource) or objects (the symbols of the resources). He can write the PCs below each painting. The person then imagines walking around in this "resource gallery", and can stop in front of each painting, let himself feel the resource, move on to another, etc. This is a great way to activate a set of resources.

g. Resource follow up

In subsequent sessions, the helper should reassess the resources installed (specific or general) to verify the effect of the resource installation on the person's stability (to see if the resources "hold").

When the person is ready for the phase of confrontation with a specific target, the helper can start the session by asking the person to select the resources (that have already been installed or new ones) that he or she needs to face the difficult event and reinforce them in the TAT pose/in EFT/with REMAP points.

h. The Sponge protocol

Simple form of resource use, adapted from the Wedge Technique, HAP 1999 by Brigitte Hansoul

This protocol is simpler than the previous one. It sets up three resources to deal with the same problematic situation. The SUD of the stressful situation is considerably reduced by connecting to positive networks.

Without even treating the negative, this procedure can be used to allow fragile patients to feel stronger in a situation, for example when the therapist thinks it is premature to treat the negative "head-on", or when the timing of the session does not allow it, or when the situation the patient is facing is imminent. If the time remaining during the session to work on the negative is too short, it is not recommended to bring the already fragile patient back into contact with the negative target. This may temporarily destabilise him rather than strengthen him to face what lies ahead. As mentioned above, keep in mind that this does not mean that the negative situation is being addressed.

Protocol:

1. Look for a stressful situation and ask for the SUD.

2. What qualities would you need to better cope with this stress?

Identify three specific qualities such as: strength, inner calm, ability to set limits, etc.

3. What quality would you like to start with?

Take the quality that the person chooses (or that evokes the most affects in him/her).

4. Has there been a situation in which you have noticed that you have some of this quality?

Let the person clearly describe a situation that he/she remembers and for which he/she shows some positive reactions.

5. What is the image that best describes this situation?

Look for the image that evokes this affect the most.

6. Where in your body can you notice a positive reaction when you connect to this situation/image?

Look for what body sensations the image causes and let the person locate these sensations in his or her body.

7. Get in touch with the image... and the body sensation. Are you in contact?

If so: "Think about that and tap (or stimulate a REMAP point, or take the TAT pose...)" for 10 seconds.

8. Then ask: **How is it now?**

Ask specifically if there is a change in the body sensation.

If it has become stronger, do another stimulation.

If there is a spontaneous affect bridge/associations to negative material, look for another situation in which the person had this quality.

9. Perform steps 7 and 8 for all three qualities.

10. Get in touch with the three qualities: (name all three) - **Are you in contact?**

If yes:

11. Look again at the stressful situation... and notice how disturbing it seems to you now from 0 to 10

Normally, the SUD has decreased significantly.

i. *Examples of Resource Installation*

(1) *Example 1: Experiential resource*

Part 2: Advanced Clinical EFT

1. Situation and required resources

BRIGITTE HANSOUL (therapist): What is the situation/event or person in relation to whom you want to make a resource?

PATIENT: I'm in an informal group. We had an official meeting where I had to defend our position, I found myself in a meeting where we distributed the roles; a colleague had to bring forward the technical aspects, she said she would be 5 minutes late and in fact, she came half an hour late.

We ended up at a meeting without these technical details.

I was in the role of managing the meeting, but I didn't have the elements and there was this void, this empty place next to me, the group pushed me to take this role and didn't behave according to our strategy to create the atmosphere for the other party to discuss with us; they were aggressive and the other party said: we will not discuss again!

I was not given the means to conduct the meeting and found myself in this position, super upset, angry, with a role where my task was not made easy.

She came later, made her arguments, it was against our strategy!

B: So the situation for which you would like a resource is....

P: In relation to this group where I have a role and where I am not respected, even if it is not formal, I would like to be respected and that everyone takes the responsibilities that we had given each other within the group.

B: You don't feel your role is respected and that makes you experience things...

P: Yes, unpleasant things, and I find myself in a situation where I wouldn't go if I knew in advance... we had worked on this for a year and I wouldn't have invested myself if I had known!

B: When you think about this situation, how disturbing is it?

P: At 8.

B: In this situation, what quality would you need?

P: My difficulty is to express myself in front of the group on why that annoys me, why I am upset; I make up a scene of what they will answer: if I approach this subject, it will be minimized by some, ridiculed by others...

B: The kind of quality you would like to have, how would you formulate it? You would like to express your opinion to the group?

P: Insist even if others minimize or ridicule me and remain faithful to what I am going through.

B: How would you like to feel in this situation?

P: Stronger, I feel weakened when it is minimized by others.

B: Faithful to your experience and stronger... Does one aspect speak to you the most?

P: Feel stronger, not really stronger, but stable in relation to my experience and the expression of my experience, more anchored.

B: More anchored in your experience to be able to express it. Either we take this resource: feeling more anchored, or we see what you need as a more precise quality to feel more anchored... it's up to you to tell me: more anchored is good, or sub-qualities is better for you?

P: Feeling supported.

B: Can we choose that feeling? If you feel supported, could you stay anchored in your experience and express it?

P: Yes.

2. Available resources

B: We're going to start from a situation where you felt supported. Is there an experience that comes to mind? Or the image of someone supportive?

P: A meeting that my supervisor was leading, there was our team and also another team with their supervisor. I had a different opinion and I couldn't speak to the supervisor of the other team, my supervisor gave me the opportunity to speak and supported me in the affirmation of what I was bringing even if it was difficult for the other team to hear.

Part 2: Advanced Clinical EFT

3. Feeling the resource

B: When you get into this situation, what do you see?

P: The meeting table, the supervisor of the other team facing me and my supervisor on the other side.

B: And when you feel supported, what do you hear?

P: He gives me the opportunity to speak and says to the other person: I have noticed that my colleague has a different opinion, I suggest that we listen to her, that we let her express herself.

B: And when you hear him say that to you, what do you feel?

P: A certain strength in me!

B: Where in your body?

P: In the plexus.

B: What about the emotional feelings?

P: I feel grown up, as if I stood up straighter easily; my voice is free, stable; there is some relaxation even if the situation is a little stressful.

B: Where do you feel this relaxation?

P: Generally in my muscles.

4. Installing the resource

B: What I propose you to do (bilateral tapping on GB34) is to connect you to this moment: you see this person in front of you, your supervisor who says: I propose that we listen to our colleague, you feel this strength, you let yourself grow, you feel this relaxation.

What did you feel?

P: More relaxation, a joy.

B: We do it again (tapping); you see that person again, your supervisor saying... and you feel that calm, that relaxation and you feel the joy.

What did you feel?

P: A feeling in my head as if something was coming back into place, a physical impression.

B: Once again (tapping): still in front of this person, your supervisor, this relaxation, you feel yourself growing, something is taking its place....

What did you observe?

P: This same expansion, but deeper; a while ago it was more up here and now it has also happened down there; there is a certain lightness.

B (tapping for 10 seconds): You see that and you can hear your supervisor: I propose that we listen to her; and this expansion down there, the lightness...

P: This expansion goes all the way to the base chakra and I feel rooted, I feel anchored.

B: Okay (tapping for 10 seconds), that feeling: anchored. What did you observe?

P: I am standing and I feel quite big inside.

B: Has it changed since the last time you tapped?

P: Yes, I grew up inside.

B: Okay, take that, you see and hear that, I'm standing, I've grown up. What's showing up?

P: That's great! I want to laugh - and a little lightness to it.

5. Strengthening the resource

B (without tapping): And when you feel like that in this lightness, what are the words that talk about you and say how you feel?

P: Really me! I am not in relation to others, but really in myself.

B: And how can you say what you say about yourself: I am myself? What would you call that?

P: It really comes from me!

Part 2: Advanced Clinical EFT

B: And when you put yourself in this situation and you say to yourself: it comes from me; what do you feel in your body?

P: A pleasant warmth, everywhere, and as if alive in the body.

B: We're going to do EFT tapping - get into this situation, tap, change at the rhythm you want, let yourself feel... and say to yourself: it really comes from me, and you let yourself feel the sensations in your body... What did you observe?

P: Nothing in particular, it was just pleasant.

B: And how much "it really comes from me" sounds real to you between 0 and 10?

P: At 9.

B: We do it again, saying "it really comes from me", feeling this warmth, the lightness, feeling alive in my body...

P: There's a very small voice that can't really believe that it can be like that.

B: What does it say?

P: It's not possible, or rather: it's going to change.

B: It is important that we accept this part, because she has other experiences, she seeks to protect you; we can thank her for having this concern to protect you with this speech she gives, and ask her if she would be okay to experiment and see what happens if she observes and intervenes if she wants.

P: Yes.

B (tapping): It really comes from me, the heat...

How did it go?

P: The first part was a child part, and she is ok, but another part says "we are not quite sure", it is an older part of the intellect, she is not ok.

B: This part is based on lived experiences... ask her if she is okay to let all these experiences slip into the container so that we can experience something else, another point of view?

P: Okay.

B (tapping): It's really me, it really comes from me, warm, alive...

P: It works now, I have seen several parts united, together.

B: How much would you say, between 0 and 10, "it really comes from me" sounds real?

P: At 10.

6. Projecting the resource into the future

B: Can you imagine yourself in your group with this feeling "it really comes from me", alive, warm, and you say to yourself: it really comes from me?

(Tapping GB34 for 10 seconds)

B: How did it go?

P: Well, I was completely relaxed and not at all in the feeling of having to assert myself but just to talk about how I experienced that, I can even joke and bring lightness into this.

B: We'll do it again, put yourself in this situation: it really comes from me, lightness, warmth...

How did it go there? Is there anything different?

P: No, the same thing.

7. Checking the SUD

B: When you think about this situation, how disturbing do you still feel it is?

P: I still feel a little tension in my chest, it's not so disturbing anymore, it's a little doubt as to how I'll position myself.

B: How much is the disturbance?

P: At 2, and I feel much more rooted, but I doubt about being able to express myself.

B: Either we do EFT on the remaining 2, or we do a resource on what is missing as a resource to be able to express yourself (end of the time available for the demonstration).

(2) Example 2: Relational resource, model

1. Situation and required resources

BRIGITTE HANSOUL (therapist): Do you have a problem situation or a person with whom you find it problematic?

PATIENT: In any situation where I am in a relationship, whether in a group or with a single person, except for my spouse, I am always on guard, I control myself, I judge myself, I criticize myself, I am not relaxed in company, I have trouble being simply myself, as if I am not well enough, and then, in general, I am very tired. I only now realise that it is because I always wonder what to say or not to say, what to do to please others, to be good with people.

B: And so, since we're going to measure a SUD in relation to that, can you take a particular situation?

P: Yes, I am with a friend at the restaurant, a friend with whom I get along very well, who is not at all into judgment and when I leave the restaurant, I am exhausted.

B: We're not going to take the next moment when you're exhausted, but the time during the situation.

P: Yes, actually, I'm very tense!

B: When you go back to that moment, how strong out of 10 do you feel the disturbance?

P: In terms of tension, I'm at least at 8.

B: And when you think about this situation at the restaurant, what qualities do you think you need to deal with it?

P: I just want to be myself, no one asks me of anything else. Just chatting together, exchanging. Besides that we're friends, it's not at all someone who will make a judgment, it's me inside who's not well, I feel inferior; I just want to be myself, be calm and talk.

B: You would like to be calm....

P: And relaxed.

B: Calm and relaxed, and what would you like to think of yourself, you said you feel inferior....

P: I'm just different.

B: That's by contrast, because you said you felt inferior, otherwise, how would you like to be, behave, be there with him?

P: On an equal footing... if you want to take specific points, he may be a better trainer than me, but he has more experience and that doesn't bother me in itself, it's normal and maybe in therapy I do more... but we don't care, I don't want to always be in this "being better or worse", we're just here, that's all.

B: So, you'd like to feel...

P: Present and have my place... yes, that's it.

B: And so, in relation to that, you would like to be yourself, to feel that you are calm and relaxed, to feel that you have your place, to be present... so what are the specific qualities that you feel would help you on that path? Be calm...

P: Having more confidence in myself and in my ability to interact with him, to be able to feel interesting, rather than not being important.

B: In terms of your self-confidence in order to have your place, one of the important things would be the fact that you might feel interesting...

P: It feels weird, because when I say: feeling interesting, I feel like I want to put myself in the "More" position.

B: How would you put it, then?

P: To have the right to simply be myself, to have the right to simply be there...

B: Okay, and if we take that as a quality, this feeling of having the right to be there, to be yourself, that's it.

P: Yes.

2. Available resources

Part 2: Advanced Clinical EFT

B: Do you have in your experience, your background, any moments when you could feel that?

P: Just recently, otherwise I don't see any others, at my mother's bedside, I had the feeling that I had the right to be there and to be in my place.

B: This one is very recent, but are there other resources from which we could start that seem more accessible or stronger to you? It could be someone you know, a role model, someone from your history, from a movie, an imaginary character, who really embodies this feeling for you: I have the right to be there, I have the right to be myself?

P: It's difficult...

B: Do you know anyone who is like that?

...

B: Or would there be a symbol, an element that you can see through: I have the right to be there?

P: Oh yes, I have a friend who is a yoga teacher and when he is in his yoga workshop, he is really in the unconditional welcome of people, of what they are, and he is really in the right position, he is in his place.

B: Okay, so, what speaks best to you as a resource, the experience with your mother or to connect with that friend?

P: Connect to this friend.

3. Feeling the resource

B: Okay, think about this friend, when you imagine him like that, do you see him particularly in a certain position?

P: I see him in the yoga classes, when he is welcoming the people: it's personalised, there's a kind of energy that comes from him, you feel welcome and so he gives everyone a place.

B: Okay, when you see him in that greeting, what image do you have?

P: He is smiling, he is calm, present, no rush, he takes things as they are...

B: If you want to connect, you can close your eyes, you really look at him now, you connect to this image of him, at this moment, you see him in this reception, with this image of him, calm, smiling... what do you feel in yourself when you see him like that?

P: I feel welcomed, unconditionally, I feel calm, as if there were something warm, pleasant.

B: And this something warm and pleasant, how do you feel it in your body?

P: It's more like I'm wrapped up. As if his voice, his gaze, the energy he radiates surrounds me.

3a. Checking the resource (optional)

B: Take this image, you feel this warmth, this energy, you feel calm and welcomed; when you are connected to all this and you think about your friend trainer, how helpful it is to feel welcomed, calm about the situation with your friend, from 0 to 10, where 0 is not at all helpful and 10 is totally helpful.

P: If I'm connected to this... I actually don't have a problem if I stay with this warmth, this calm...

4. Installing the resource

B: It's helping at 10, so it's already very good.... now just start looking at your yoga teacher again, Fabrice... look at Fabrice, you see his energy, he's calm, smiling, you feel this warmth that surrounds you, you feel unconditionally welcomed...

P: I have a parasitic interference... sorry.... I'm jealous!

B: Are you jealous that he could be like that?

P: Yes.

B: Do you have your Container and your word from the Basic State?

P: A milk tank, and I don't have a Basic State word, I can't do it.

B: I would like you to think about your container and let slip inside everything that has led to you feeling jealous earlier, everything that has led to these parts of you being activated in this jealousy, all the experiences you've had, all the experiences that have led to this, you let all this slip into your milk tank... and you tell me when it is done.

Part 2: Advanced Clinical EFT

P: Okay.

B: Now think back to Fabrice as you did earlier: you see him smiling, welcoming, and you feel welcome, you feel that energy, that warmth, that calm in you and while you're doing that, you can take the TAT pose, just by connecting to that, that warmth that envelops you, that calm.... that's it, you can let go.

What do you notice in yourself?

P: There is both this warmth and then a point, I don't know what it is.

B: Put your attention on your container: there is a part that expresses herself there through this point, ask her if she would agree to let slip into the container everything that has led to her being activated, knowing that by developing this resource, this will surely help her as well, knowing that if she leaves us room to develop this resource, you will also be able to take better care for her. Ask if she agrees with that.

P: Yes.

B: Pay attention to your milk tank and let slip inside everything that has led to this point, all the experiences, all that this part has lived, let it slip in...

P: Okay.

B: When you think about Fabrice, do you feel okay?

P: Yes.

5. Strengthening the resource

B: We're going to take up the TAT pose again, and again you connect to this image, you see him welcoming, smiling, you let yourself feel the warmth, and you can say to yourself: I'm unconditionally welcomed, ok, you can relax... tell me, what did you notice when you made this pose?

P: As if calm settled in and I tell myself spontaneously, raising my arms: thank you, life!

B: Take the pose again and connect again to this image of Fabrice, and say to yourself: I am unconditionally welcomed, feel the warmth... and you can relax...

P: As if I were rolling in a ball, like bears when they play in the grass....

B: Did you have the feeling that it was getting worse?

P: There was something more cheerful!

B: Okay, we'll do it one more time. Take a pose, look at Fabrice, welcoming, smiling, feeling the warmth, and... you can relax...

P: It's as if there was love settling in...

B: How do you feel that physically?

P: Wellness, something warm that sets in... it flows...

B: Let's take the pose again, Fabrice, I'm unconditionally welcomed, feel the warm love that flows... you can relax.

P: There is something negative coming to me, a part that wants to punish me and says to me: you have no right to that.

B: What do you think... Do you want to have a dialogue with her? Do you want to communicate with her?

P: Not really....

B: So, think about your container, think about that part that came, and probably for good reasons, telling you: you have no right to that! She's certainly protecting something. Tell her that we heard that she had fears and that you certainly have experienced things that generated those fears, and ask her if she agrees to let them slip into the container so that you can discover something else and that you will take her into account, you are taking her into account, as you have heard the fears she has. Ask her if she just wants to give you a little space to let you experience this resource, experience something else and see what that can do for you...; would she be okay with that?

P: She doesn't want to give up completely.

B: What is she afraid of?

P: That I may die.

B: She's afraid you may die. And why is she afraid that you may die if you experience this love....

Part 2: Advanced Clinical EFT

P: Because I could start being happy and I can't, that's what she says.

B: She's afraid you may die if you go through this, if you start being happy... do you understand the connection for her? Can she explain?

P: It's a loyalty to my mother who never laughs; and if you laughed, when you were a child, she would get angry.

B: We understand that for this part, having joy, being happy is associated with something going wrong, there is a danger for her.

Bring your attention to your container and let slip into it all the experiences you have just spoken about and all the ones that would be in your unconscious in relation to this association of joy and danger, let all these experiences slip inside and tell me...

P: She's okay for now.

B: Think about Fabrice again, take a pose, see Fabrice welcoming, smiling and let yourself feel this love flowing, being warm... and you can relax... how is it going now?

P: I am lying with my arms stretched in a field of flowers, the sun is beautiful, that's me...

B: And when you are lying like that and thinking: I am unconditionally welcomed?

P: I am smiling.

B: Okay, and if you always imagine yourself there and you say to yourself: I have my place, I have the right to be there, I have the right to be myself, how true does it sound between 0 and 10?

P: It's okay.

6. Projecting the resource into the future

B: And when you keep this connection and turn to your training friend, how does it work?

P: I am smiling and he is smiling too.

7. Check the SUD

B: Is there still a disturbance when you meet with your trainer friend? In your body?

P: There could still be a tension at 1 maybe... no, it's okay.

(3) Example 3: Symbol resource

The demonstration I made with Stephanie, which is transcribed below, is interesting in various ways.

A. It demonstrates the importance of taking the time to **specify the situation and the nature of the resource** being sought. The latter is not easy for Stephanie to identify. I help her by making suggestions to her while ensuring that she looks for what precisely matches her need.

B. This is a case of a **resource that must be "nuanced"**: Stephanie needed a resource of strength but was afraid that it would make her inhuman. I therefore suggest that she look for a model that has strength, but also humanity. She evokes male family figures, but they obviously do not have the required qualities. So, I dismiss them. As having a tender heart is associated with the idea of being fooled, and Stephanie can't find a resource that combines strength and humanity, I'm about to manage differently, when her unconscious brings her the image of a resource that combines both aspects: a bear, which can be strong and tender at the same time.

C. During the installation of the power resource, a part arises that is very insecure and is afraid of being in danger of death. I take the time to make a **specific resource for this part** too insecure to be easily put aside. We'll use a dome of light there. Once this security is in place, I return to where I was in the installation of the power resource (the bear).

1/ Situation and required resources

a. Situation

BRIGITTE: Choose a situation in your life in which you would need resources.

STEPHANIE: I risk going wide... do we need a specific situation?

B: Yes, a situation where you have found yourself in difficulty and you feel that you need resources.

S: It's related to my divorce procedure, we're in process of liquidation of the shared property, we sold the house, my ex is blocking me from receiving my share, the Public Center for Social Welfare doesn't want to give me money because I'm independent. In a month, my accounts will be at zero. I experience a lot of injustice, because the money from this house is a considerable amount to which I am entitled. If it continues like this, we'll have to go before the judge, I'm entitled to it. It represents a lot of energy and a lot of potential, because I have almost nothing left to live on and my children live with me, there are four of us involved but I am responsible. And, already last year, I almost stopped school to get a job. What happened two weeks ago also called that into question. There are many issues behind this and a whole life situation for me and also for my children. This money is like having an energy ball in front of me and I can't integrate it into myself. I'm entitled to it and everything drags on. The house has been sold since June and I still don't have my money. There are a whole series of events that are causing everything to fall behind. My ex changed his lawyer who died two days later, and everything always happens to block and delay. No one expected that at the meeting, that he would block me from receiving this money, and I see it as a great injustice.

b. Required resources

B: It's really this feeling of injustice, because there's this considerable amount of money, this ball of energy that you can't integrate because it's blocked. When you think about that, what resources would you need to deal with this situation in its current state?

S: I need my lawyer.

B: Okay, and your lawyer is a resource for you, do you feel you can really count on him?

S: Yes, but what I have been struggling with in this situation and for the past year and a half is the process of justice which is very, very slow. We will starve to death before justice is done, we're in a mess.

B: What can help us is that you first identify the qualities, the resources, I don't know, courage, patience, strength or... what would you need to feel in yourself as qualities, so that the <u>situation seems more bearable to you or so that you can do things as you want?</u> (A)

S: I don't know, because I don't have a choice: I must have courage to stand up, so I still find it, otherwise I wouldn't be here; it is the same with patience.

What I miss the most is a support, a prop to hold on to. I really find myself in the position of a little girl who calls for help and who doesn't have that crutch, that prop next to her, so she feels completely alone and helpless. There is a lot of helplessness in this situation.

B: What you really need is this resource to be supported, to have a prop because you feel like a little girl.

S: In fact, I have all the capacity to be this prop myself, but there is a whole situation that makes me not enough. We have to bring in the justice system and this is done very, very slowly, going on for months in a row.

B: What you're telling me is that you have the ability to support yourself and you know that you can use these abilities normally, but that here, because it blocks, as you have to bring in justice, there's really this powerlessness. It's difficult, that's true: because it blocks, you don't know how to use your own resources. They're not enough and so you feel helpless. I understand that you usually have internal resources that help you deal with things, but here they're affected, right?

S: They are affected and it is above all the duration that makes it hard, it lasts too long.

B: What would you need since it lasts and since it doesn't depend on you that the outside blocks?

S: What I miss most is <u>stability,</u> from time to time I fall and then I go up the slope, as if I clung to all my resources and it is okay, I continue, I have hope, I move forward and I continue and then there is an event that takes on more importance and that makes disappear everything that has made me do all I could to hold onto it, and it is as if every time I have to start climbing again. What I lack is something stable: it seems that I have found some strength and then, as it's been going on for so long, I regularly fall back into the hole, into the ditch, so for ten days I've been a little bit in this ditch again.

B: Could we say...?

Part 2: Advanced Clinical EFT

S: What I'm missing is the ladder... the ladder that holds. I find the ladder, but the ladder seems to be regularly pushed back into the hole.

B: I hear two things: that in a moment like this when you feel like you're in the hole, you need this ladder as a support to come out; and at the same time, that every time you manage to climb the ladder, something happens, it falls apart and then there's a feeling - which one? Discouragement? What would you say?

S: Powerlessness, injustice, no matter how much I hold on to my resources, there is always something new, something stronger, that tests me, a stronger opponent, and I can't handle it.

B: I'll tell you what I think might help you and you try to test inside yourself, you tell me if there are ideas that resonate, something that we could boost as resources. First of all, you tell me that you have the inner resources, so we could already use them to boost the moments when you felt them and when you noticed that they were effective; that's the first thing we could take.

The second thing is that you tell me you need a ladder, a support at a time when you have the feeling of being on the bottom, so there, we could take as resources some images, symbols of support, something that helps you and allows you to feel supported.

The third thing I see as possible is that when you tell me that this comes back, the opponent is stronger: we could take an experience you've had where, despite the fact that everything falls on you, you've gotten away with it, a resource that would be of the order of "even when everything seems to be going wrong, it ends well".

What do you feel would help you the most?

S: The last idea, I don't understand it very well, I would go and look for it in an experience?

B: Don't worry about where to look for it. You would be able to feel today that even though it has fallen on you again, for the 10th time, you have climbed up; and that you can have hope and certainty that you will start again, it will be fine. Because that's kind of what I feel in what you're telling me, it's that when you're in that hole, there's despair: it's too much now, I don't have a ladder, it's not going to be okay.

Tell me what you would need most in all this, or in anything else that would come up to you?

S: The 2nd point, inner resources, symbols... this, I have already developed quite a bit, it helps me a lot but, in fact, deep down inside, I think I am always looking for something external. I manage to climb back up the slope, I have resources inside, but I'm constantly looking outside.

B: You mean that in trying to use models, there is something that maintains the fact that you are not strong enough inside?

S: Yes.

B: How would you like to feel inside in this situation?

S: Almost unshakeable, without being inhuman. No, stronger, I'd like to feel strong!

B: What would you like to think of yourself? (PC)

It could be just that (I am strong/I feel strong), but see if it also comes in other forms...

S: In this situation?

B: Yes, if you were unshakeable and strong, what could you say about yourself?

S : In fact, it's paradoxical because feeling strong is also being able to manage all emotions, and partially I also attribute this to an inhuman side, a robot ; I want to be stronger to live all that remains to be lived and, at the same time, I have a part of myself that says I want to remain human... I am afraid to close myself to life, to others, to completely close my heart to everything, I am afraid to close myself off to everything else and not enjoy life if I am strong and unshakeable like that at the emotional level. My fear is there.

2/ Available resources

B: We could check and see if in your experiences or in the people you have been communicating with, you have someone who is strong but always in contact with their emotions, not inhuman. Firm, strong but always in contact with themselves and their emotions.

S: The images of strong people around me are my father and my grandfather on my father's side; at the same time, my grandfather, I only saw him vulnerable once, at the end of his life, and I discerned a human side. He scared me all my childhood, he was a very strong person who succeeded in everything, unshakeable in life, but that could not be reached from the heart's point of view, he was hard. My father doesn't have that hard side, but he never shows anything. For these two characters, the only time I saw their vulnerable side was when they had physical problems, like kids...

B: These are not good resources for us now, so would there be a symbol, an image that gives you that impression...?

S: Where I combine strength with a tender heart?

B: Yes, would you see an image, a symbol, a divinity that would represent that?

S: I don't think so, I really have the association that when you have a tender heart, you get taken advantage of, that's what I've been going through since I was a little girl...

B: Here, we have two options: we can do a little TAT on the negative belief "if you have a tender heart, you get taken advantage of", so that it gives us an opening, and then we can make a resource.

The other thing we can do is that in resources, sometimes we divide the different aspects we need and make a resource of each one. We could make being strong a resource, even though for you it would be too inhuman. Then, we could make one more resource, not the tender heart, given the way it sounded, but rather a resource of humanity, so that you can really feel that the two are present; just because you have one, it doesn't mean the other isn't there.

I think... tell me, do you have a feeling about this?

S: I think I found a symbol, in fact, a totem that combines both: the bear that can be very strong, very powerful and at the same time, the bear is also this soft toy for kids, the teddy bear.

3/ Feeling the resource

B: Great! Let's take that. Tell me: when you connect to this bear, what do you see? That bear that is both tender and strong? (V)

S: I see a brown bear standing upright in all its power, on its hind legs, who at any time can decide to use its strength or to calm down, cuddle up and be gentle.

B: We're going to focus on what you feel when you see it like that, in all its strength and also in its ability to decide what to do with it; when you see it like that, what do you feel? (K)

S: It's like a prop settling down all along my chest, in fact, it gives me strength... and at the same time my heart remains open. It's really the right symbol.

B: Your heart stays open, you feel like a prop at the chest level. And what feeling does that give you, what emotion? (E)

S: It's like I'm getting more power, actually.

B: And when you regain power, how does that make you feel?

S: I feel safe.

B: Safe.

S: And as a result there's peace too, because if I feel strong and safe, I can be at peace.

3a/ Checking the resource

B: We'll see for now, if you think about the blocked situation "things don't depend on me", and you connect to these words: it's like a prop in my chest, my heart remains open, I feel safe, at peace, I find my power, how helpful are these words in your situation: 0 not at all, 10 very helpful?

S: I feel like saying 6.

4/ Installing the resource

B: Okay, we're going back to the image of the bear; you connect to that image, you really let yourself be won over by that prop feeling, your heart remains open, feeling of safety, peace, "I find my power"; just stay with that and tell me how it feels.

Part 2: Advanced Clinical EFT

S: I want to go towards that, but it's like having a ball in my stomach, there's fear, fear that it won't hold, that it's not possible.

B: There is a part of you that can connect to this force, so that "I find my power again" is really about yourself, and there is a part of you that is afraid that this won't hold, and that necessarily is triggered when you stay in contact with the resource.

S: It comes almost at the same time, actually!

B: You had your Container yesterday: a train carrying away what needed to be reprocessed. Close your eyes if it helps and focus your attention on your train. And all the experiences that have led to that part being activated and being afraid it wouldn't hold, all the experiences in your life, all the imprints that have led to that, you just let them slip inside your train.

S: The opposite of yesterday is happening, my train remains motionless, because for months, every time something happens and things get better, something even stronger happens, it's as if my train is waiting for the continuation....

B: Exactly, everything you just told me, everything that happened, all those memories, let them slip inside the train so that now, we can do this resource, let them slip there. And we can reassure the part who has experienced all this, we can tell her that we understand that she is afraid, that she has had these experiences and that we can, for the moment, let all that past slip into the train.

S: ... It is calming down.

B: Put your attention on your bear, his strength, you see him like that, standing upright. And let yourself go and feel this prop, your heart that remains open, this feeling of safety when you see him like that. He can decide to use his strength, or he can decide to be tender-hearted. The feeling of peace... Look how it feels.

S: I'm more there now than I was before, but there's still a little something blocking it.

B: What do you feel?

S: Like a bar, there (chest), it's as if the power, the force could go up to there (chest) and then it gets stuck.

B: (C) This feeling, do you have any idea why it blocks?

S: I think that...... the fear that it's not enough... it's almost the fear of dying, that if I can't get out of this mess, the end is death; that I would have no other way out but this one, the fear of reaching the very end...

B: It's really a part of you that's very, very insecure, it's the survival that's wondering if it will all be fine, so I think it would be important to make a resource of security for that part of you.

Do you have a security resource, do you have a moment when you felt secure, a person who really made you feel secure, it's about having confidence in the future, feeling secure about the future?

S: No, not really, with my therapist we have installed security resources, I have symbols for physical security, for security at home, it's true that that's where the problem lies, it's the security for the future, that I can face things.

B: What would be the image of security for you, the opposite of what you're telling me, if you had to cut an image out from a magazine, an image that represents this total security?

S: The image that comes to me is to install a white dome over me and my children, to be under this white dome, a dome of light with the protection of the whole universe, in fact.

B: Now connect to this white dome that protects you and your children and tell me how you feel?

What does it make you feel in your body?

S: Something I often find in meditation, I am used to this white dome, but it's true that sometimes I don't think about putting myself under this white dome and immediately, it's as if it were there, I'm flooded with light, with calm, there's no more problems, everything's fine.

B: Flooded with light, calm, everything is fine.

In your body, is there calm? Where do you feel it in your body, how do you feel it in your body?

S: It's really like a shower, which also penetrates the heart.

Part 2: Advanced Clinical EFT

B: Okay, so you take the TAT pose. And you connect to that, all that you have just said, "there is this dome that is there, that protects us, that floods us with light", you feel this shower in your heart, and everything is fine. How are you feeling?

S: I want to say: everything is fine...

B: How much do you think this sounds true, "Everything's fine, I'm safe", when you're connected to this resource?

S: I want to say 10, but there is a very small part that remains sceptical, I would say 9.5.

B: Okay, you're back in the pose. Okay, let yourself go in order to feel this shower of light, this dome, this calm, your heart (pause). There, you can now release. Has that changed from 9.5?

S: Yes, it's 10.

(Back to the primary resource.)

5/ Strengthening the resource

B: Okay. Go back to the image of the bear, and reconnect with the image of the bear, straightened up, feel its strength and let yourself feel in your body the effect it has on you, the prop, the feeling of security, peace... and tell me how it's going now.

S: For me, it is as if all the qualities of the bear were in me, I am the bear. I am a lady-bear!

B: Great, we take the TAT pose, and you let yourself go in order to feel exactly what you just said there. All the qualities of the bear are in you, you are the bear, security, strength, peace, the heart that remains open (pause). There, you can now release. How was it?

S: Good.

B: Can you feel it's amplifying more?

S: Yes.

B: So, we'll do the pose again. The same thing, you connect to the bear, to yourself, to this feeling of being the bear, security, peace, feeling of a prop, I find my power back (pause)... And you can let go.

How much do you think all this sounds true, here and now, when we are doing it?

S: At 10.

6/ Projecting the resource into the future and 7/ Checking the SUD

B: I would like you to connect to the situation that is blocked because of justice: your ex blocking you, the feeling of injustice, and when I say these words, this bear that you are, with a feeling of a prop along the chest, the heart that remains open, security, peace, "I find my power back"; how much is that helpful in this situation? 0 not at all helpful and 10 very helpful...

S: I feel good, either it will be a bear that is stronger than me, or I am stronger than him, we will see!

B: You feel calm.

S: I feel that I have more weapons, I feel equal with my opponent, I do not feel superior to him, but equal to equal. I have the same cards as my opponent in my hand.

B: Thank you, Stephanie.

F. The targeting

The targeting work is done from the most general to the most specific, identifying in the following order:

- the problem and the theme;
- the specific event;
- the worst moment;
- the criteria of the target:
- image of the worst moment,
- emotions,

Part 2: Advanced Clinical EFT

- sensations,
- negative belief,
- SUD.

1. General problem

When treating a difficulty experienced by the patient, targeting specific facts is very important (especially in EFT and REMAP). A failure of the technique is often based on a lack of precision in the choice of the treated events.

Indeed, the dysfunctional network is made up of the traces of specific **events** experienced at a specific time, in a specific place, with specific people ("When my father called me an incapable person in the kitchen when I was 6 years old"), and not by general concepts ("My father belittled me all the time").

First, we will identify the patient's general **problem** ("I had a father who belittled me"), then, within this problem, we will focus on specific facts: **a particular situation or event**.

The treatment must target these specific events, not concepts.

2. Specific event

The target has the structure of a single memory (or a network) encoded in memory database and must therefore be a **specific event that has been experienced**, that can be dated, and not a concept.

Example: "When my father came home two hours late and hit me on my 6th birthday."

3. Finding the centre of the target

For some therapeutic methods (EMDR, EFT, REMAP®), the more precise the target, the faster and more effective the treatment. Hence, you should look for the centre of the target, that is, the "worst" part of this memory. In the Movie metaphor, this is the worst moment of the movie that you could summarise by the title of the movie or this scene.

The more the patient focuses his attention on the worst moment of the memory, the faster the treatment of the memory will be.

Here are the aspects that allow the patient to be connected to this centre:

- Im: the image of the worst moment of the memory;
- NC: the most disabling negative belief/cognition associated with the memory;
- E: the emotion (several can be accepted; however, identify the strongest one);
- K: the physical sensation;
- SUD.

The SUD, calibrated with this set of aspects, could be higher than the one previously found for this target! The explanation is very simple... The person is connected to the point felt as "the worst", and therefore to the maximum intensity of his current resonance to the memory.

IMG 10

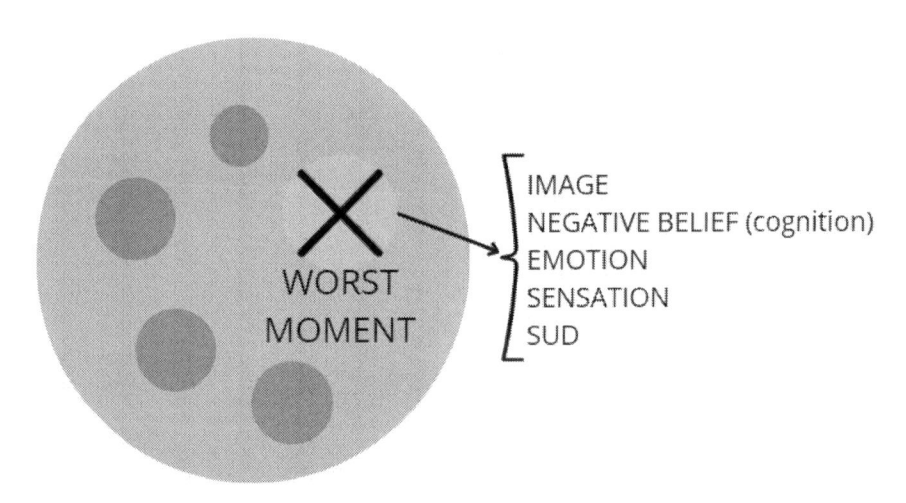

IMAGE
NEGATIVE BELIEF (cognition)
EMOTION
SENSATION
SUD

WORST MOMENT

4. **Finding the image of the worst moment**

Source: Shapiro, EMDR

This is the visual image associated with the worst moment of the event. Most of the time, the strongest trace, the most important thing about an event is what you see in your head when you think about it.

More rarely, what comes to mind is not the visual image, but rather the auditory memory of words that have been spoken, or of noises (in an accident, for example), or the physical feeling that has been imprinted in us.

In this case, find, if possible, the visual image that accompanies the auditory or kinaesthetic memory, and focus on the whole. By extension, this set will then be called "the image of the worst memory".

Questions:

What is the worst image you see when you think about that?
Or
What is the image that represents the most difficult moment?
Or
What is the first image that comes to you spontaneously when you think about this situation?

5. Identifying the negative belief (cognition) of the worst moment

Source: EMDR

These are the beliefs that the person has about himself when he thinks about the worst moment.

We are looking for the belief that underlies the current negative experience of the memory. To find it, we try to meet the following **criteria**:

- irrational;
- preferably formulated in "I" form (1st person singular);
- still valid today;
- relative to the most important aspect of the emotion (emotional resonance);
- generalisable: broader effectiveness.

Four main categories

This belief can be related to one of the following areas:

- lack of **security;**
- lack of **self-esteem;**
- responsibility/culpability;
- lack of **choice.**

These categories follow the developmental chronology: first of all, the baby needs to have a sufficient sense of security (survival). Then, the issue will be about its image of itself: who am I? Who am I to the other? (Self-esteem) The themes of guilt/responsibility and lack of choice come later at the developmental level.

Questions

When you think about this image, what do you think of yourself?

When you think about this image, what are the words that come to you that say something negative about you?

When you think about this image, what does it say about you?

When you think about this image, what conclusion did you draw about yourself because of what had happened to you?

When you think about this image, what conclusion about yourself coincides with this feeling/emotion? (According to what the patient said)

What are you afraid that people will think of you?

Adapt your questions to the situation; some are more helpful than others in a given situation.

See the "List of Beliefs and Cognitions" below.

6. Specifying the emotion of the worst moment

It is the emotion felt by the patient **when the patient is thinking about the worst moment**: fear, anger, anxiety, worry, guilt, frustration, discouragement, shock, etc.

There may be several of them. In this case, it is useful to ask the patient to specify which one is the strongest, even if all the emotions mentioned will be repeated during the protocol.

Part 2: Advanced Clinical EFT

As seen above, there may be the reminiscence of an emotion from the past and/or a current emotion that was not present in the past.

Question

When you think about this image of (repeat the situation) and these negative thoughts (repeat the NC), what emotions do you experience?

(If there are several) Which emotion is the strongest?

7. Specifying the physical sensations of the worst moment

It is the localization of the physical sensation felt **when the patient is thinking about the worst moment**: headache, ball in the throat, knot in the stomach, discomfort in any part of the body, etc.

Question

When you think about this image of (repeat the situation), these negative thoughts (repeat the NC), and you experience this (these) emotion (s), where do you feel it (them) in your body?

8. Asking for the SUD of the worst moment

It is the SUD felt by the patient when he is thinking about the worst moment and is connecting to the emotion(s) and physical sensation(s).

Question

When you think of this image of (repeat the moment), these negative thoughts (repeat the NC), and you experience this (these) emotion(s) and (these) physical sensation(s), how much between 0 and 10 do you feel the disturbance? With 0 for no disturbance at all and 10 for the most disturbance you can imagine?

9. List of beliefs and cognitions

NEGATIVE BELIEFS	**POSITIVE BELIEFS**
Safety / Survival	**Safety / Survival**
I am in danger	I am safe and secure

I am going to die	I am safe and secure
I am not going to make it	It's over, I survived
I cannot defend myself	I can (learn) to defend myself
I am defenceless	I can (learn) to protect myself
I can do nothing	I can do something
I cannot trust myself	I can trust myself
I cannot rely on my judgement	I can rely on my judgement
I can trust no one	I can choose whom I trust

Responsibility / Guilt	**Responsibility / Guilt**
I am guilty	I did the best I could
I did something wrong	I did the best I could
I should have done something	I did what I could
I should have known what to do	I did what I could
I could have done better	I did the best I could
I am not reliable	I can make mistakes, but I am reliable

Part 2: Advanced Clinical EFT

Self-esteem	Self-esteem
I am not good enough	I am someone good
I am worthless	I have value
I am not good at all	I am worthy
I am not important (insignificant)	I am important
I don't deserve to be loved	I deserve to be loved
I don't deserve love	I can receive love
I don't deserve to...	I deserve to ... I can have...
I don't deserve to be happy	I deserve to be happy
I only deserve bad things	I deserve good things
I deserve trouble	I deserve to do well
I deserve to die	I deserve to live
I am incapable	I am capable
I am a failure (I'm going to fail)	I can succeed
I am stupid	I am intelligent
I do stupid things	I can learn
I am weak	I can be strong
I am bad, monstrous	I am a good person
I am a bad guy	I am good even with the mistakes I have made
I am horrible	I am good as I am
I am unworthy	I am respectable
I am ugly	I am ok as I am
I have to be perfect	I can be myself
I have to be perfect	I can make mistakes

Possibility of choice	Possibility of choice
I am stuck, a prisoner	I am free

I don't have a choice	I have a choice now
I have no control	I am in control
I cannot have what I want	I can obtain what I want
I cannot succeed	I can succeed
I cannot trust anyone	I can choose whom I trust
I cannot stand it	I can (learn to) manage it
I cannot accept it	I can choose to accept it
I am incapable	I am capable if I want to

Part 2: Advanced Clinical EFT

III. Simple trauma: phases of the treatment

The distinction between simple and complex trauma has been described in the first part of this book.

Here are the phases of the treatment plan for a simple trauma or problem: patient who does not have a complex trauma and for whom the therapist can therefore target and treat the centre of the problem (the most intense event and its roots):

1. Anamnesis protocol (below).

2. Treatment plan: decide the order of the targets to be treated (below).

3. Preparation (Therapeutic rapport and alliance, Safe Place, Container, Basic State): see above.

4. Treatment of targets according to the treatment plan: see chapter "Treatment plan".

A. Anamnesis protocol

By Chantal Bailly for Therapeutia and Yves W.

First, if it is possible at this moment of the therapy, keep in your mind, during the anamnesis, also to try to find the different parts related with the problem (see Ego States, IFS and SEB). Exiles (wounded parts), Fireworkers (OCD, mentalization, phobia, addictions, excessive behaviours) and Managers (control parts)

1. What is (are) the problem(s)? (Present)

- Behaviour? Sickness? Emotional problem? Trauma? Belief?
- If several, what is the **most serious** or **urgent problem** to be addressed?
- **What** is this problem **about**?
- What are the **circumstances** and the **triggers** of the problem?
- How **often** does the problem occur?
- **Why** is the patient consulting **now**?

- Redefine the problem(s) in clear, precise and acceptable terms.

   2. What is the history of the problem? (Past)

- When did it start? Does the client remember **the first time**?
- List different **memories** related to this problem (network) and identify the **most charged**

memories responsible for the dysfunction.

- What is the most painful memory, where was it **the hardest**?
- When and how did the problem **last occur**?
- What other problems can this problem be related to?
- What is the client blaming the problem on? **What is his interpretation**?

   3. What solutions have already been tried?

- Has he seen any **doctors, therapists**? Did he take any **medication**? Which ones? Has he been **hospitalised**?
- On the other hand, what has the patient already tried by himself?

   4. Exploring psychological and social resources

- Is the client surrounded by people? Does he have a family? Or is he very isolated?
- What is his type of life? What kind of studies has he done? What kind of work?
- Does he have favorite activities in his free time? Hobbies? Dreams? What does he like to do?
- Does he appear to be well anchored in reality? Capable of introspection? Stable or very fragile? Self-destructive? Suicidal?

   5. Defining the healing objective(s) (Future)

- Define realistic and accessible objectives in terms of positive behaviours or beliefs.

- Future scenario: how would you like to imagine yourself in the future in a similar situation?

6. Designing a treatment plan

(See the chapter of the same name)
- Stabilisation and therapeutic alliance, reinforcement of **resources**, if necessary.
- Choice of problems, symptoms, **targets** to be treated as a priority.
- Work on the past, the present and a projection into **the future for simple traumas**.
- **Re-specify the treatment plan if you are confronted with a complex trauma.**
- Choice of the **techniques** to be used: listening and ACP, SEB, TAT®, EFT, REMAP®, Logosynthesis®, IFS, CFT, etc.

7. Evaluating the treatment

- See the objectives achieved. Ask **the client for an evaluation** of his or her treatment, what he or she has resolved and how satisfied he or she is.
- **Personal feedback** from the therapist.
- "Goodbye" and end of therapy.

B. Treatment plan

1. Choosing the problem

As the anamnesis establishes, the first step is to identify the different problems or themes brought by the patient, and then to select the one to be addressed first.

Usually, the patient is asked which problem is the **most serious or urgent to treat**.

2. Checking if the problem is isolated or networked

It is a question of determining **what other problems can be related to this problem.**

The isolated or networked nature of the problem is investigated.

See the chapter "Case Conceptualisation" for the example of phobia.

If you suspect a networking nature of the problem, then you should target the **most influential aspect of the network** in question, respecting the rigorous restrictions if the patient has a complex trauma profile. See the chapter "Complex Traumas" below.

3. Logic of the three periods: the past, the present and the future

The logic of conditioning painful emotions and associated negative beliefs (an event of the past that conditions current events) leads to the following psychotherapeutic approach:

1) Process the dysfunctional memories from the **past** - etiology.
2) Process the triggers of the **present** (conditioned triggers).
3) Address the fears of the **future**.

Some of these targets would be mentioned by the patient during the anamnesis. The others should be searched for and processed in the order given by the Past/Present/Future protocol: PPF protocol.

The elements involved in this protocol are detailed below. The protocol itself is summarised further in the text.

a. The level of the present

Present trigger

Part 2: Advanced Clinical EFT

When an event could not be "digested" by the AIP, a dysfunctional memory network develops in the past. This would manifest in the present in the form of any situation that has an element similar to the undigested situation from the past. It is like in Pavlov's dog conditioning experience where a "bell" would activate the dysfunctional network of the past. The reaction of the present will therefore be disproportionate, since it is not adaptive.

The current event that triggers the dysfunctional network of the past is called "present trigger".

Example: A patient had a violent father who beat him and screamed frequently. These memories are stored dysfunctionally, which means that their emotional and cognitive content (the NCs) remains active. The mere fact that, in the present, someone raises their voice is a bell that reactivates the whole reaction of fear and submission felt by the child at the time. This reaction seems irrational and disproportionate if it occurs when his boss raises his voice a little at a meeting in order to be heard in a lively debate.

Other present triggers can be:

- any aggressive behaviour in others;
- anyone who raises their hand, even to hail a taxi;
- music, smell, residential area, physical similarity, language accent, etc.

When the patient talks to us about his "present triggers", they have necessarily already occurred and theoretically belong to the "past". But, as these are the things that are happening in his daily life, they are called "present".

From a theoretical point of view, one could say that this "present" of the present triggers actually includes the recent past (as opposed to the older times of the past that can no longer be considered part of the patient's current situation).

Establish the present triggers: what are the circumstances under which the problem is occurring today?

As our emotional functioning is eminently conditioned, the event of the past that has conditioned the present is the "fire under the pot" of our current emotions. It is difficult to try to prevent the pot from boiling by trying to cool it if the fire is still lit underneath. **It is therefore necessary to address the emotional roots of current events.**

b. The level of the past

(1) Past triggers

A past trigger is simply a former present trigger

As time passes, the "present triggers" become "past triggers". Actually, events never constitute the source of the problem (the Source/Root Memory), but they ring a bell, that triggers it. They are therefore "triggers" and not "source/root memories" (see below). And as sometimes they took place fifteen years earlier, they deserve to be called "past".

Establish the list of the different **memories** related to this problem (network) and identify the most charged memories responsible for the dysfunction.

The first time, the worst time (the most painful), the last time are the main targets of the past (but not necessarily the source targets, see below).

If no memory prevails, ask the patient to create a worse memory.

(2) Source Level and Source (or Root) Memory

(a) Definition

The Source Memory (or the Source Level if it is a network of memories) is the one that is at the root of the cause-and-effect chain: it is the one that, chronologically, **first** undermined the AIP (what we could call "digesting" the event) and **led to the formation of a dysfunctional network of memories**. All other future dysfunctional/targeted networks derive from this one.

- The patient is sometimes aware of the Source Memory and then spontaneously evokes it:

E.g.: *"I startle every time someone makes a sudden move near me. It reminds me of my father who used to beat me."*

Part 2: Advanced Clinical EFT

E.g.: *"I can't watch a movie with children anymore since my niece passed away."*

Sometimes the patient does not know that his or her symptoms are the result of a Source Memory; the targets of the past that he or she delivers do not contain the Source Memory, but rather the "past triggers".

This is the case for patients with attachment disorders, whose lives will be enamelled with situations that constitute past triggers and then present triggers, such as: death of a loved one at age 10 (past trigger), first romantic break-up (past trigger), threats of separation in the current couple (present trigger).

It is not always clear whether targets from the past are past triggers of an older Source Memory, or whether they constitute the Source Level.

What should make you think it's a trigger?

If the patient has reactions (in the present or the past) that are disproportionate **and not everyone would have these reactions in such a situation**, it is probably because the situation itself does not justify such a reaction, and it is a previous dysfunctional network that is responsible. This is a **trigger**.

When you suspect that past targets delivered by the patient do not reach the Source Level, you can use the **float back technique**, which allows the patient to go back to the source.

In case of an early childhood Source Level (attachment disorders), a float back in a state of normal consciousness may not be sufficient, and hypnosis or other methods of access to the unconscious should be used.

(b) Identifying the Source Memory

This can be done by direct questions, if the patient has not spontaneously mentioned the Source Memory or the Source Level.

Once the target has been specified - the negative belief (NC), the emotion (E) and the physical sensation have been identified - ask the patient:

- When you feel like that (quote E) and think about yourself (quote NC), what does it send you back to in your past?
- When did you first have these negative thoughts? (NC)

- When did you first feel the same way? (E)

It is important that the patient **does not respond in a mental way**, with what he "believes" or "thinks", or has analysed in the course of other therapies, but rather that he responds according to his **inner feeling**.

If the patient remains mental, use the float back technique which accentuates on passing through the feeling.

(c) The Regression Bridge/Float back technique

The technique of the Complete Regression Bridge or "Float back" (which literally translates as "letting oneself be transported into the past") is used to identify the Source Level or Source Memory when the patient cannot lead us there spontaneously or through direct questions.

In the first part of this book we have seen the Affect Bridge technique which is less accurate than the Regression Bridge/Float back. The Affect Bridge regresses "following" the emotion. Float back regresses "following" the **association** of the emotion, the physical sensation and the negative belief.

According to Pavlovian conditioning, when an event activates a bell, it will evoke the same internal reaction in the patient: NC, emotions, identical physical sensations.

However, the SUD of the time will not necessarily be reproduced (extinction phenomenon) in the same way. What matters to us is the trace that is still active today!

The perceptions of time will also not be activated, except in cases of severe trauma with dissociation (flashbacks of veterans, for example).

The elements that are common to the past and the present are therefore: NC, E, K.

By connecting the patient to these elements (releasing the image) and by "following them back" like following a red thread to the past, we reach the Source Memory.

If the patient evokes a series of situations rather than an isolated or precise memory, the term Source Level is more appropriate, in which the most intense or representative Source Memory should be sought.

Part 2: Advanced Clinical EFT

(d) Regression Bridge/Float back protocol

Specify the **starting target** by its usual elements: **Im, NC, E, K, SUD.**

Tell the patient (float back): **Think of this image of (repeat the situation of the starting target).**

Now, when you feel (quote E) with these thoughts (quote NC) and this sensation (quote K), and you let your mind go back to the past without thinking, to the first time you felt like that... what comes up? (Or: At what age was the first time when you felt like that?)

Let the patient describe the situation that comes to mind.

In general, the person will have a spontaneous image and, from there, you will almost always find a specific period of time or an event from which you will verify that the type of situation, the emotions, the sensations and especially the cognition are the same.

If it is a context or a set of memories (identification of the centre of the memory network), **say:** *What is the most disturbing situation among all this? The one that resonates the most now?*

Specify the target of this Source Memory:

- Im (image of the worst moment of the Source Memory);
- NC (must be the same as the one from the trigger);
- E (same or sometimes modified compared to the past);
- K (same or sometimes modified compared to the past);
- SUD of the Source/Root Memory.

N.B. The negative belief is a powerful organiser of memory networks, which is why it is a good "red thread". Note, however, that this is a cognitive element that does not occur until the age of speech.

When the Source Memory is located in the stage of very early childhood, we can follow the physical sensation alone which is present in the encoding of the earliest memories.

This is what is done in hypnosis with the *Somatic Bridge* - a cousin version of the Affect Bridge that uses physical sensation instead of the emotion of the Affect Bridge.

When searching for later targets, it is preferable to take into account the NC, in order to stay in the right associative network.

IMG 11

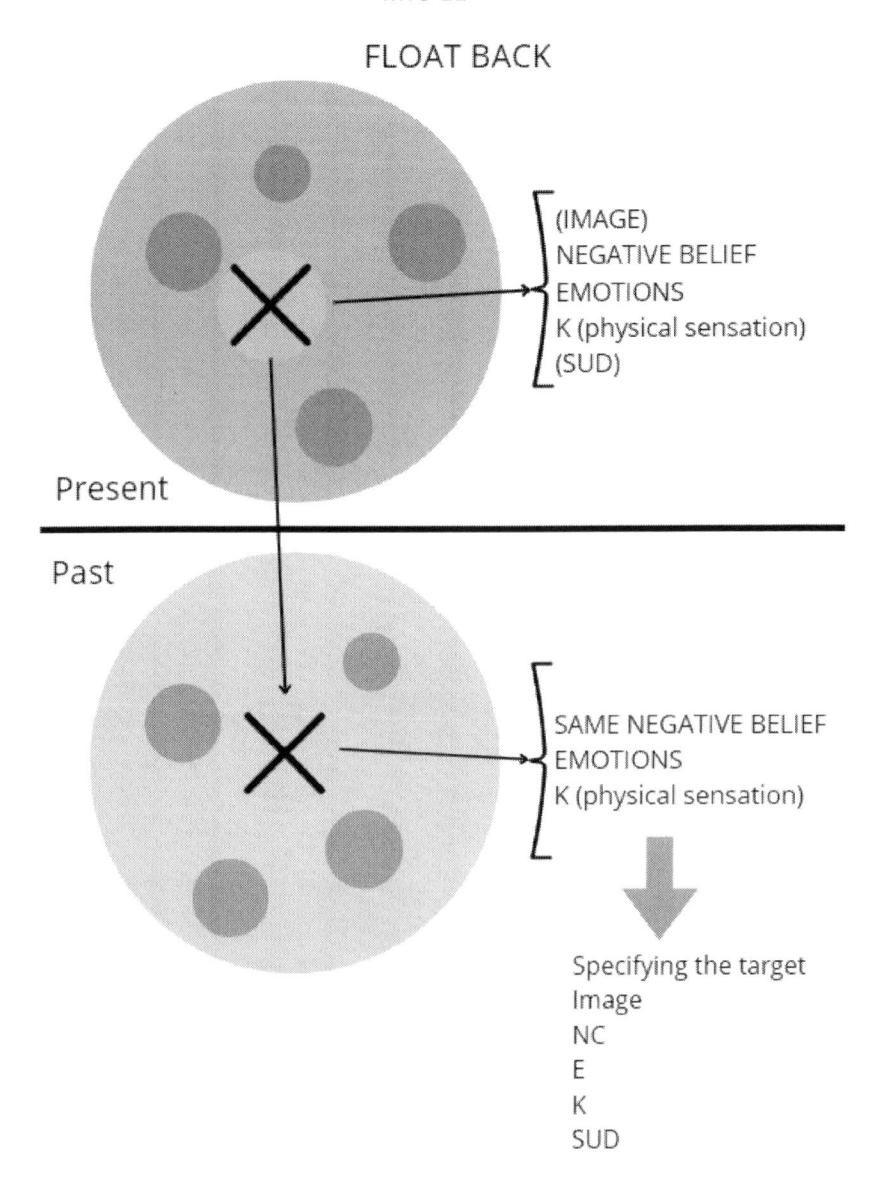

FLOAT BACK

(IMAGE)
NEGATIVE BELIEF
EMOTIONS
K (physical sensation)
(SUD)

Present

Past

SAME NEGATIVE BELIEF
EMOTIONS
K (physical sensation)

Specifying the target
Image
NC
E
K
SUD

Part 2: Advanced Clinical EFT

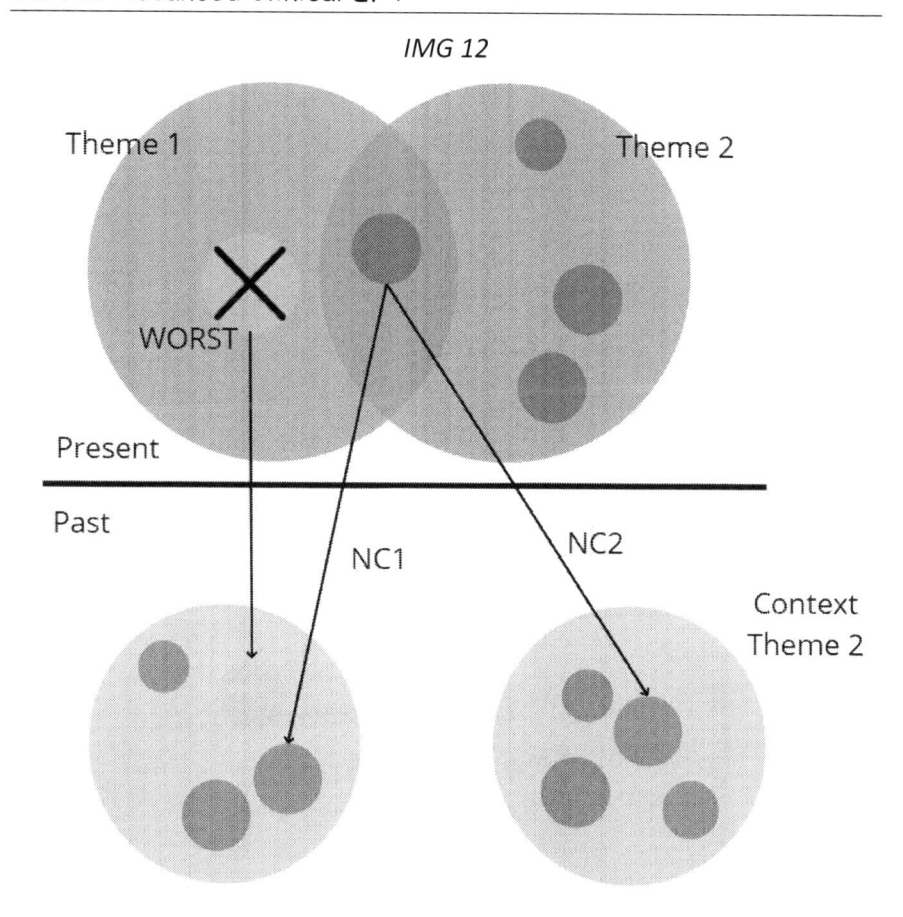

IMG 12

c. The level of the future

(1)   The future as verification

If the patient has started from a present or past problem, when all past and present targets are already disabled, it is essential to ask the patient to project himself into the future and check that all is going well there too.

This makes it possible to remove certain remaining blockages, beliefs, etc.

If such blockages occur, treat them as normal targets.

(2)   The future as a healing objective

When the patient does not bring concerns for the future, you ask him/her during the anamnesis protocol: When you think about the problem you described earlier, how would you like to imagine yourself in a similar future situation? What could you say to yourself that is positive or constructive? What would you like to be able to say to yourself?

And this allows us to verify whether this objective is achieved after treating the past and present targets.

(3) Concern for the future

Sometimes, the patient directly targets a concern about his or her future.

E.g.: "I have a meeting in a week and I'm very stressed, it's not going to be okay."

We treat this as a target:

- What is the worst of his/her anticipation?
- Specify the target (Im, NC, E, K, SUD).
- Seek the source of his/her anxiety in the past:
    - What makes you think it's going to go wrong?
    - What did you experience as an event that has programmed you to think that way?

We thus find present triggers or Source/Root Memories and we follow the standard protocol related to them.

4. Choosing the first target on which to do EFT (for simple trauma)

a. Establishing the targets provided by the patient

In the anamnesis, identify three aspects:

- - **Present**: the present triggers.
- - **Past:** the past triggers,
    - the Source Memory if known.
- - **Future**: future anxieties,

- healing objective, how the patient imagines himself after the treatment.

b. Finding the first target by keeping the following rules (for simple trauma)

Start from the oldest level

Exception: when there is a more urgent or much more important target.

In case we have a Source Memory, it will become the first target.

In case we have a present or a past trigger, we will then do a Float back to get back to the Source Level.

Take in this level the worst, the strongest or the most painful memory.

If this is not possible, if no memory is worse than the others, choose one or imagine how the worst would be.

5. Treating all the targets of a given level

a. General principles

As we have seen, we start a priori from the oldest level.

The goal is to disable all targets of the concerned level.

This is the only way to "move forward" to the more recent level.

This is the condition for "healing" the networks of dysfunctional Source Memories, and for relaunching AIP in a cascade, from the oldest to the most recent levels.

Targeting the worst memory and the centre of the target, is a strategy for maximum effectiveness. **It often happens that by disabling the centre of the worst memory, the whole level is disabled.**

Otherwise, we continue reprocessing the next targets at the same level, according to the principles of the Tabletop, the Oil Stain Effect and the Tree in the Forest metaphors.

b. Verification of the complete deactivation of the level

Find out if there are still some active, i.e. disruptive, targets at this level:
- by measuring again the SUD of all the targets that had been identified in this level;
- if there were **no other targets** (for example, in the case of a float back that led directly to an isolated Source Memory), the following question is asked:

When you think about this theme (quote the theme in the context of the level), are there still any memories that seem disturbing to you?

- ▶ If there are some left, they are treated one by one in the following sequence ("treating in the order"):
- the worst one/ones in the descending order of SUDs;
- the first one;
- the last one.

Actually, by the **Generalisation effect** (the Oil Stain effect), treating the few strongest memories will allow a deactivation of all the others (cf. the Tabletop metaphor).

- ▶ If there are no more, we go back to the previous level.

c. Going back to the previous level

Here too, the same **rule** is applied: **"the worst, the first, the last"**.

- If we have identified the worst memory of the previous level (in case of float back), we start by measuring its SUD and then treating it if necessary.

Then we continue with the rule "the worst, the first, the last" until the Generalisation effect works and all SUDs are at zero.

- If we haven't identified the worst memory of the previous level, we do that in order to be able, once again, to apply the rule "the worst, the first, the last" until all known SUDs are at zero.

Be sure to **check that the level is completely deactivated** (see above) before **moving forward to the next level.**

d. Future scenario

Part 2: Advanced Clinical EFT

Have the scenario of the future imagined and check that everything is going well.

"I would like you to imagine yourself doing/reacting..." (ask the patient to imagine that he or she is in the previously problematic situation, this time in the future and going well, to check that he or she is able to live it without being triggered by the old triggers):

a) if staying positive, reinforce (TAT poses, EFT, REMAP points);

b) if disturbance, assess:

- if you have to reprocess an event from the past,
- if it is just an anxiety about the new/the unknown.

In both cases, specify the target (Im, NC, E, K, SUD) and treat it.

Re-imagine the future scenario and check that everything is going well.

If something negative occurs again, repeat from point (b), then double-check.

If it's all positive, reinforce with tapping.

6. Summary of the PPF protocol - past / present / future

The PPF protocol brings together the sequence of steps to be followed in treating past, present and future targets.

1) Identify the conscious targets of the different levels. Measure their SUDs.

2) For each level, take the worst memory (with the highest SUD) and specify its target (Im, NC, E, K, SUD).

3) Make a float back if necessary, to reach the Source Level.

4) Treat the Source Level (the past):
   - (identify the worst moment, specify its target and) treat the Source Memory;
   - check that the level is completely deactivated (if not: treat the other memories);
   - move forward to the level of previous triggers (past or present).

5) Treating **past triggers** (if any).

Proceed as for the level of the present triggers.

6) Treating present **triggers**:
- treat the worst one, the rest of the worst ones;
- check that the level is completely deactivated (if not: treat the other memories);
- move forward to the level of the future.

7) Treating the **level of the future**:
- treat anxious expectations, if any

AND/OR
- make the **protocol of the future scenario**.

7. Examples: transcriptions of demonstrations

a. *Searching for the Source Memory and float back*

BRIGITTE (therapist): Do you have your Container?

PATIENT: An iron biscuit box and the word "well-being".

B: Do you have a Safe Place?

P: Lake Geneva.

B: What do you like about it?

P: The clear view, the calm, the soft pleasant sound of the water, and the fresh air.

B: What would you like to work on?

P: This morning, when I asked you a question, I felt a certain unease, I felt that I was blushing up and I was a little surprised by this. (Present trigger)

B: When you think back to this morning, do you have any idea what might have triggered this, why might it have been triggered this morning when it's usually fine?

P: I don't know, but I think it started the moment you answered me and I saw your face, with what I interpreted as an interrogation. (Worst moment)

Part 2: Advanced Clinical EFT

B: Okay, so you have this image of me with this question in my eyes? (Image)

P: Yes, and I thought that you were thinking: what does he mean?

B: An emotion when you connect to this image?

P: An anxiety....

B: Sensations in your body?

P: In the plexus, with a feeling of emptiness too, a feeling of narrowing, almost the desire to disappear.

B: And the negative thought about you... stay with that feeling, that emptiness...

P: I wasn't clear again, it's not understandable, I don't know how to express myself.

B: And for you, what does that mean for you if you haven't been clear again, what do you conclude about yourself?

P: I'm a lousy and in that relation, I didn't manage to be clear.

B: What does that mean for you: "I didn't manage to be clear"? Why is that so important to you?

P: Perhaps a certain risk... the relationship is a place that can be pleasant and nourishing, but also a place where one can be hurt.

B: Telling you that you haven't been comprehensible sends you back to that risk of being hurt, so how could we formulate that idea? Stay with your feeling... I'm.... I'm... I'm lousy... I'm in danger? I'm vulnerable?

(When there are self-esteem and safety issues, safety prevails, it is the most frightening.)

P: Being vulnerable is a risk, not a fact.

B: If you go back to this moment when you see an interrogation on my face, and you feel at the same time "I am vulnerable in relationship", how much do you think this is disturbing now? (SUD)

P: At 5 or 6.

B: If you go back to that moment when you see it on my face, when you say to yourself "I'm vulnerable", the anxiety, the feeling in your stomach, the narrowing, the desire to disappear, if you let yourself slip into the past with all those sensations, as far as it takes you... let what comes to you come to you... and tell me what shows up in your mind. (Float back)

P: Many situations... yes....

B: Tell me what went through your head.

P: All situations with my father... where the consequences could be significant, and he didn't know how to handle the situation, and that affected me. (Source Level)

B: You have a lot of them, tell me: does one or the other seem stronger, more emblematic for this kind of situation?

P: They are all strong... but the examples are: we broke a glass, there was yelling, the slap was quite strong, excessive, or if we hurt ourselves, we would get another one because we were crying...

B: I understand why you are activated by this question on my face, it reminds you of your father's reactions, this insecurity...

You told me about these two typical situations....

P: He was decompressing at home.

B: What if we had to deal with the most emblematic situation?

P: The second one: I hurt myself, I fall, he doesn't understand, he tells me to calm down, I don't calm down, I feel pain and I get a slap, he says "so that you can cry for something"...

B: And in this scene, what is the image you have, the worst one? (Targeting)

P: My father is both panicked and angry, a mixture of the two.

B: You can see him.

P: Absolutely unkind in his attitude.

B: How do you see that?

P: By his verbal and physical aggressiveness, there is no sweetness.

B: And when you see your father, what do you feel like emotion now?

Part 2: Advanced Clinical EFT

P: A very big internal vibration.

B: And an emotion too? Are you feeling sad?

P: A mixture of sadness and anger.

B: And what you're thinking is....

P: I don't belong here, I'm not loved, what the hell am I doing here? I shouldn't have existed...

B: How much does it activate you between 0 and 10?

P: At 10.

B: Put your attention on your father's image, his aggressiveness, I don't belong here, I'm not loved, I shouldn't have existed, and your vibration: can you think about these other situations from the past with your father, can we take the one where you broke a glass...?

P: There are others coming... we could spend the night... (a "tabletop" with many legs - Gary Craig's metaphor)

One... several... with me or not...these are flashbacks... (network activation) I feel anger and my heart beating fast.

Brigitte's comment: The Container remains active throughout the session/demonstration. At the end, all the remaining disturbing material is placed in the Container to close the session.

If the session had continued, we would have searched for the strongest target associated with the present anger and then we would have deactivated it. Certainly, we would have had to treat several of them so that the level of the past would be desensitised before returning to the present.

b. Wasp phobia: Float back and reprocessing of the Source Memory

BRIGITTE (therapist): Tell me, speak to me about this wasp phobia... the story...

PATIENT: According to my parents, when I was around 6 months of age, I was stung, but really on the corner of my eye, by a wasp; we lived in the countryside, every year there was a wasp invasion and I was regularly stung, the last time on the corner of my lip, about twenty-five years ago.

(Memory from when he was 6 months old, but it is a reported memory, so, a priori - we can't work on it because I suppose there is no E or S = Source Level; then another memory from twenty-five years ago.)

P: I don't really like eating outside, especially in summertime when wasps are more concerned with humans than anything else, I am extremely vigilant during meals or aperitifs.

(Present trigger, to be checked when we finish dealing with the past.)

P: If I think about a meal outside and I even see a single wasp approaching, and especially when there is a risk, I am scared; it is probably due to this sting in my eye, even if I don't have any personal memory.

B: What you're telling me is that if you think about a situation where you're at the table and there's a wasp approaching, it's stressful?

P: Yes, yes, yes.

B: How much between 0 and 10 here?

P: The more I think about it, the higher it goes... my palms are sweating... it's 8. The first reflex, when I see something approaching, is... an abrupt gesture and a withdrawal.

(Present trigger)

P: I can feel it just by talking about it.

B: It gets active... What are the real memories you have of being stung?

P: On the corner of the lip twenty-five years ago, I remember it, in Francorchamps, in the back of a red car.

(Past trigger)

B: And this is the last time?

P: Yes.

Part 2: Advanced Clinical EFT

B: Do you have any other strong, stressful memories of being stung or very scared?

P: No.

B: And when you think about twenty-five years ago in Francorchamps and you recall that moment?

P: Strangely enough, it's less stressful, it's in the past.

B: How much would you say?

P: At 3, I was so surprised then... It's not so much the fact that I was stung that causes me a problem; it's rather the fact that I risk being stung... and that's the irrational part...

B: And what do you fear in the idea of being stung, what worries you about the fact that you might be stung?

P: The impression of risking terrible suffering far beyond reality, because I've already been stung by horseflies without realising it, and that doesn't bother me, whereas it seems terrible for some people, so compared to wasps, there's really something irrational about it.

(Normally, the protocol includes a present trigger and then past triggers or Source Level, but here we have a Source Level that is not a real memory and a past trigger at 3.)

B: What I suggest you to do is that, although the situation twenty-five years ago has a relatively low SUD, we treat it first; even though you tell me that the worst thing is the risk of being stung rather than the fact that you have been stung...

P: If I imagine that I'm eating and a wasp is coming, I'm more emotionally affected than when I think of Francorchamps.

B: So we can start one way or the other, either deal with the past where you were stung, or with the past where you were afraid of being stung... if we had access to the original event, we would treat that one... and if you imagine yourself as a baby stung by that wasp, does that stress you?

P: Yes, a little.

B: How much?

P: At 7.... if I imagine that...

(If he had said he didn't feel stress, we would have started with Francorchamps or present triggers at the table, but he has a SUD as a baby: it means that his brain is activated when he imagines this baby situation.)

B: Describe to me a little bit what is stressful, how you feel this stress in your body, the images you have...

P: I imagine my cradle, what I feel is an alert level with heart palpitations, a little sweating and some sort of escape or anger reflex towards the wasp.

B: What about when you imagine yourself as a baby?

P: Now I feel anxious that I can't react.

(He had gone out of the Source Level again, a baby is not preoccupied with trying to kill the wasp, I have to take him back to the baby.)

P: I'm panicking but I am unable to act...

B: And so, palpitations, sweating, at the moment as well?

P: Yes.

B: And do you have an image?

P: I see a huge wasp on the right, disproportionate in size....

B: We're going to start on that, and during the tapping you stay in touch with that moment, that image; I'm going to repeat from time to time a keyword that connects you to that - what should I say?

P: The wasp.

B: The emotion you have?

P: Fear.

B: Eyebrow Point: "Even though I have this fear because of this wasp, even though I have this fear when I see this wasp approaching, even though I have this anxiety of not being able to react"...

(tapping)...

B: How did it go and what's left now when you connect to this scene?

Part 2: Advanced Clinical EFT

P: I felt relaxation and, gradually, this image got smaller in size, it had a less frightening face, not nice either, but a little bit like the face of someone who would laugh without necessarily being mean, like a comic book when I was a kid; the image is less scary, mentally I can almost let the wasp come to me without worrying too much, but it still doesn't feel nice.

(We can see the change in perception as the treatment progresses.)

B: And when you get back to the same starting situation, how much do you think you feel upset, stressed now?

P: At 4.

B: What does 4 represent? What do you feel is there?

P: There could still be some danger, not immediate; I don't know how to react, but I wonder what I could do...

B: There could be some danger and you should be prepared?

P: I don't know what I should do.

B: A worry?

P: Yes, what I feel is much less than 7.

B: It's okay, it's subjective.

Where is it physically, in your body?

P: A bit of warmth, sweat in my hands....

B: Anything else in your body?

P: No, at the heart level, it's fine.

B: And what word would you use to describe the emotion, is it still "fear"?

P: Risk.

B: And what emotion does this risk give you? Fear?

P: Concern or anxiety.

B: Even though I have this concern because there could still be some danger, even though I have this anxiety of not knowing what I should do, even though there is this risk....

(tapping)...

P: What is quite extraordinary is that I started from the risk by visualising the cradle and now I see only a tiny risk there; I mentally accepted the idea that this wasp could settle on my face and then I could imagine a wasp in front of me by seeing your yellow Bic pen without it causing me a problem... it seemed bearable to me to imagine a wasp, a mixture of reconstruction of the past, past risks and future risks, a mixture of everything, without it creating a problem.

B: What if you reconnect to that moment in the cradle?

(Always return to the original target)

How much stress do you feel?

P: My mental and rational side says it must be 1, a basic scepticism.

B: You feel 0, but....

P: Yes, that's right....

B: And you no longer feel any stress in your body?

P: I quickly get the image of the cradle and it is much more peaceful.

B: There is still something left since you said: much more (persistence).

P: There's a little something left, yes.

B: Tell me, how do you feel there's something left?

P: A small pinch in the heart and a low level of alert (if we accept this, we risk missing what's left, always aim for 0). I visualise the wasps spinning around my head....

B: And the fear you have is the fear of what?

P: Fear of aggression.

B: Even though I still have this pinch in my heart because I'm afraid of being attacked, even though I still have this low level of alert, even though I'm still afraid of aggression when I see these wasps spinning around my head... (tapping)... What's left?

P: I am much more relaxed, and during the tapping I have this desire to be in summertime to see how I accept the risk... and on a physiological level, a soothing feeling, even when I switch the different images in my head; I

Part 2: Advanced Clinical EFT

feel extremely calm... 0.5, with a background of Cartesianism that would never be taken away from me.

B: Can you think about Francorchamps in that car again? (Going back to the past triggers, the level above the Source Level.)

P: I try to think about what happened, but it doesn't bring back emotion, I think about everything in an extremely detached way.

B: SUD?

P: At 0!

B: Can you go through all your memories from the last few times, see if anything else is still active?

(All memories of fear of being stung = past triggers, check that the whole level is deactivated before going further.)

P: No, nothing, even when I think of huge hornets, it's fine.

B: You were telling me that you wanted to be back in summertime, imagine it's summer, you eat outside and there's a wasp coming... near your face, what does that do to you?

P: I will always have a reflex to chase it away, it's normal, but a slight gesture of avoidance, not an abrupt gesture of safeguarding.

(He chases the wasp but that's normal, it doesn't mean that he's activated, at the level of the present triggers it's okay, then let's make the future scenario... imagine being outside without wasps and see if he can remain serene.)

B: Imagine that you are eating outside, there is no wasp, and observe if you can stay outside and enjoy the time, the moment, the meal...

P: My intuition tells me that the wasp will soon come and there is again a little vigilance, I will not be totally....

B: In reality, is there often a wasp coming or not?

P: In reality, much less than I fear.

(If he said there are a lot of wasps around, it would be normal for him to think that this will happen, but since he tells me the opposite, it's still a sign of stress.

B: Let's take a look at this....

P: Yes, there are years when there are almost none.

B: Even though I'm sure a wasp will come and I feel vigilant, even though it's sure a wasp will come soon...

(tapping)...

P: As I went along, I was expecting it less and less and then I didn't care if it would come or not, no more emotional stress at all, the images of wasps were showing up, and nothing.

B: How do you feel right now at the table?

P: Very good!

c. Demonstration on a case of insomnia with comments and questions and answers

Therapist/teacher: Brigitte

Patient/student: Sylvie

Thanks to Gaetana Vastamente for her transcription, proofreading and organization of this report.

SYLVIA: My sleep problem: I wake up early, but most often I can't fall asleep.

BRIGITTE: Since when?

S: For a long time; several times in my life, it has lasted for several months to the point that I couldn't sleep at all, and the first time it happened on a long-term basis was after Mom died, I was 18 years old; after her suicide, I had no reaction, I was relieved of her death, but I couldn't sleep for months and fell asleep three months later (point 1).

B: What is the connection you would see with the sleep?

S: I have experienced other situations where there was a link with motherhood, the mother-child relationship.

For example, I had my first child easily and for the second, I did very heavy treatments that kept me awake until I reached a stage where I hadn't slept for months (point 2).

Part 2: Advanced Clinical EFT

It also happened to me three years ago when one of my sisters made a suicide attempt; I repeated the same phenomenon (point 3).

My sleep is better, I have worked on it in therapy but it remains fragile; currently, I have been unemployed for more than a year, my life is not financially easy, I always have the impression that I am not sleeping; I do not think but I do not sleep, and it has consequences, I am also depressed.

    (Brigitte returns to Point 1)

B: If we go back to the first time, the death of your mother, explain to me how you learned about it and how this sleep problem developed.

S: I was a student, I came home one weekend, I wasn't talking to my mother at that time.

My father and sister were looking for my mother, they had gone to look everywhere. I was alone at home, the police called and said she was found dead in the woods, and my first reaction was relief, I said it to the others...

B: At what time of the day?

S: Around 3-4pm.

B: And when did your sleep disorders start?

S: The same day, I didn't sleep, and neither did the following days.

B: And how did you feel?

S: At the time, relieved, I thought it was easy; I continued my studies, supported my father, my sisters, until I started feeling anxiety.

B: Tell me.

S: I didn't know how to reason them, I didn't know how to put them into words.

B: You are thinking of one particular day...

S: Yes, I hadn't slept for too long, and one day, in the middle of the forest, I disconnected, and it fell on me, I was panicking, I was afraid to die...

B: Do you think that a part of you might not have been relieved but had difficulties with her leaving?

S: Clearly, I had hopes, she had been depressed, she had tried to commit suicide when she was pregnant with me, she didn't talk to me, she never touched me, never a kind word, but in my head, there was always hope: one day this will change! When I have children... but then I realized this eternal lack, that there would be no one to replace her either.

B: Did you also feel this realization of the eternal lack in an emotional way?

S: There must have been a time when there was emptiness, fear of not being able to hold on... fear of letting go, this is quite unconscious... fear of falling asleep.

B: In your life as well?

S: No, in my life, I have learned to let go, but unconsciously there are apparently things I can't let go.

B: That's more like what you're thinking: you're thinking that maybe you don't sleep so you don't let go?

S: Yes, but when I don't sleep, I don't think; I observed that these problems come when there are events related to the mother-child relationship, I didn't have sleep problems when I lost my job.

(Brigitte takes charge of Point 3)

B: When you go back to your sister's suicide, what is the worst moment?

S: When I hear it on the phone from my other sister, I feel bad, I tell myself I have to call a friend, then I get myself together, and a few weeks later I can't sleep and my life is no longer manageable, I feel anxiety, that's what's hard.

B: Can we go back to that time when you first learned it on the phone? What's the worst image of when you found out?

S: Something like a collapse: that's not true!

B: And when you recall that moment, what's in front of your eyes?

S: I'm in my room, in front of the mirror, thinking: I don't want to collapse. I go to the bathroom, look for sugar...

B: You see your image in the mirror, you feel this collapse, and what emotion do you feel now?

S: I feel alone, more and more alone.

B: What emotion do you have? Are you sad?

S: At the time, rather shocked, sadness does not come immediately, first there is the shock.

B: And today, when you stand in front of the mirror, is that the shock that you feel?

S: Yes, the ball in my throat and a knife in my chest: not again, damn it, that's enough!

B: "Not again" means "not again what"?

S: It's heavy, I've had enough, it's not fair!

B: And when you think about that now, how much between 0 and 10 does that affect you?

S: At 10.

B: And when you think about the moment you heard on the phone about your mother's death?

S: Less, at 5-6.

...

S: She was dead, and I am finally living!

B: So, the first time you didn't sleep was after your mother's death and then your sister's suicide attempt?

S: Yes, and in the meantime too, when I had the treatments for my second child, I went for months without sleeping.

    (Point 1: Brigitte returns to the level of the past/Source Level: the mother's death)

B: I suggest you start, even if the SUD is lower, with that moment when you received the call for your mother. When you think about that moment, what image do you have?

S: I'm under the staircase, sitting on the armchair.

B: Do you remember the worst moment of this shock?

S: It's dark, I'm sitting, there's a wooden chest, the wall...

B (tapping):

Even though I felt this shock, when I heard that my mother had passed away,

Even though I didn't sleep after that and I don't really know why,

Even though I felt a shock but mostly relief...

Put your attention on this moment of shock....

this shock...

...

Nose: this relief....

...

Breast: I felt relieved...
Eyebrow: relieved because I didn't have a relationship with my mother...
Eye: even though for a part of me it was the end of a hope...
the end of hope....
I felt alone....
the end of hope....
I feel alone....

...

I'm alone...
I feel collapsed....
no one...
I am alone...
no one...
I'm alone...
this shock...

When you think back to that moment when you got that phone call, tell me what comes up, how does it look like?

S: I can feel the country air, the birds, it's hot outside.

B: What about your disturbance that was at SUD = 6?

Part 2: Advanced Clinical EFT

S: It is at 2.

B: What's left?

S: A small ball in the chest.

B: Anything else when you think about it then?

S: I let go, I feel in my body that the relief is marked by a relaxation of the muscles.

B (tapping):

Even though I still have that small ball,

Even though I still have that small ball,

that small ball....

...

When you think back to the moment you get the call, what's going on inside you?

How much disturbance do you feel?

S: None, zero.

> (Brigitte returns to Point 3)

B: If now you think about the phone call for your sister and you get back to the moment when you look in the mirror, that shock, how much between 0 and 10 do you feel it's disturbing now?

S: SUD = 8.

B (tapping): Even though when I see myself in the mirror, I feel this ball in my throat, this knife in my chest,

Even though I feel this shock and I feel alone,

> this shock
> I feel alone
> this shock
> knife in my chest
> that ball in my throat
> this shock

>   this shock
>   I don't want to collapse.
>   I don't want to collapse.
>   this shock
>   That's enough, oh, not again.
>   I've had enough.
>   this shock
>   I'm afraid of collapsing.
>   I don't want to collapse....

B: When you think back to that moment when you first learned it, you look in the mirror, tell me where are you now? What's still there?

S: A tension in my neck and another small ball.

B: Between 0 and 10?

S: At 4, there is a contraction in the jaw, in the neck.

B: And emotionally? Earlier you said "I feel alone", how is it now?

S: I still feel alone.

B: When you think about that moment?

S: Yes, I feel alone.

B (tapping): Even though I have this ball in my throat and this tension in my neck and jaw,

Even though when I remember this moment, I feel alone,

>   when I get this call (I say this to make sure she's properly connected to that moment)
>   informing me about my sister's suicide attempt
>   I feel alone
>   I feel alone
>   this tension in the neck
>   tension in the neck
>   tension in the neck
>   tension in the jaw
>   I feel alone
>   I feel alone

this shock
I feel alone...

How much would you say is left now?

S: A slight ball, I'm much more relaxed, I feel... alone, and then, we're always alone?

B: And the slight ball, do you know what it says?

S: Maybe a fear, maybe a fear of collapsing, I don't know.

B: Does it speak to you or is it in your head?

S: No, it speaks to me.

B (tapping): Even though I have this fear with this ball,

Even though I'm afraid of collapsing,
Even though I still have that ball of fear,
>   when I think about this moment
>   when I heard about my sister.
>   I have this ball.
>   this fear
>   this fear of collapsing
>   this fear of collapsing
>   this ball
>   this ball of fear
>   this fear
>   in this ball
>   this fear in this ball
>   this fear
>   in this ball...

Think back to the moment you learned it, that phone call, you see yourself in the mirror, how much disturbance do you still feel?

S : SUD = 0.

>   (Brigitte addresses Point 2)

B: When you think about when you were doing this treatment for your second child, does something stay heavy?

S: No, I had this child.

(So no trigger for the present/recent past)

(Brigitte: test of the future.)

B: When you can't sleep at night, do you get apprehensive about that, do you think "oh my God"?

S: Before I used to, but now I accept it, I read, I meditate.

B: So now, when you think about your nights, you don't have any negative emotions?

S: No, sometimes, but I still have a good day.

DEBRIEFING

I normally demonstrate on something emotional for the didactic aspect: you can see better how things evolve.

What Sylvie brings is not an emotion, and we don't have a present trigger with a particular emotion. So, we couldn't make a float back.

I did the demo anyway because there were some interesting things...

Sylvie quickly told us about her problem in the present: the sleep, but I couldn't do much of that, no SUD... no present trigger.

Sylvie says it started when her Mom died and then tells us about other events. First her treatments. Then her sister's suicide attempt. Since there is a triggering event, I assumed it was related, but it's not certain, there may be many other factors.

There was a theme for her, but I wondered why it manifested itself in the sleep; I tried to dig for other elements, to tap on them... And in addition, when her mother died, she felt relief! So, it doesn't meet the usual criteria for trauma. It's not easy, we have to keep investigating.

I asked the question about the parts... for whom it might be difficult... since she says she feels good but doesn't sleep.

I got to the hypothesis that the negative belief with the mother is "I am alone", whereas she said it only after, for the sister, as well as "I am afraid of collapsing"... I even used words that she did not say for her mother but for her sister, in case that was the unconscious link.

Part 2: Advanced Clinical EFT

I treated the target related to the mother. The emotion was shock, we can accept that as emotion in traumas...

I said, "even though I felt a relief", in case she had felt guilty for feeling it... I could have made her talk about this guilt, if the SUD hadn't decreased, I would have dug into the guilt.

What was very positive was when she was able to say, "I am alone, and aren't we always alone?" She had enough internal security resources. There was no intensity/SUD in relation to the treatments.

I treated what was related to the sister by targeting well.

After that, I didn't have any present triggers... I asked her if she was anxious about not sleeping = the future. If she had said yes, I would have tapped on it.

Questions from students

     1. We could have tapped on something positive, e. g.: I can now let go in my sleep without danger...

B: No, because even if tapping on the positive strengthens a highway of neural connections between the present and the positive aspect, the path of neural connections to the negative aspect is still there and the patient can follow it again; it is therefore necessary to first remove the wrong path.

If we treat the negative, we remove the connections that lead to the negative experience, so there is only the positive neural path that is there and that can be followed, and we can then reinforce it by tapping with positive phrases.

     2. Should we always start with the oldest past trigger even if its SUD is lower?

B: No, we start with the strongest trigger (the sister) unless we have the impression that there is a cause-and-effect relationship: in fact, she did not feel this collapsing with her mother, but I assumed that if she did feel it with her sister, she had felt it with her mother.

3. Why were you stopping in short rounds?

B: It's when I thought it was worth checking up her current state. And I calibrated so there was apparently nothing left.

Debriefing the next day

Sylvie: The rest of the day, I was tired but calm; in the evening, I went to a lecture and usually, after an evening that is not calm, I sleep even less well, I even have a ritual: reading, meditation.

Yesterday, I went to bed without a ritual and I slept right away. We'll see what happens next.

Thanks to Brigitte for the gift, the field, the group, I felt the kindness, the respect, the empathy, I felt comfortable to be able to expose this.

Analytical diagram of Brigitte's demonstration

Future *Fear of not falling asleep*
No

Present   *- (no triggers)*

Past   *Sister: 10*   8
0
                                                            ↑
                                                            |
            Treatments for 2nd child

            Mother: 5-6 (lower SUD   ⟶   *0*
but supposed cause-and-effect relationship)

Present: no trigger, makes the connection between sleep disorder and mother-child relationship.

Past (no float back possible):

Part 2: Advanced Clinical EFT

1. first time: the mother's suicide: relieved but not sleeping the first night and for months;
2. treatment for her second child, no sleep for months;
3. attempted suicide of the sister.

Treatment

Past:

- Point 1: a part is relieved and a part is "always hoping that one day it will change", realization of the eternal lack, nobody to replace her.
- Point 2: the emptiness, fear of not holding on, of letting go, of collapsing, fear of falling asleep... that's what she says to herself rationally, but no emotional experience.
- Point 3: worst image: I see myself in the mirror.

I feel a collapse, it's not true, I can't collapse.

I am alone, more and more alone = NC.

E: the shock (this can be accepted as an emotion in traumas).

K: ball in the throat and knife in the chest.

SUD: 10.

Brigitte starts with Point 1, even though its SUD is lower, because it implies a cause-and-effect relationship.

Assumed NC for Point 1 = I am alone.

It uses the words of Point 3.

The SUD of Point 3 has dropped to 8.

Then she treats Point 3.

Point 2: no SUD.

Present: Okay.

Future: Okay.

8. **Transcriptions of supervised and commented student sessions**

a. Therapist - Deborah session

Transcript of a supervision session during therapist training. Two students are doing the exercise: Lara, the "therapist", and Deborah, the "patient". Yves supervises and takes the role of the therapist at the end.

THERAPIST: Even though I have experienced many things, I accept and respect myself.

> Even though it is quite normal that my head is a little empty, we have revised many things, we have seen many things and have lived many things, I love and accept myself...
> Even though I have experienced all this, I love and accept myself, and there's another way of looking at it, I do my exercise as I am, I don't have too much tension or stress anymore, and I'm going to be completely relaxed.

DEBORAH: Sabrina comes up to me and says, "If I do the exercise with you, you will do it quietly." I told her "no, it's clearly no, I won't do that". Just thinking about it irritates me. It hits me again, I am asked to keep quiet, I am not allowed to speak.

T: If I understood correctly, you are quite activated by this, are there any other emotions?

D: The emotion is revolt, anger.

T: Is there a place in your body where you feel this anger, this revolt more strongly?

D: Here, and I'm hot.

T: On a scale of 0 to 10, can you put a number?

D: I'm going to say 9.

T: Do you remember the first event in your life when you felt that revolt, that anger?

D: The first one, I don't know, but it's clear that it's part of my experience because at home, I had to keep my mouth shut with my father.

T: With your father. Do you remember the first moment when it happened, a special moment when you could experience that and you still remember it today?

D: The first one, no. I can't separate the first one, it was all the time. However, one event that I find very symbolic of this is that he yelled at me because I had polished my nails and had rings on each finger. He made me take that off. I don't know what he told me anymore. I went up to my room, I revolted, so I hit my closet because it had to come out and, in no time, he went up and he hit me. I think it's really... It's in the sense that I might not have done it on purpose, he's down there, he doesn't know. He just hears a noise. There was not an ounce of doubt for him... it's at that point, what. It's the extreme. There is no room for doubt, there was no question as to whether it was that (it is true that it was a result of that, but this is not the question).

T: If you could make a little movie of this anger, as you would.... of this anger you feel now?

D: A movie?

T: You would be the director and you would make a film. How would you do that? The event you had with your father?

D: No, I don't know. It's difficult.

T: We're starting, are there any other events that remind you of this anger besides this event with your father?

D: With my father, it was all the time. I just had the right to shut up, otherwise... I couldn't express my dissatisfaction.

T: Even though I have to shut up all the time, already with my father, and I still have to shut up, I don't have the right to express myself even today, I accept and respect myself...

> Even though anger rises when I am asked to shut up, to keep silent, I accept myself...
> Even though the rage and anger are there, just by thinking about what happened yesterday with S., I...
> this anger
> this anger

> I'm asked to shut up.
> I can't express myself.
> I can't be clean.
> this rising anger

D: It annoys me because I didn't say the word "clean", it's already starting.

T: I heard the word "clean", sorry.

> *(This is a reminder how important it is to use the client's words correctly)*

> this rising anger
> this anger
> I have no right to express myself.
> I have no right to express myself.
> this anger
> I have to shut up
> all the time with my father
> all the time
> I still have to keep silent.
> I'm angry.
> I'm really angry.
> I'm really sick of it.
> I'm really angry.
> this anger that is now rising
> this rising anger
> especially when I have to keep silent.

D: I don't have to keep silent, I do not want to be silent.

T: It explodes

> it explodes
> my chest where I feel this explosion coming
> and I want to... what would you want now?

D: If I let this part do its job, she would shake Miriam... it's really violent.

T: I would really like to...

D: I can't even admit that she could ask for that.

Part 2: Advanced Clinical EFT

T: Yes, I can't admit that she asked for that.

> I don't understand how she could ask for that.
> I'd want to shake her up if I saw her.
> to ask me to be silent
> I had to keep silent all the time with my father....

D: All my youth, all my childhood.

T: I still remember that event where I put my rings, my nail polish.

> I'm angry.
> I'm really angry.
> I'm really angry now.
> it rises up, this anger
> I want to explode.
> I want to shake Miriam...

D: I'd shake her up, she doesn't even realize it.

Besides, I didn't take that target because I didn't want to impose that anger on Sonia, and it was really a mess!

T: It's a mess...

> It was a messy day yesterday!

D: No, there have been many beautiful things.

T: Many beautiful things, but I'm angry...

D: This part, yes.

W: This part is angry... what would she need to say?

D: That she has the right to speak, I have the right to take my place.

T: I do have the right to take my place...

> I really have the right to take my place...

D: In that part there's not an ounce of possibility that I am not given my place.

T: And the anger is here.

D: Yes, if I am not given my place, she's angry... which obviously doesn't please the other parts.

T: This anger is here...

> this anger
> I want to shake Miriam
> maybe I would have done it...

D: No, never... I have to keep living with myself.

T: I have to live with myself...

> The anger
> this anger
> take a deep breath
> how do you feel?

D: I don't know, I don't have the feeling that it's changing.

T: It doesn't change much. When you think about the anger, where is it on a scale of 0 to 10?

D: If Miriam came to me again and asked me the same thing, I would react in the same way... although my way wasn't... I just said "no", I wouldn't do it, that's all. But it would still put me in that state, if I think about it.

T: Do you feel a more sensitive part?

> Even if S. were to come now, I would probably still feel the same way...

D: If Miriam came now, I would react in the same way.

T: And the anger is here anyway, I accept and respect myself...

> Even though this anger is there, and if Miriam came to me now, I would still have this anger, I accept and respect myself...
> Even though this anger has been there all the time....

D: No, not all the time, I guess I wasn't born with it.

T: Since my father made me...?, I accept myself...

> that anger is here.
> the anger is there

Part 2: Advanced Clinical EFT

if I see Miriam, the anger is here...

D: With her cheesy look, wanting to be pitiful (it's not nice), that irritates me too, but maybe it's something else.

T: It annoys me, that cheesy look....

D: No, it's something else, it's another target.

T: Yesterday, it was anger...

how could she ask me something like that...

D: Above all, it's no, I won't do that when I managed to listen to her, ask her if she's worried and help her get past her worry, but I didn't give her a shred of space and I don't know how she took it, but at the time, it didn't worry me at all.

T: How could she ask for something...

D: I can understand why she asked for such a thing, it's just that asking me not to express myself as I want to express myself is "no".

T: That's "no"...

D: I can no longer keep silent.

T: I can no longer keep silent...

D: No, I don't want to keep silent anymore... yet I sometimes keep silent, but for that part, it's horrible.

T: It's really horrible...

D: ... to keep silent, yes.

T: I don't want to keep silent anymore...

I don't want to keep silent anymore.
I had to keep silent all the time,
I should no longer remain silent...

D: No, because I am no longer in danger, I can express myself.

T: I'm an adult now, I can express myself...

D: Yes.

T: Miriam asking me that?

D: No, it's no... it's "fuck you, what".

T: Yes, it's fuck you, no is no...

> I have the right to express myself
> I really have the right to express myself....

D: I don't tolerate being asked to be silent... it's mostly that, because I do express myself, but the reaction comes when I'm asked... not to be able to express myself about what's there... to pretend... no, I can't pretend anymore.

T: I can no longer pretend....

> No is no.
> ?
> No, it's no.
> it's really no....

D: I will not keep silent.

T: I will no longer keep silent...

> No is no. It's no.
> I will no longer keep silent
> I can't stand being asked not to express myself...

D: No, I can't stand it... it's unbearable.

T: Unbearable....

> it's unbearable.
> asking me not to express myself
> it's unbearable.
> No is no.
> I will no longer keep silent
> it's unbearable.
> I will no longer keep silent
> ...

D: I will no longer be silent anymore, that's not true, it's just unbearable.

T: It's unbearable...

> to ask me to keep silent

Part 2: Advanced Clinical EFT

> I will no longer keep silent...

D: But if I keep silent, every time I'm afraid of being hurt, I keep silent.

T: I will no longer keep silent...

D: But it's unbearable for that part... so it's a mess.

T: No, it's no...

> this anger
> the revolt....

D: My body can't take it anymore, it's sick of it, it would like to be relaxed.

T: This anger is here...

> the revolt
> it's unbearable.
> No is no.
> I will no longer keep silent
> No is no.
> it's unbearable...

D: I don't know if it will ever be bearable someday.

T: I don't know if it will ever be bearable...

> this anger
> unbearable
> No is no.
> No, it's really no.
> I will no longer keep silent...

D: It sounds false, this thing, "I will no longer keep silent".

T: How do you feel?

D: My whole body is vibrating.

T: When you say "it seems difficult for me to say that I will no longer keep silent"...

D: No, because it is not true.

T: Even if you don't want to keep silent, it won't be possible.

D: No, because you can't say everything, not just anyhow.

T: It's difficult.

D: No, it's okay. It's just that it's difficult for that part to be obliged to do it because it wouldn't be right.

(Change of therapist: Yves takes over)

Y: Even though it's totally natural that I'm angry...

> because it's unbearable.
> and I'm tired of being told to keep silent.
> and it's normal for me to be angry,
> it's unbearable that Miriam comes to me and asks me that.
> just like my father...

D: He didn't even ask me to.

Y: And it's unbearable....

> and now we're in a training where we should say the things
> and I'm told "I hope that you will not say the things"
> it's unbearable.
> it's an abuse.
> it's an abuse.
> and it's normal for me to be angry
> I'm angry.
> I'm angry.
> I feel lost.
> I was like a little girl.
> I didn't know what to say.
> I said no because it's unbearable to be asked that, because I'm no longer a little girl, I have the right to say "no"...

D: I don't know if I was a little girl.

Y: I'm angry....

> I have no right to express my anger
> but I have the right to express my anger
> there are parts of me that say "you have no right"
> there are parts of me that say "you have the right"

> I'm angry.
> I have the right to say "no"
> I said "no" to Miriam
> I couldn't say "no" to my father
> I didn't dare say "no" to my father
> I wouldn't have known how to say "no" to my father.
> but I was dying to say "no" to my father
> I'm also afraid
> I was very scared.
> parts of me who are afraid to say
> it's not appropriate, you can't say
> this is not to be said
> I have to be careful.
> but it's not necessarily true that I have to be careful
> we can't say everything, not just anyhow
> and if that wasn't true...

D: Yes, it is true.

Y: And if that wasn't true....

D: Yes, it is true.

Y: And if that wasn't true....

D: No, we can't say everything.

Y: And if that wasn't true... Even though I'm very scared and if that wasn't true...

D: Yes, it is true.

Y: And if that wasn't true....

> even though I'm really very scared.
> I was told that you can't say....

D: It's not that I was told.

Y: I was hit on to say "we don't say"

> they didn't let me experience things.
> I was not allowed to express my emotions.

and even if I expressed myself against my closet, they would come and hit me
it's not fair.
I couldn't be asked that.
Miriam couldn't ask me that.
she doesn't measure the impact of her words
It's not okay for me.
I told her "no"
it's normal for me to say "no" to her
I have the right to say it.
I have the right to say it to her.
I have the right to put flowers in it
I have the right to leave thorns there if I want to
it's up to her to manage her thorns
it's not my thing not to speak up
I may have the right to speak up
I may have the right to learn to speak up...

D: I do speak up.

Y: I also have the right to say to my parts who say "no" that I don't have the right to speak up, to those parts that say I don't have the right to speak up...

D: I don't follow anymore.

Y: I may have the right to tell the parts who say I don't have the right to speak up...

that I may have the right to speak up
I have as much right as they do.
I just need to find a balance.
even though I want to hit them with something rude
because they've been blaming me for enough years.
They have been whipping me up.
even though they think I'm ruining Lara's session, that's not true
and if that wasn't true
I accept and respect myself
all my anger
this ton of anger
this pool of anger

Part 2: Advanced Clinical EFT

> this ocean of anger...

D: This universe of anger.

Y: And if it was partially mine...

D: It is mine.

Y: And if it wasn't just anger...

> and if it could be anything other than anger
> what would that be?

D: Energy.

Y: Um... okay...

> all that remains
> the universe that remains
> the galaxies
> the suns...

D: Except that anger is not the universe, nor the galaxy, it is rather bombs, weapons, things that kill, things that hurt.

Y: Bombs, weapons...

> I would have shaken her like a plum tree
> I would have hung her from the ceiling.
> to hooks
> do you realize what you just told me
> you don't listen to what I'm telling you
> We've been meeting for two years and you still don't know
> You don't listen to me...

D: I've never told her anything.

Y: I've never told her anything...

> but I accept and respect myself
> Take a deep breath. How do you feel, calmer, less calm?

Yves' comments

I'll explain why you got lost. At first, you didn't understand each other well when you said "if it was a movie" and the sentence is "if it was a movie title" to get a keyword. You have superbly found an affect bridge, that is, the past and the connection to the past, but you have not targeted anything specific. So, Deborah's unconscious doesn't know what it's tapping on, it's tapping on 50,000 things at a time and so the SUD can't change. It's too vast.

You could have said, "If you were to symbolize or represent the episode with S., what could we call it? The stupidity, the misunderstanding, the anger... and then in particular, what is the most difficult moment? The moment you hear her say that, the moment you see her face, the moment you realise what she's asking you to do? "What is the most difficult moment", and therefore fix the most difficult moment. When you do that, the unconscious knows what you're referring to when you tap.

And every time you have finished a round, you say "go back to the basic event, the basic image, and observe how you feel at the level of your SUD?" Now it's not stuck.

Here, we have something particular, as it is a trauma that affects the childhood things, and we must recognise that. You didn't do that, and it should have been done right away.

When you were tapping, you said "the anger", but you have to say "and it's so normal to be angry" because it's true. That is what this part needs to be able to release the pressure. After that, all the work is to go and negotiate with the other parts, those who say, "but no, no", "I'm really afraid to say everything". It is to gradually bring them to reconciliation, acceptance and living. This is a whole job that does not necessarily have to be done in one session. Here, it was really to say "I recognise that you have the right to be like that" and, as soon as we start doing it, the SUD goes down.

Let's check the points. There are two points where Deborah was not precise enough: on the eyebrow, under the eye. It's exactly what we deal with, the security, the insecurity, etc. Bladder 2 is insecurity, it is one of the most important points in relation to what is being treated. It's not for nothing that she tapped just next to the point, she can't do it. It was necessary to fix that, to hold the point.

The second point she couldn't tap well was the Stomach: fear is on the cheekbones. It's normal, these are parts of her that say it's too hard to touch, so I tap anywhere. When you observe, do not hesitate to say "I

Part 2: Advanced Clinical EFT

notice that you are not quite on the point". It should not be forgotten that the point includes the space of 1 cm in diameter around the point.

At one point, you were trapped, because as you were looking for what to do next, I think she took the lead in the session. She was the one saying all the stuff and you were following, repeating. But it is also a defence mechanism: I take the leadership, which we will call the mind to make it simple, and I keep my thing. In that case, you speed up the pace. That's what I did, I accelerated the rhythm and at first, she couldn't follow... I keep on throwing the lines. Even if she says no, I go through her defence, but without forcing it. The goal is to activate both the part that says "no" and the part that needs a "yes". I gently desensitise the one who says "no" and feed the one who needs this "yes".

At one point, Deborah said: "Yes, it is true... yes, it is true" and I only insisted on saying "and if it was not true" because it is the part that needs it not to be true that is fed by it. Even though the parts need to say "it's true" because that's how they survived at one point. I am not in opposition, I do this with a smile on my face, I am not getting angry. The parts that needs to be heard in there, is nourished.

She said, "No, not all the time, I guess I wasn't born with that", it's clearly a defence mechanism. I make it intellectual, I trivialise it. There are Psychological Reversals here.

She says, "S. was cheesy" and then she says, "it's another target". No, I don't think there is another target, it's another aspect of the same target, it's her side "she's pugnacious compared to Miriam who is a victim, so obviously that irritates her, since in her life story she had to fight to get out of it, "I'm strong""; so it's like a mirror in S. who has the same injury but expressed differently: "I'm the poor little mouse" against "I'm the lion". Obviously it activates her fully. That's another aspect.

This kind of thing, you point it out: "Even though S. annoys me when I see her complaining like that, whereas I'm fighting, I had to fight to survive, I accept and respect myself." It is to recognize once again the parts that are there, that have expressed themselves.

"I will no longer keep silent, it's not true, but it's just unbearable." These are Psychological Reversals, blocking or limiting beliefs. She gave you a whole list of Psychological Reversals. Why it got stuck here, it is because at the base, it was necessary to target more specifically, a precise moment, an image, so that you have a guiding star, a point on which you can measure your SUD. Your SUD, you measured it on 10 targets and so you thought that it didn't move. Yes, everything moved, but you couldn't measure it.

Secondly, check carefully if the person is tapping well. Is it everywhere or on certain points? If it's on some points, what do these points mean? This is not just some innocent coincidence. I will make her hold this point, I will insist longer.

All the Psychological Reversals that Deborah mentioned, we have to work on them. Even though blah, blah, blah, blah... Even though it's unbearable... Even though parts of me say I can't tell myself... Even though other parts say you still have to keep silent because you can't say everything, I love and respect myself... And if all that wasn't true or if it was something else, what could it be...

You just say "what if..." even when the SUD is high. By the way, you made an open sentence: "And I can't... and you didn't finish the sentence and that's great. And she was lost.

In reality, you don't expect the person to answer. You say, "and if it was...", "the anger", "and if it was..." and you don't complete it because the Unconscious will complete it. Her mind may say to itself, "What did he mean, why did he say that?", but you don't care because her Consciousness will do its job, but the Unconscious is challenged, it is connected to a root and it will automatically complete the sentence.

Even if that doesn't come up, as sometimes it comes and sometimes it doesn't, but you mark some points, you gently break through the defence.

In summary

Great, apart from the lack of specificity of the target: image, emotion, sensation, you had to pick a precise moment of the scene (and from there the cognition) and then make an affect bridge with the past. There, you make a therapeutic choice where you decide to work on the scene from the past by creating a link with the current target during the tapping. From time to time, you could have said "S." You didn't make that choice; you were

Part 2: Advanced Clinical EFT

tapping on both at the same time. So, the SUD cannot decrease because the work is not targeted enough, its scope is too wide.

Below, you can read an example of poor targeting, not because the phrases or elements are bad, but because we are dealing with a complex trauma. That's why the treatment plan should have been different (see the chapters on the treatment plan and the difference between simple and complex trauma).

b. Carla - Aurélie demonstration

Yves supervised the session. Aurélie takes the role of the therapist and Carla takes the role of the patient.

Before the tapping begins, please tell the patient: "If something comes up during the tapping, it is important that you can say it and feel totally free to add things yourself or to tell me if what I say is not okay for you!"

CARLA: On Friday, I was already starting to get signs that carrying everything was too much for me, I went a little crazy, that surprised me, it's not typical of me, what happened?

My day had been hectic, in the evening Thomas was difficult, I was hungry, he was tired, it wasn't going well, I couldn't do it, I was at the end of my rope.

I said it to Stéphane, who had had a drink with his colleagues, but I have difficulties with making clear requests. I wanted him to calm Thomas down and he prefers to let him cry. I said: I'm going to do it myself; I had Thomas in my arms and I screamed! Thomas screamed too; I did worse than well.

This really upsets me because it has never happened to me before. (Carla cries)

> Yves: I suggest you tap on the Karate Chop point.

AURELIE: What is the emotion? Sadness? Discouragement?

CARLA: I'm exhausted, I'm afraid: how will I manage if it happens again, will I be able to carry it out?

> (Comment: we could have dug here. Why does she have to carry everything by herself? What is the negative belief behind it?)

A: That's the strongest image, I guess... Title?

(Comment: Aurelie assumed and Carla agreed, okay.)

C: That's too much.

Yves: Look for other emotions and each time measure the SUD.

A: When you see yourself screaming with Thomas in your arms, do you feel guilty?

(Comment: according to our common sense, we can propose logical emotions.)

C: Yes, at 9 because it was worse than good, I feel responsible.

A: The sensations?

C: It's in my chest and belly.

Yves: No need to ask for sensations, we can see that she is connected but it is important to look for all the emotions: anger against yourself, against Stéphane? Helplessness? Guilt? Shame? Look for the strongest emotion and then ask where it's felt in the body.

C: Anger against Stéphane, yes, because I couldn't count on him, and against myself for not having asked more clearly.

A: Against Stéphane, and what is the SUD?

C: It's strong against him, because we talked about it in the evening and he didn't understand, at 9.

Yves: Make it clear that 10 is unbearable and 0 is ok.

A: And the guilt?

C: At 9, I'm not able to express things correctly.

A: Anger against yourself?

C: Yes, at 9.

A: Other emotion? Shame?

C: No, it can happen, but I'm afraid that it will happen again, that I won't be able to endure, to manage, and I'm afraid that I'll make things worse for Thomas, the fear of myself.

Part 2: Advanced Clinical EFT

A: How strong?

C: And at the same time, I was also afraid because I didn't recognise myself at all.

A: How strong here and now?

C: Everything is strong, at 9 too.

Yves: You could tell her: and this fear of yourself, have you ever experienced it at other times in your life? What about the anger? To look for older roots, is there fear of losing control?

C: Fear of myself: no; fear of losing control, it's my personality, I always want to manage everything on my own.

A: What about the anger towards Stéphane?

> Yves: In relation to Stéphane, expand to other times in her life, the goal is just to find out why. This can be another root = I have not been acknowledged...

C: The lack of support in this situation reminds me of a lot of things related to Thomas, I managed a lot on my own at the hospital, maybe there are things accumulated, that I didn't feel supported enough, acknowledged. For me, it would be a form of support if he recognised everything I do and yes, maybe there must be anger towards him because I don't feel recognised. And there is an injustice: the mother is a mother and therefore she should care for the child... but that's not fair, we are two parents, just because I'm the mother doesn't mean I have to carry everything.

A: There is an injustice...

C: Yes, it's a bit strong but it sometimes makes me angry, it makes me feel a little lonely at times, like I have to carry everything in relation to Thomas.

A: Angry outbursts before, in your life?

> Yves: Observe her, she is more and more calm, therefore less connected, so make her think about the basic situation and which emotion comes first?

C: "I've had enough" and anger.

> Yves: Which one is the strongest? Is it towards you or Stéphane?

A: More towards Stephane... a part of me accepts that I can be at the end of my rope.

> Yves: You can start and connect the different emotions, use the words she used.

A: How angry with Stéphane?

C: At 8.

A: Even though I have this anger, it's too much...

> Yves: Specify with Stéphane, be specific!

A: Anger towards Stéphane, he went for a drink when I needed him...

C: I can't help defending him, he had made dinner.

A: The anger, he doesn't understand when I need him, it's too much...

A: If you go back to the original situation, how angry are you with Stéphane?

C: It has decreased, I can still feel it in my stomach at 6.

> Yves: Before asking for the SUD, always ask what came up during the round, to integrate it afterwards: images, emotions, sensations, people?

> Be careful to repeat the same words: she was okay with him going out for a drink...

C: I always tend to defend him, hard for me to legitimate my anger against him, it's not okay to blame him when I have my responsibility too...

> (Comment = Psychological Reversal)

A: Emotion?

C: Angry with myself, I blame myself for not expressing better what I need.

A: How angry is the anger with yourself?

C: At 9 with myself, in the chest.

> Yves: It's the anger that has risen but before that, there is a Psychological Reversal-> Sore Spot: Even though part of me thinks I have no right to be angry with him...

Part 2: Advanced Clinical EFT

Use her own words, otherwise she could oppose during the stimulation of the points.

Associate the anger against herself and Stéphane in the tapping.

Be careful to ask what came up during the tapping.

And an important aspect of the beginning is Thomas -> to be included in the tapping too; there are three aspects, three main roots: anger against Stéphane, anger against myself and poor Thomas, and behind all this there are several possible cognitions: I am helpless, I am a bad mother, I am alone and abandoned. To name but a few. These are aspects to be taken into account during the tapping phase.

It is better to stay on the main root: anger towards Stéphane, say this aspect most often during the tapping and from time to time we introduce the other two aspects. Do not forget to (re)check everything at the end. The SUD must be at zero!

If you do this, it will be faster than doing only one aspect at a time, but you will have to make sure that all these aspects are desensitised.

Comments and questions

Marc: She doesn't make Carla repeat the phrases after her?

YVES: It is probably always better to have them repeat aloud so that you can also check that the person is repeating what you are proposing and not other words that could paralyse the desensitisation process. If the person is not able to do it, ask them if it is difficult... or offer to say it for them, and when they feel ready, they repeat. Ditto if the person does not know how to tap, ask to tap on him/her.

Marie: What about the cross-legged position?

YVES: This is not important in EFT. The electromagnetic energy or field does not stop when your legs are crossed. It's an urban legend.

Sabrina: They don't both have the same tapping rhythm; should the therapist adapt?

YVES: No importance, unless you give a specific rhythm especially to keep the person in a comfortable working window. The principle of tapping is as follows: the faster you accelerate, the higher the connection to the feelings. This is especially indicated for people who tend to cut themselves off from their feelings or who dissociate themselves from the problem to be treated. On the other hand, if people tend to be too high in their emotions and feelings, and risk falling into an abreaction, it is important to slow down tapping or even just rub the points to slow down the stimulation.

CARLA: There is also the anger against Thomas; I can't blame him, so I throw it on Stéphane.

> Comment: Four aspects: anger towards Stéphane, herself, fear for Thomas and anger towards Thomas.

AURELIE: Anger towards Thomas, at how much?

> Yves: No, not here, she's going to miss this. It's better to integrate it into the tapping.
>
> Think back to that evening and your anger against Stéphane, use his words again to immerse her in the event and when it's over, check all aspects.

C: I remember what triggered it, the mayonnaise jar was emptied all at once, it was too much.

> Yves: Start again, she's well connected, but include the Psychological Reversals she gave you.

A: Tap on the Eyebrow point: "Even though I don't allow myself to be angry with Stéphane and Thomas".

> Yves: Repeating the same thing three times = EFT1, better: integrate the other aspects into it, say her words: I can't help defending Stéphane...

C: Even though I can't help defending Stéphane,

> Even though I'm angry with Stéphane,
>
> Even though I don't allow myself to be angry with Thomas,
>
> Even though I'm afraid for Thomas,

Part 2: Advanced Clinical EFT

> Even though I'm afraid of myself...
>
> Yves: write down the exact sentences, otherwise, if using other words, the person can bring up resistance.

A (tapping): Are there any things that are coming up?

C: The "it's too much" was much calmer, it didn't resonate anymore.

A: If you think about Friday night, the anger against Stéphane?

C: At 5, but I tell myself I'm not sure he understood, I'm afraid it will happen again.

> Yves: 5 is a lot, she doesn't seem angry -> and how do you feel this 5, where is it in your body? Is that anger? Or frustration? Or fear? What makes you think it's anger?

A: It's true that I feel more relaxed... I don't know what's going on.

> Yves: We are at a crossroads of the session: either the anger has disappeared and there are the other aspects and possible other ones, or the anger has decreased and the other ones are there, or she is not connected. First try to reconnect her by retelling the whole scene with her words.

C: There is still anger, but especially the fact that I am not supported.

A: Frustration?

C: Fed up, in our relationship, it's always the same, we don't see things the same way.

> Yves: Another event in your life that illustrates this even more strongly (= an event that has an impact on the starting event).

A: Yes, Thomas' medication, Stéphane is very supportive of medications, and I am not at all.

> Yves: Do a round on this, integrating the other aspects as well, then check if the starting scene changes. We are on another root: anger towards Stéphane for another reason.

C: Even though not ok with Stéphane about the medications...

...

A: I also feel lonely because I can't assert myself enough.

> Yves: Anger against myself because I can't assert myself enough: linking the two aspects.

C: Less and less angry with Stéphane.

A: Guilt? Anger with myself?

C: I guess there's none but there's still a knot in my belly, I don't know what it is.

A: At how much is the anger against Thomas?

C: I have a little something in my stomach, I don't know if I'm angry.

> Yves: She doesn't seem angry; we'll check at the end.
> The stomach = fear, the plexus = will, ability to assert oneself.
> Do a round on the fear, which was one of the aspects.

A: Think of your anger against yourself, against Thomas.

C: Something in my stomach, against myself: at 3, but I have the impression that in order to go to 0, I have to talk about it with him.

A: And the fear of yourself?

C: It's okay... a little knot, 2/10.

> Yves : During the tapping but not during the setup, you can introduce other supposed aspects, maybe...

If this session were to be repeated, we would first check the quality of the therapeutic relationship between the therapist and the patient. Then, we would try to reconnect the patient with her Self (see the notion of the Self in the treatment plan for simple and complex traumas) and finally we would swing between the trigger that was targeted at the beginning of this session and this Self or the useful resources that we would have reinforced or installed.

Here, it is clearly necessary to continue with the other cognitions that will probably refer to other scenes. We are not dealing with a simple trauma, nor a bump in life, but with a tangle of "small" wounds or abandonments that have sensitised the client and caused an insecure attachment disorder... The real root behind all this is to be found in this area if we want to achieve sustainable and perceptible improvements with the client in her daily life... To continue therefore!

C. The steps of a session

1. The phases of a typical session

When treatment is in progress, each session can be done according to the following scheme:

1. Eventual **stabilisation** (Container...)
2. **Evaluation** (of the results of the previous session)
3. **Determination of the** next **target** (the same target if the session is incomplete, or continuation of the treatment plan)
4. **Treatment** of target(s)
5. **Closing** (and stabilisation if the session is incomplete: SUD > 0)

a. Closing of a session

(1) Complete session

A session is complete if the SUD = 0.

The closing of a complete session does not require anything special.

However, the patient can be offered the option of going to his or her Safe Place for a few seconds.

(2) In the event of an incomplete session: stabilisation

A session is incomplete if the SUD is > 0.

Stop in a calmer moment, if possible.

If the patient is still active, it is necessary to allow him/her to calm down before leaving the office.

Several techniques can be used:

1) - **In case of moderate SUD**: Container/Basic State, Safe Place, Safe box.

2) - **In case of high SUD**: Quick REMAP - Stimulate each of the points for one minute until relatively calm.
3) - **Find a positive moment or aspect of the session**

When nothing else works, it is often a good way to connect the patient to something positive at the end of the session. It is rare that the patient cannot find anything positive.

"What positive thing did you learn today?"
- Identify and specify the target (Im, PC).
- Reinforce (TAT® pose, EFT tapping, REMAP® points).

b. *The next session: evaluation*

For each new session, it is important to check how the results of the previous session were held.

(1) *Complete session*

Check that the SUD is still at 0.

(2) *Incomplete session*

If the previous session was incomplete: **resume by re-evaluating the target "now"**.

Part 2: Advanced Clinical EFT

IV. Complex traumas

A. Structural Dissociation of the Personality

I explained the difference between simple and complex trauma in the first part of this book. I used a simple metaphor, that of the house whose foundations are, or are not, solid enough.

The explanation below is more clinical and takes into account the theory of the Structural Dissociation of the Personality: **O. van der Hart, E. Nijenhuis, K. Steele: *The Haunted Self (2006/2010).***

In the case of complex trauma, there is structural dissociation of the personality: the patient's "Self" has fragmented into "parts of the Self" during his or her life, with the existence of an ANP (apparently normal part) and one, or often more, EP (emotional parts).

It is quite simple to understand what is a ANP/ "apparently normal part": it is the patient's personality as it presents itself to you when the patient is "normal", that is, in his or her usual state, as opposed to the "abnormal" state in which he or she is when he or she is recalling a painful situation in a lively way. For example, when a patient who was abused at the age of 9 (touching) comes to you on her first appointment, she may seem quite "normal", that is, the impact of the abuse is not visible in her behaviour here and now, and if she does not tell you about it, you may not know anything. It's her ANP.

Emotional parts are those parts of the patient's Self that have experienced a trauma and have remained "frozen" in the experience of that trauma in the past. In the example above, there is an emotional part who is 9 years old and reacts like a 9-year-old girl, with a little girl's voice. This part of the Self will come to the forefront if the therapist targets a memory of the abuse. When the "bell", presiding over the revival of the network of memories of that time, was agitated, it is the emotional part, the sub-personality "containing" those memories, that manifests itself. Suddenly, the "normal adult" patient in the therapist's chair turns into a little girl who cries in distress and fears for her physical integrity. By definition, a trauma is an event that exceeds the person's ability to cope. This means that the 9-year-old girl could not cope with what happened. **The emotional part therefore does not have the resources to deal with the treatment of the targeted abuse.**

B. Modification of the treatment plan in case of complex trauma

The treatment of **simple traumas** is done with the three-step protocol: first the past, then the present, and finally the future.

In the case of **complex traumas**, due to structural dissociation and lack of resources of the different parts, treating one part is not always bearable for the other parts. It is also common that the treatment of one part is not transferred to the other parts. This is why, treating traumatic experiences is **not** effective (even if the SUD decreases or drops down to 0 for a given traumatic scene), and sometimes re-traumatises the patient.

Below I detail the steps to follow:

- stabilise the patient: initial stabilisation;
- treat targets by making a **reverse protocol**: treatment protocol adapted to complex traumas by:
    - making specific resources for each of the past targets,
    - using the Container before each target treatment,
    - adapting the exposure level.

1. Initial stabilisation

The initial stabilisation consists in not starting the treatment of the negative aspects at first but taking a certain number of sessions (in case of a heavy complex trauma, this can take months) to stabilise the patient and bring him to a state that will finally allow him to approach the negative.

Here are the different stabilisation methods:

a. *Installing the Container and the Basic State*

This is essential and preferable to a simple Safe Place/Safe box.

b. Affect Regulation techniques

Teach the patient techniques to help contain the affect/emotions (EFT, REMAP®, Mindfulness, taking distance in hypnosis, symbolisation...). This gives him a feeling of security and above all can be used in case of an emotional surge once you start with the treatment of sensitive targets.

c. Stabilization through general resources

Even if the therapist knows the general theme of the traumatic targets because the patient mentioned them in the anamnesis or the first sessions, he would have to refrain from targeting (looking for the worst image...) because the patient is too fragile for that. It is not yet time to make specific resources for these traumatic targets.

We start by making general resources that can help the patient feel better in his daily life: if he lacks self-confidence, we make resources on this theme, etc.

This phase is prolonged or shortened depending on the patient's ability to move to the next step. Your clinical experience, as you work with complex patients, will guide you in determining whether you need to stabilise more or whether you can move on to the target treatment phase.

Optional: connect the patient to the Self.

N.B. The strengthening of the connection to the Self is the subject of a separate course on the therapist-patient relationship in the therapist overall training. It is not described in this book. However, you will find some guidance on this subject in Yves' review article "How to build a treatment plan", at the end of the book.

2. Specific adaptations for complex cases

For complex traumas, all the finesse is in the therapist's art of allowing the patient to stay within the window of tolerance. Dissociation, abreaction or phobia of confronting the trauma are the pitfalls that make it very difficult to deal with traumatic targets.

Therefore, for the treatment of targets with the reverse protocol below, the following two methods should be used to modulate the contact with the trauma.

a. Using the Container

Important: Before reprocessing a target, always start by using the Container. Actually, it soothes the patient's psyche and puts him in the best conditions to confront the trauma.

Method:

1) Let "everything that needs to be reprocessed" slip into the Container.
2) Treat the target.

b. Exposure levels

I transcribe here a very useful contribution from Hélène Delucci, which makes it possible to regulate the intensity of the patient's exposure (contact) to the thought/memory to be treated. It is taken from an EMDR protocol that Helen called the "Gearbox", which is intended for the treatment of complex trauma. This protocol contains many clinical aspects and procedures that are outside the scope of this book.

Nevertheless, I have extracted for you two aspects of this protocol that are simple to apply and will make your life much easier when dealing with complex cases. The first of these aspects, which I develop here, is the use of a modulation of trauma exposure. The second is the "treatment of future fears" and is discussed further below.

Modulation of the exposure:

When treating a target, you can use a gradual exposure (contact) of the patient to the thought/memory to be treated.

c. Minimum exposure: the pendulation (CIPOS)

Remember, pendulation (see "stabilisation") is used to reduce the extent of SUD, dissociation and trauma confrontation phobia. It consists in asking the patient first to think about the trauma for a few seconds, then to reorient themselves in the present. Then, the patient is led to swing between the trauma and a resource.

N.B. Since you are in a case of complex trauma, you have necessarily installed general resources and then resources related to the trauma before treating it.

d. Average exposure: Im + K (no NC)

Working only on the worst image (Im), the emotion (E) and the physical sensation (K), without the negative belief (NC).

Actually, it seems that it is the fact of focusing the person on a beam of components (Im, E, K, NC) of the trauma that tends to activate it, and therefore brings a risk of destabilisation. **Cognition** seems to act particularly as an organiser (negative cognition is what "brings memories together" into a network); targeting cognition is therefore the same as targeting an entire network. That is precisely what we are trying to avoid at this stage.

We will therefore only process the image and the physical sensation associated with the targets (the precise identification of the emotion is not necessary. It is often fear). This helps to separate the components and reduce the risk of connecting the traumas.

e. Maximum exposure: Im + E + K + NC

Conventional reprocessing with all the criteria of the target: Im, E, K, NC.

Comment

Thus, we can start with a pendulation. If the patient treats the targets easily, try with medium or maximum exposure, and go back if they cause too much distress or make the treatment too difficult.

When you become familiar with these exposure levels, you can use them flexibly throughout your sessions: you intuitively try an exposure level and then modulate according to the result.

3. The reverse protocol

In the case of simple trauma or targets that do not exceed the ability of patients to cope with them, we have seen that the following principle is used: get to the root of the problem at the maximum intensity for maximum effectiveness.

In the case of a patient with complex trauma, it's the opposite: intensity is what we're trying to avoid, because we have to stay within the window of tolerance, and it's not easy.

For the simple trauma, the order was as follows: Past - Present - Future.

In the reverse protocol, we treat in the following order:
- the future;
- the **present** triggers;
- the trauma (**the past**) comes last!

In other words, we go from the least traumatic to the most traumatic.

a. The future

There are two types of targets that can be treated for the future:

(1) Desensitising future fears

Adapted from Hélène Delucci by Brigitte H.

Stabilisation has an impact on daily life, and it is often the primary objective of patients with complex trauma. The work on the future is proposed in the reverse protocol because it causes less destabilisation than the work on the present triggers or the past events.

It is useful to **reduce realistic or hypothetical fears about the future**, and in particular **about the treatment.** This leads to an improvement in daily life, helps the patient have confidence in the therapy and reduces avoidance.

When it comes to dealing with the difficult events of the past, fears often arise:
- fear of dissociative parts,
- fear of being destabilised,
- fear of slipping into depression,
- fear of going crazy,
- fear of death,
- other fears of the future.

Part 2: Advanced Clinical EFT

Asking questions directly allows the patient to talk about things he or she would not have mentioned, such as the fear of decompensating or going crazy.

Question: "Do you have any anticipatory fears, concerns that could block the therapeutic process?"

Procedure

It is possible to treat fears by specifying the target (Im, NC, E, K, SUD) or not (without making a precise targeting).

Unspecified fear

Question: When you think about this fear (for example, of decompensating), what comes to your mind now?
Im: What image do you have in your mind when you think about this?
(No questions about the emotion since it is, of course, fear.)
K: physical sensation.
SUD

Reprocessing (preferably in REMAP® or EFT)

In EFT

Setup: "Even though I have this fear of..., I can understand myself and I accept myself."
Tapping: "This fear of..., this fear of..."

In REMAP®.

- use the 4 points of the emergency procedure;
- ask the person to focus on the image and the physical sensation, and stimulate;
- ask the patient to note if the sensation decreases when the point is stimulated;
- if so, let it decrease until it doesn't change anymore and then go to the next point;
- otherwise, proceed directly to the next point.

By stimulating one of the EFT points or by TAT pose

Do steps 1 and 2:
Step 1: "Everything that led to this fear has happened."

Step 2: "Everything that led to this fear has happened, but it's over now, I don't need to be afraid anymore. I no longer connect or identify with this fear."

If necessary (very intense fears or fears that activate dissociative parts), use the pendulation **(CIPOS)** beforehand to lower the SUD.

Classically targeted fear for the future

As for a classic target for the future, look for: Im, NC, PC, E, K, SUD.
The PC is the opposite of the NC. Ask for the VOC.
And treat with EFT, REMAP® (or TAT®):
- treat the target until SUD = 0;
- check the VOC of the PC;
- strengthen the PC up until 10 (as you do with a resource).

(2) Desires for the near future

What objective in everyday life does the patient want to achieve? These are emotional or behavioural goals that would help him improve the quality of his life. We see what is blocking and treat it as a **concern for the future (see above in "Future Level", "Treatment Plan").**

It is about taking **small** steps, **small** steps forward.

Ex.: I have a meeting in a week and I'm very stressed, it's never going to be okay. I would like to feel more relaxed, be able to answer my boss and not break down if my colleagues look at me with a strange face.

We treat this as a target:

- What is the worst in her/his anticipation?
- Specify the target (Im, NC, E, K, SUD).
- Treat it.

b. The present triggers

We look for what triggers the patient in his everyday life and treat these sources of stress as normal targets **without using float back** because we do NOT want to address the trauma at this stage.

Any present trigger in the patient's life, even related to the trauma (but which is only the trigger, it is not the trauma itself), can be reprocessed by:

Part 2: Advanced Clinical EFT

- **pendulation (CIPOS)** between the target of the trigger and the resource;
- determining an **image** and a **physical sensation** (no NC) and desensitizing until SUD = 0;
- according to the standard protocol **(Im, NC, E, K, SUD** and treatment).

c. The trauma / the past

(1) Principles

The past will only be dealt with when the patient has been stabilised and is able to cope with the reprocessing of the present triggers.

Actually, if he is too destabilised by the work on them, it is a clear indication that he is not ready to deal with the targets of the traumatic past.

Begin by addressing past targets that are moderate and see how the patient is able to address them without dissociation or abreaction.

Remember that when processing a target, you must:

- put everything in the Container first;
- make specific resources for this target.

(2) Specific resources for the chosen past target

This involves using the protocol for specific resource installation described in the chapter "Resources", slightly adapted as follows in the next paragraph.

Identify the resources needed for a current problem

- Think about the memory of the past that we will treat.
- When you think about this situation, what is your degree of disturbance between 0 and 10? (SUD)
- When you think about this situation, what qualities, resources or strengths would you need?
- What would you like to think of yourself in this situation? **(PC - positive cognition/belief)**
- How would you like to feel? (emotions/sensations)
- What would you like to be able to do? (behaviour)

N.B. It is important here that the positive belief of the resource is the opposite of that of the traumatic target. Actually, this is how the resource will have the greatest impact.

Build one or more resources related to the target to be treated.
They can be used when using CIPOS/pendulation.

(3) Pendulations and continuous adaptation of the protocol

Once the patient is stabilised and resources have been made available for the first past target, treatment can begin. When dealing with old trauma, it is often necessary to alternate trauma treatment with resources or stabilisation (Container). Whenever the patient is overwhelmed by emotions, the Container is used to calm the patient, and you resume the treatment of the target using the modulation of the degree of exposure.

The use of **CIPOS/pendulation** is extremely helpful.

For past traumas, we will therefore go back and forth during the same session between:

- the Container/Basic State;
- the resources related to the trauma (alone or during the pendulation);
- treatment of trauma targets;
- ego states activated by the traumatic material;
- ego states activated in the transference relationship (patient-therapist).

(a) Ego states activated by the traumatic material

If a part of the Self is activated by the traumatic material, one can for example do surrogate EFT for this specific part: You stabilise the patient (the Container). Thus he/she establishes contact with his/her "apparently normal part", and we can ask him/her if they agree to do a surrogate EFT session with us (the therapist) for the activated part.

But the simplest way is to use the Container and "let everything that led to the activation of this part slip into the container" (see the transcriptions of demonstrations in the "Container" section). The path is then clear and we can continue with treating the target.

Part 2: Advanced Clinical EFT

(b)   Ego states activated in the transference relationship (patient-therapist)

Patients with a complex trauma profile often have parts that are activated in the relationship with the therapist, by transferring affects related to their parental relationships (or other dysfunctional relationships from their childhood). It can be a transfer of lack of trust, of fear of not being understood or rejected, etc. It is important, and sometimes unavoidable, to recognise and treat them, because the feeling of security here and now with the therapist is a *sine qua non* condition for the progress of the treatment. It is often very relieving for patients that the therapist welcomes their fears, recognizes them, and takes them seriously to the point of treating them. It is very therapeutic, because it is what didn't manage to happen in the past with their parents or other adults involved (calming their emotions in the relationship and returning to a feeling of being safe in the relationship).

(4)   Remarks

In the case of complex trauma, it is often successful to initially follow the objectives brought by the patient, even if they do not include an approach to the underlying problems.

If we first follow the patient's initial objectives, it is frequent that once they are reached, the patient fixes others. They are then more confident and know that they will be able to maintain sufficient control of the situation. Patients with complex traumas who do not wish to prolong therapy beyond their initial objectives are rare.

The therapist can present the therapeutic model and options to the patient (fundamental therapy versus "surface" objectives), who can then choose what is best for him/her.

Example: Michel, a long-time depressive patient, consulted after suicidal ideas related to the potential breakdown of his relationship. Michel did not get involved with the fundamental treatment, which seemed too far away from his direct need: managing his chaotic emotions towards his wife. On the other hand, he is very pleased with EFT's rapid progress on the most painful targets on a daily basis. Once these targets have been treated, Michel asks by himself to do a thorough work on his abandonment fears.

C. Examples of sessions

1. Complex traumas and attachment disorders - targeting and reprocessing

Yves (therapist) - Sébastien (patient)

YVES: We're going to treat this accident you had when you were a child, can you remind me how old you were?

SEBASTIAN: Nine years old, November 1960.

Y: Can you reconnect with the emotion you have when you hear a siren, when there is a flashing light?

S: Yes, it's funny, the Belgian sirens don't make the same effect on me, they make hoo hoo... the sirens that affect me, they make this pimpon noise with a specific frequency...

Y: Just now, you were at 3/10.

S: Yes.

Y: Even though I have this fear of the unknown, of what would happen to me when I had this accident at 9 years old...

S (taking the initiative): Even though I didn't want to say where I live because I didn't want my parents to know...

Even though my worst image is this blue flashing light with this siren pimpon sound, I had a very big headache and this cop who asked me for my address, I didn't want to give my address...

    blue flashing light, when I hear the pimpon sound, I freeze for one or two seconds...

Y: When he hears the pimpon sound, he freezes and becomes absent, even while driving. He was on a bike and got hit by a car.

    blue flashing light, that cop questioning me
    I fainted as soon as I told him.

Part 2: Advanced Clinical EFT

It was an accident, it was dark, it was raining.
I put a flashlight on my bike and they didn't see me
blue flashing light
that cop questioning me, as soon as I hear the pimpon sound, I freeze.
I didn't want to say my name or address
blue flashing light, I felt very sad and I even wondered how sad this boy should be to attract their attention in this way.
(Y: his parents never cared for him, diplomats and travelling...)
I didn't want to say my name or address, the pimpon sound, as soon as I hear this sound, I freeze.
I was very scared, I had a very bad headache
I'm afraid my parents will find out; I didn't want to answer the cops.
I didn't want to say my name or address
this blue flashing light, I can still see it turning before my eyes, I can still hear this siren
I have a headache, a terrible headache, I'm afraid my parents will find out.
I fainted, I was hit by a car, I can't stand the noise of ambulances, I really freeze, for one or two seconds I leave the present moment.
a fear and a very great sadness, I was afraid of being yelled at too, but I wanted my parents to take care of me
that cop questioning me, that blue flashing light, the siren

Y: Breathe well, how are you feeling right now?

S: It was like going through it again, like a journey, I saw the pictures again, moments, I saw the cop's cap, the rain, his voice, the flashing beacon turning.

Y: If you think about the event now, the emotion you feel now, how much is it now? Is there anything else?

S: No, it's quite calming, quite relaxing, as if it had been evacuated.

Y: Do you still have a physical sensation, a little bit or not?

S: No, less, but still a little out of the present.

Y: You say less, so there's still a little bit left?

S: I think about it, it's a little obsessive, there's a bit of a compulsion phenomenon, sort of.

Y: Do you think you need this a little bit, that it's part of you?

S: No, I think maybe I need to reattach to that memory... I feel a little bit of an emotion... I have some tears in my eyes, a little warmth, a little heartache, it all comes when I say that I reattach to that memory and I can't let it go even though I know it's something that hinders me a little, like there's something that's afraid to express itself if I let go of all this, so I hang on to it. When I have an emotion, it's the emotion of that unsaid thing; but I don't know what it is. Anxiety maybe, but I can't say what it is exactly. I feel like I'm hanging on to this event, I'm holding on to it.

Y: We're going to work on that.

Eyebrow point (EB): Even though I have this feeling in my throat, this heartache, this warmth, as if I were attached to these memories a little, I can't let them go, as if part of me were afraid to let go, because she's afraid to let go of everything else at the same time.

Even though a part of me is afraid to let go of that memory because of her fear of letting go of everything else and I feel a little anxious about it.

Even though a part of me doesn't know what the unspoken thing of that memory is.

Even though a part of me is afraid of no longer being nostalgic about this childhood and what I missed during this childhood, as if I were giving up part of my identity.

I can't let it go.

it's a part of me, it's a part of my life, I don't want to let it go.

I'm afraid I won't be the same if I don't have the same emotion anymore, that blue flashing light, the cop's cap.

a part of me is afraid to let go, it's been so long since I've been having this anxiety with me

I don't know who I'll become if I let go of this anxiety, I'll have to take better care of myself.

Part 2: Advanced Clinical EFT

I'm afraid I don't know who I am anymore, the voice of the cop, the blue flashing light, the siren.

> all that fear, all that fear of letting go of that memory
> all that fear
> the blue flashing light
> the blue flashing light
> the fear of letting go of that memory
> all that anxiety, all that memory represents in my life
> and if I allowed myself to get rid of it now
> and if I allowed myself to let go now
> and if I gave myself permission to live free now
> all that's left of my problem
> all that's left of that blue flashing light
> all that's left of this siren noise
> all that's left of this nostalgia, the abandonment, the presence of my parents
>
> all those unsaid things, all the things I wish I could have said to them, all the things I didn't allow myself to say to them, all the things I didn't want to say to them, all these aspects of my communication, all the things that make me a communicational being, all the things that made me have a career in communications, and if I freed myself from all the unnecessary weight of the past?
> all that's left...

Y: Breathe well. If you think about this accident, do you still have an emotion about it?

S: Yes, one that comes after the accident, but one that is rather positive.

My mother finally came to see me. In fact, it's an accident with multiple scenes, I do realise that: the shock of the car, I go under the car, the ambulance and everything, that's a life being torn apart; just after, there is my mother in the hospital, I am in a bed, in a rather reassuring place, calm, I feel less pain, less nausea, I am in my bed late at night, I open my eyes and the doctor and my mother are above me and I am happy, I have a huge smile and a big bump on my face, as I am told... I stayed two weeks in the hospital and there I succeeded! I did it right, it was a won episode... but there's a next chapter, can I talk about it?

Y: Yes, we're going to come back to that, but if you just think about the accident, do you still have a negative emotion about it?

S: No, I'm calm now.

Y: Okay, so the second part is about your mom...

S: Yes, Mommy comes, but during the second visit to the hospital, I was in the children's room, there were 15 beds with children in them; it's Sunday, all the parents come to visit! It's generally an emotional event, all the parents come, they bring stuff, and I'm the only bed in the hospital room, I'm the only one who's alone, all the others have their parents, brothers, sisters who brought them toys, chocolates, and Nader is on his bed, there's no one there and it lasts, the visit lasts an hour; and I start crying around 4:30, I start crying and my mother gets there at 4:55, too late! And that really got me... there's the return of the initial wound... She arrives, she's all happy, she arrives all smiling, she doesn't understand; for her, she didn't arrive late, she came to say hello to me, but for me, she didn't come when the other parents came, she didn't come when the other parents were there, she came when she wanted.

Y: And how do you feel about that?

S: Well, a little sadness, but at the same time, a little anger.

Y: And the worst image? Is it when you see the other parents who are present?

S: Yes, that's what hurts, it's not jealousy but it pushes the nail in, why not me?

Y: What about your emotion right now?

S: It's funny, I didn't expect to see this image coming up like this, at 4-5, yes.

Y: Is it more like anger?

S: Yes, sadness and anger, it's not abandonment.

Y: And the emotion that seems strongest to you, is it sadness or anger, or disappointment perhaps?

S: Yes, sadness and disappointment, not anger, sadness, emptiness... and even more so when mother arrives, because even with her presence, she can no longer do anything for me, I am really condemned, there were many things before that that made me feel this thing so strongly, my birth, my mother's absence, for reasons we know, she had lost her daughter, she was unavailable when I was born... one year after my sister's death.

Y: Should we work on that a little bit?

Even though I felt a little betrayed by my mother because I was waiting for her visit to the hospital and all the other parents were there, I was the only one alone...

Even though I feel a little sadness, a little anger, especially disappointment and a little bit of abandonment, I feel like I'm unworthy, I'm different from the others...

Even though she arrived five minutes before the end of the visit, it was too late for me,

> the parents' visit, my mother was not there
> all the other parents were there with oranges, gifts, I was alone
> Five minutes before the end, my mother arrived but I had been crying for so long, so disappointed, so abandoned
> I feel a little angry.
> I feel a little angry, a big disappointment mostly, I felt abandoned by my parents, especially by my mother even though I know she was doing her best because she had lost my sister
> all this disappointment, especially when she comes and I don't even feel happy to see her, it was too late
> all that sadness, all that I feel about it, I'm all alone
> no one is there for me, I start crying
> I started crying, my mother wasn't there, no one else was there, I was all alone
> all the conscious and unconscious reasons I have for feeling sad
> everything that led to what happened
> all that disappointment, all those parents who were there for all the others and me, no one
> I felt completely abandoned, I'm unworthy, as usual, I'm unworthy

as usual, I am different from the others, I have this image of all the other parents present and I feel different
and I feel completely different.

Y: Breathe well, how do you feel now, what did come up?

S (coughing): It's liberating for me (coughing), it reconnects me (coughing) in a very permissive way, in the good sense of the word, to things I've never said to myself, these are very simple sentences that allow me to take my child in my arms and that creates a bond, a connection.

Y: If you think about the disappointment, what do you feel is left?

S: Not so much.

Y: How much?

S: 1/10.

Y: Do you have a place in your body where you feel that way?

S: Still in the throat, the sternum.

Y: And is there a special feeling?

S: It's the thing that gets tight in the throat, some sadness, I don't know how to say this.

Y: And do you have a particular image that has come up?

S: Plenty of images, I saw the beds in the hospital again, my mother in a beautiful coat, she dressed up to go out, to appear, she didn't put on jeans to see her son... I see that, but another image came to me, it's Anne Lise, because I don't want her to experience the same thing.

> (Y: It's a very borderline person, constantly afraid of being abandoned, he's a bit of a saviour, they're no longer together.)

S: There is that support in my childhood, that damaged bond, I want to restore it, but I took the wrong target and, instead of repairing it in myself, I wanted to repair it in her... that was a part of our relationship...

Y: We're going to take the Sore Spot point, a slightly more painful area, down on the outside, a neurolymphatic reflex area, don't press hard, just feel a little pain, the idea is to get your circulation moving again, to detoxify your body.

S: Even though I saw my mother dressed up to be seen, and I still have a little tightening in my throat...

Even though I still have this little tightening in my throat, at the top of my sternum...

Even though I had the impression that my mother had dressed up more for herself than for me, and that it was like another betrayal for me, something other than her true presence...

Even though that made me understand that I may have tried to reproduce this with Anne-Lise, that I wanted to avoid it for her, or to repair what she hadn't had because I hadn't had it myself...

Even though maybe I should have helped myself instead of trying to help her,

> this tightening in the throat
> in the top of my sternum, tightening in my throat
> I saw my mother who had put on a beautiful coat, who had dressed up more to be seen than to be with me.
> all that is left of my disappointment and sadness, this tightening in my throat
> that tightening in my throat that keeps me from saying the things I feel
> this tightening in the throat
> at the level of my sternum, these difficulties in saying the things I've had all my life
> tightening in the throat
> tightening in the throat
> and if I could free myself now
> and if I gave myself permission to communicate fully, all that's left of my tightening in my throat
> all that's left of my tightening in my throat
> all that's left of my tightening in my throat
> all that's left of my tightening in my throat, I'm freeing myself from it now...

Y: Take a good breath...

S: Um, um... (coughing), something that means... it's interesting, I thought of Anne-Lise again, one word seemed to have a double meaning, as if all of a sudden my unconscious freed me, the word that sounds both like "tightening" and "oath". Why do I have a tightening, an oath, what does this bind me to?

Y: If you go back the hospital, all the other parents, your mother... is there anything left of that?

S: Um, um... (coughing). There must be something left... Um, there's not much left, there's a spot in the throat, like a word I shouldn't say, I don't know what, there's something, like a spot.

Y: We'll move on to that right away.

S: Even though I have this spot in my throat that prevents me from communicating...

Even though I have a word that gets stuck in my throat or aches that get stuck in my throat...

Whatever the reasons for these words and aches, I accept myself...

Even though I have carried these words and these aches for so many years and I may be a little afraid to let them go, because I may be a little afraid of the vivacity of these words, of the age-old nature of these aches,

> words, words and aches
> those bruises in the heart, all those bruises in the body, words and aches, the fear of saying, the need to say, all the fear of saying, the need to say
> fear of saying, all these words and aches, the fear of saying, the fear in my throat, all this fear in my throat
> all that it points to in my throat.
> all that it points to in my heart
> all that it points to in my body
> all that it points to in my words, all that it points to in my aches, all that remains of this tightening
> all that remains of this oath, all that binds this oath, all that this oath has bound me to
> everything I haven't allowed myself to say, everything I'm not allowed to say, I'm freeing myself of it now

> all that's left, the little that's left
> all the little that's left
> all the conscious and unconscious reasons for which it's left, all these words and aches, all that remains of this oath, all that remains of these words
> everything I can let fly away to free myself
> and if I gave myself this permission, to free myself from all this right now

Y: Take a good breath... how are you feeling right now?

S: We always want to say better but I'm thinking... I feel connected, that is connected to myself, and then the word oath... maybe the oath I took was not to disturb, I made a pact not to disturb, not to make my mother unhappy, not to be disturbing so that she would not be unhappier. If I drew attention by distracting her, by seducing her, I got results, so there were two things... I had to disturb her in a good way.

Y: If you think about the episode, do you still have an emotion?

S: The episode of the bike and the hospital room, the arrival of my mother? No, I'm okay, I see her smile, I see her smile, and I see her out of context, I see a smiling woman coming and I don't even look at the watch to see if it's too late or not; when she arrived, she was smiling, she was beautiful, radiant, it was like a fairy coming, a fairy in the hospital.

> (Y: We really see the reprocessing of the information... she has become a fairy.)

Comments: The client is a person with a strong mind, he analyses, he thinks a lot, that's why, at the beginning, I repeated all the sentences, all these words: the cap, the flashing light, it was raining... to put him back in the context, to connect him with his emotions.

During the second round, he was disorganised at all levels, and then everything was more or less ok, it was due to the emotional rise; it is also a way of checking that we are still on the root even if the patient doesn't seem activated: the fact of seeing his body reacting is a way of detecting that we are on the root.

If the SUD does not move, you have to ask yourself if you are still on the root or if there is a disorganization that makes your intervention no longer effective.

But as long as the SUD moves, you can continue.

Emphasize certain points according to the emotions present during tapping; refer to the table of points that show some links to the emotions.

2. Complex case, complete regression bridge (float back) and other advanced techniques

Below is a session that integrates the elements of a Regression Bridge, with many technical points.

Demonstration: Sarah (teacher)/Yves

SARAH is a teacher who experienced a burnout. She suffers from attachment disorders, which gives rise to symptoms of very low self-esteem, a need for constant recognition and a tendency to take everything on (too much), hoping to receive recognition or signs of affection that she lacked during childhood.

She has difficulty saying "no" and, as a result of this burnout, she has lost all the confidence she had acquired thanks to her professional qualities. She would also like to leave her profession as a teacher to start therapy activity, but the employment agency sends her SMS messages inviting her to take up, at short notice, a temporary position in a school.

YVES: How can I help you?

SARAH: It's about what happened two days ago at home; before, I used to have full confidence in homeopathic remedies and since my burnout, I've lost that reflex. My child was sick on Thursday night and I only thought about it on Friday night. I would like to regain my confidence in what I believed or knew before my burnout!

> (Here, I will start to see if I can create an affect bridge by using reconnection to emotions to specify my starting target: either the event in question (current), or an older event that would have the same memory traces.)

Part 2: Advanced Clinical EFT

Y: What do you feel like emotion? Anger? Anything else?

S: Yes, a little anger about no longer trusting homeopathy, no longer having these reflexes and staying like that without doing anything!

Y: Are there any other emotions? Guilt? I couldn't help my child? Shame?

S: There is mostly anger against myself, and also guilt.

Y: And the strongest? If you think about your daughter on Thursday night... Is Thursday night the most difficult moment or Friday night? Or some other time?

S: I want to find my mechanisms again.

> (The patient has difficulty staying on the scene and keeps on engaging in mental activity. It may be a defence mechanism. I will therefore bring her back to the situation by suggesting that she review the movie of the event while asking her for the worst image, the most difficult moment in order to reconnect her to the problem (to get out of a dissociated state) and also to check if the person's psychological state allows her to go deeper into the problem.)

Y: If you think about this movie, what's the worst image?

S: It was on Friday, when I realised: "Why am I only now thinking about the remedy I used to give before?"

Y: Do you have a precise image?

S: In the morning, when I woke up.

Y: Take this image and tell me what emotion is there.

S: ...

Y: A sensation in your body?

> (The connection to the emotion seemed difficult, so I switched to a sensation to check if the person is associated or dissociated from her problem. In case of dissociation, there can generally be no sensations.)

S: There, when I got up?

> (Here again, it is important to check that the connection is "here and now", because otherwise it is only a memory in the mind that would produce little effect if you started tapping. Then you could not be sure if the person is sufficiently associated with his or her problem to be able to reprocess it! This would lead to either incessant rounds or the person coming back to you and saying that nothing has changed.)

Y: No, now: get back into the scene, what are the emotions or sensations?

S: The feeling is that I have to go, some impatience...

> (This is not a sensation, but a feeling related to an emotion in this case, and, as a result, it confirms that she is associated with the problem.)

Y: Do you have it now?

S: Yes.

Y: Where is it in your body? Any general tension? In the shoulders? In the stomach? In the plexus? Where is it now?

> (Again, these questions allow us to check and deepen the connection to the problem.)

S: It's difficult, you tell me to go back there and I'm here today.

Y: That's it... Today, what do you feel? Now, when you are thinking about the situation?

S: I get angry, I am restless (reappearance of emotions of nervousness and restlessness).

Y: Between 0 and 10?

S: At 8.

Y: Are there other aspects when you think about that? Any other emotions or associated images?

> (And there, after having sufficiently reconnected her to it, another aspect appears because it is more related to the beliefs underlying the problem.)

Part 2: Advanced Clinical EFT

S: My self-confidence about everything, for example: in class, I couldn't do this or that, I don't have self-confidence; it irritates me!

Y: Is the anger stronger about that or about your daughter?

S: The anger is for everything, for the totality!

> (It is important here to specify again the exact target to start with in order to cover the need to be specific enough.)

Y: When you think about this class, is the anger you feel stronger than the anger of Friday morning?

S: Yes.

Y: We won't be able to bring the event with your daughter to zero without working on the school because it's a stronger root.

S: I want to do it right.

Y: Anger or frustration?

S: Anger 15/10.

Y: Worst image?

S: When I was forced to go, when I received the SMS.

Y: Is that anger?

S: Anger, frustration, being tired of it.

Y: The strongest emotion? Is it "I am tired of it"?

S: Yes, tired of being dragged from one side to the other, life catches up with me, I have to adapt again to what is being imposed on me.

Y: Disappointment?

S: Yes, I'm sick of it!

Y: Do you have a precise image?

S: When I receive the SMS.

Y: If we used a movie title, which one would it be?

S: Who am I, where am I going? Who am I? I'm lost!

Y: Karate Chop point: Even though I'm lost when I think of this SMS...

Even though I'm disappointed because I'm out of the line I have set for myself...

Even though a part of me is angry, frustrated and irritated because I think that's it, I'm unlucky again, I'm going to end up losing self-confidence, I accept myself completely...

> Eyebrow: I'm lost
> Side of the Eye: I'm lost
> Under the Eye: I'm lost
> Nose: I'm not going to be able to cut it off
> Chin: I'm lost
> Collarbone: I lose my reflexes, I didn't even think of helping my daughter
> Under the Arm: I'm lost, I can't do what I want when I choose a line
> Under the Breast: something gets in the way
> Thumb: I'm lost
> Index Finger: who am I, where am I going, I am lost
> Middle Finger: I'm lost
> Little Finger: SMS, I'm lost
> Back of the Hand: totally lost
> Eyebrows: I lost my benchmarks.
> Side of the Eye: I lost my reflexes, I'm lost
> Under the Eye: I'm lost, I lost my benchmarks, I lost my reflexes
> Under the Nose: I'm losing my good reflexes; I'm not going to be able to cut it off
> Chin: I'm tired of it, I've had enough, I don't want to answer this SMS
> Collarbones: I'm lost
> Under the Arm: I'm angry, angry with myself.
> Under the Breast: I'm lost, SMS, I'm lost...
>
>> (At each point, we repeated a reminder phrase, "I'm lost," and a different aspect to speed up the desensitisation - 3 rounds).

Y: Did anything come up while we were tapping?

Part 2: Advanced Clinical EFT

S: On Thursday, when I arrived at school, I received a call from my daughter's school and then from the other girl, I was no longer a good mother, I didn't know how to take care of my children.

Y: Okay, if you think about the basic image, the initial one, the one you started from, the SMS, what is the intensity of the emotion about it?

S: It's calmer: at 8 or 7.

Y: It's still huge and you talk about it calmly!

> (I noted that the difference between 15/10 and 7 or 8/10 did not correspond to the non-verbal. It is more certainly a Reversal, so I immediately resume as if it were a Reversal, probably a mental blockage of the resolution of the problem.)

S: Yes, these are good points.

Y: Karate Chop point: Even though these are good points, it still irritates me...

Even though I thought about those two calls on Thursday, and I haven't been a good mother...

Even though I'm still upset when I think about this SMS, because I feel lost, I'm torn between several things....

Even though I'm lost, angry and disappointed....

> (Resumption of EFT rounds by changing words at each point)

> I'm lost, SMS
> SMS, lost, couldn't even pick up my kids, bad mother
> I'm lost, SMS
> I couldn't go there.
> I'm lost, I'm tired of all this, I'm sick of having to always find a solution
> I'm lost, SMS
> Lost SMS, tired of being a teacher
> I'm angry.
> I'm lost.
> I'm lost.

333

my children are lost without me
SMS

I don't know what's good anymore.
not thought of the right medicine for my daughter
I'm lost, SMS
I don't want to go, it pisses me off.
I'm lost, it irritates me.
I'm sick of it.

SMS

SMS

SMS

I'm lost.

SMS

I'm lost.
I'm lost.
totally lost
SMS
lost, SMS lost, I don't know what to do, I'm stuck, I hate being a teacher
I'm sick of it, leave me alone.
I'm sick of it, leave me alone, I'm really sick of it
I can't escape it.
I'm lost, SMS
all that's left of this SMS....

Y: Think back of the image with the SMS, is there an emotional intensity or an unpleasant sensation in your body?

S: There is still tension, because I think that if there are other SMS, it's going to piss me off again!

> (Note: this is a futurization to be desensitised too. Remember to always check the past, present and future aspects of your source or root target.)

Part 2: Advanced Clinical EFT

Y: Even though I tell myself it's going to piss me off again and I'll have this tension, there'll be other SMS, with my type of luck, I won't get away with that, they'll contact me again, I'll get more SMS...

these damn SMS, there'll be more of them.
there will certainly be more.
it would make sense is there are more
There's going to be more and I won't be able to cut it off.
or maybe I will.
maybe not
all these obstacles in my way.
it's my fault.
SMS, they will come back, it pisses me off
and if it wasn't necessarily true?
and if I opened up to the possibility that it might be different
and if I trusted myself more
and if I thought faster about this medicine for my daughter
There's going to be more SMS messages.
I'm going to have to start again.
this tension in my body
all these tensions in my body and everything my body is trying to tell me with these tensions
all these tensions, and if I got rid of them
There's probably going to be 10,000 SMS, they'll only want me.
there will be 50 million SMS
the employment agency will only think of me
this totally pisses me off.
even though it's only me and I'm going to get 10,000 text messages
SMS, it might happen to me.
maybe not
I'm angry.
I'm upset about these SMS.

....

all that's left, the little that's left
if I didn't care.
I'm not even one SMS closer
It annoys me or maybe it doesn't.

335

> all that's left
> SMS
>
> I'm lost.
> all I could lose
> the little bit that remains

Y: How do you feel?

S: I'm fine.

Y: Think about the anger related to these SMS.

S: It has decreased but is not yet at 0.

Y: What do you feel?

S: Like a sadness.

Y: No anger or a little anger?

S: The desire to cry, because I really want to move forward in life, I have fought for years in teaching, and now that I want to do something else, I don't want to go back.

> (We can see here that tapping has desensitised the primary problem, that other emotions appear from then on and that we can simply sweep these aspects away little by little in order to end the session.)

Y: Even though I don't want to go back...

Even though now I feel sadness, not anger...

Even though a part of me really wants to change my life, it is quite normal that I am sad because it is my project, and if I open myself to the possibility that I could accelerate my project...

> (Here, we introduce a complementary element that is to recognise what the sad part is going through because, by recognising it, you calm it down and open up the possibility of reframing it to strengthen the resources and reprocess the initial information.

Even though there's the employment agency, if I just opened up to this idea in my head, and focused all my energy on it...

Part 2: Advanced Clinical EFT

S: It's what I wanted, but it didn't work.

> (The fact of sometimes bringing in more directive reframings as above can help to highlight the Reversals, the blocking beliefs, and thus opens up the possibility of reprocessing them - see below.)

Y (on the Sore Spot): Even though that didn't work...

Even though there are always things in my way and a part of me doubts...

Even though a part of me wants to adopt the idea that I can make this project happen...

> I can get there quickly.
> I can carry out my project quickly
> difficult for me because of the employment agency
> I'm lost.
> I could get there quickly.
> and if I was looking forward to carrying out my project
> and if I could free myself from all these doubts
> and if I connected to the moments when I feel good because of doing this job well
> maybe I'd smile more
> and if I fed on these good surprises even when I receive those SMS
> Maybe it would piss me off.
> I could put some wind in the sails
> SMS
>
> chases the dark clouds away
> long live the blue sky
> and if I wasn't as lost as I think I am.
> and if I didn't care about the SMS
> and if I thought about all the great moments I've given to others
> everything I get from my sessions with Diane...

Y: How do you feel?

S: Calm.

> (Here, we will check the different aspects treated or those that appeared during the session in order to confirm the appeasement of the event we worked on.)

Y: Think about the SMS.

S: 1/10, but it still bothers me.

Y: In your body, are you relaxed?

S: Almost, it's so deep...

In this case, this session shows that after stabilisation and some desensitisation we will have to return to the treatment plan for complex traumas and attachment disorders, which requires us to start working on strengthening the Self and, from there, to start pendulations between the Self and the resources and the present triggers. (See below "Treatment plan for simple and complex trauma".)

It is important to build affect bridges and include the different aspects in the same round (different emotions, past, present and future events). These affect bridges will make it possible to identify present triggers (in the case presented) and install useful resources before going back to the past itself. Normally, if it were a simple trauma, we would have prioritised the oldest events (roots of the current problem) then the events of the present and finally we would have visualised the future to verify that all aspects of the situation had been addressed.

However, in the presented example which is a complex case, we should, in the next session, continue to install these positive resources related to attachment disorders and lack of recognition. That is why, during this session, we have opened up the possibility of seeing things differently, less negatively. It is also very important to respect the patient's rhythm in order to avoid that he or she leaves the comfort zone too quickly or too abruptly. If the patient leaves the comfort zone too quickly, you may trigger an abreaction or dissociation, or even discourage the patient from continuing therapy. These are cases where EFT will not be as fast as in other circumstances but will empower the client by allowing him/her to work on his/her own between two sessions. It will be recommended that they work on qualities to be installed or reinforced rather than on the past itself.

V. Summary: How to build a treatment plan for simple or complex traumas

Yves has summarised in this article what has been developed in detail earlier in this book. You will also find some information on how to use the connection to the Self. As mentioned above, the connection to the Self is part of a series of courses on the patient-therapist relationship from the therapist training; this is beyond the scope of this book.

A. Working protocols

One of the main challenges that therapists face when starting a therapy is to be able to easily identify the point of origin that is at the heart of the behaviour or problem to be solved. In essence, it is all about the ways and means to be used to find the starting event (the root, heart) that is at the source of the client's request.

And, indeed, being able to quickly and accurately identify what we are facing is one of the key elements of effective therapy.

And to do that, our ability to easily differentiate between a simple trauma and a complex trauma is a very important element. At the very least, if you want to establish the best possible treatment plan.

Some basic questions should therefore be asked at the anamnesis:

- What is the client's life story? What was the place of emotional expression or acceptance in the family system?
- How did parents get involved in their children's education, what was their presence, physical or emotional absence?
- What were the life events the client faced?
- But also, do you recognise any traumatic symptoms? Any defence mechanisms such as amnesia, denial, avoidance, hyper motivity, hypersexuality, anguish or anxiety, the presence of OCD, phobias, addictions, etc.

- And are you able to work with them as efficiently or respectfully as possible? Or should you have supervision or refer the client?

In the case that I would like to explore further with you, namely how to differentiate between a simple trauma and a complex trauma, it is certainly useful and indispensable to ask the client/yourself these questions.

However, sometimes, when the client comes with a request that seems to have nothing to do with a trauma, we may make a mistake even by good intentions! Think of all those people who come with a seemingly simple request. For example, a request to stop smoking, or to reduce an addiction or a particular obsessive behaviour, or a dull and deep anxiety... This request could lead us to treat a symptom rather than the original problem. One of the clear benefits of a more clinical approach is to help us recognise what exactly we are facing, regardless of the client's request. And, through this recognition, we will be able to offer ourselves the possibility of re-specifying, redefining the patient's request by enlightening them on what more accurately refers to their symptomatology. We will also be able to restore their autonomy and give them a real grasp on their inner world through this process.

In this article, we will provide ourselves with ways to identify this type of simple or complex trauma while creating, tailor-made, the most appropriate treatment plan to resolve it.

B. Trauma

The trauma includes a physical or psychological injury inflicted on a person and its specific and general consequences in relation to that injury.

C. Simple traumas (type I)

3. Definition

A simple trauma can be defined as the trace, the emotional imprint, accompanied by sensations and a negative cognition, which a traumatic event freezes in us. In general, a simple trauma is the result of a single event that is not repeated over time.

Part 2: Advanced Clinical EFT

For a simple trauma, the treatment plan is also simple! The therapist will ideally work on the oldest event related to the problem.

You can use float back to help the unconscious and our memories effortlessly descend to this root event.

The float back is a tool that allows us to reactivate our access to older memories that would be directly related to what activates us today.

The easiest way for the float back is to start from the present trigger - the scene that activates the client today. Ask them and help them to reconnect well with the cognition, the belief that is associated with this precise and vivid scene. Then you check that the person feels a lot of unpleasant sensations, as well as the emotions associated with them.

When the person is in good contact with these sensations and the cognition has been clarified, you make him close his eyes and quickly ask him at what age he sees himself when he felt this for the first time.

If your float back is well brought in, an image comes up instantly, or sensations, or a particular thought. This very often makes it possible to identify a root scene from which to start processing past events.

When this past target is desensitised, we move on to the present to desensitise it in its turn and, finally, we will verify by a projection into the future by asking the person to see himself in the same situation as that of the desensitised past. The purpose of this "projection" into the future is to verify if, in all his Past - Present - Future aspects, the person feels totally at ease, without any further symptoms of stress. Normally, there should no longer be any doubts, negative emotions, limiting thoughts or unpleasant sensations caused by the reminiscence of one of the situations treated.

Summary of the treatment plan for a simple trauma

You will work on the past in the first place, taking the most emotionally reactive event.

Then, work on the present.

And finally, ask the client to see himself in the future, confronting with his old problem.

a) Past (Float back)
b) Present
c) Future (projection into the future)

D. Complex traumas (type II)

A complex trauma will not be treated starting with the past!

A complex trauma can be articulated in various ways.

1. Definition

The complex trauma is the result of an accumulation of traumatic events repeated over time. They may be of the same or different nature. They can be relatively concentrated in time or, on the contrary, spread over many years.

Traumas are divided into different spheres and can be identified by certain symptoms:

Acute stress, distress, brief psychotic disorders, up to one month after the trauma.

Post-traumatic stress disorder (> 1 month), chronic (> 6 months), delayed, with symptoms:
re-experiencing, avoidance, hyperarousal.

Re-experiencing = traumatic memory: repetitive thoughts about the violence, ruminations, intrusive memories of all or part of the event (sensations, pains, noises, words), sudden actions as if the event would happen again, flashbacks, illusions, repetitive dreams, nightmares, lived intensely with great anxiety and distress.

Avoidance: phobic avoidance of all situations related to the trauma or reminiscent of the event, avoidance of the thought itself, development of an imaginary world; avoidance of any painful or stressful situation, blunting of affects, disinvestment in interpersonal relationships, loss of positive anticipation of the future.

Part 2: Advanced Clinical EFT

Hyperactivity of the neurovegetative system resulting in hypervigilance, a state of alertness and control, jolts, insomnia, night awakenings, hypersensitivity, irritability, angry outbursts, concentration and attention disorders.

Dissociation symptoms that are often significant: altered state of consciousness, disturbances in memory, concentration or attention, feelings of strangeness, being a spectator of one's life, depersonalization, imaginary companion.

Complex post-traumatic stress disorder: proposed to describe the consequences for victims of repeated long-term interpersonal violence (type II trauma according to Lenore Terr). It is defined by several criteria, some of which are also part of the borderline personality:

- altered emotional regulation with marked impulsivity and self-destructive behaviour;
- disturbances of the attention or consciousness, which can lead to dissociative episodes;
- a change in self-perception, with permanent feelings of shame or guilt, and a sense of emptiness;
- a change in the perception of the aggressor, which can be idealized, for example;
- disrupted interpersonal relationships, with an inability to trust or have an intimate relationship with others;
- somatization symptoms;
- cognitive alterations with a loss of hope.

(Website on traumatic memory and victimology that I recommend: http://memoiretraumatique.org/psychotraumatismes/generalites.html)

Some people may also be more sensitive to it when combined with attachment disorders. Attachment disorders arise from a childhood in which emotional attachment has not been secure and reassuring. This will then produce either an anxious attachment or a detached attachment.

E. Treatment plan

All these nuances, all these psychic colours will make the treatment plan and the order in which we should work in therapy more difficult. This order is all the more important as it will make it possible to work in the most ecological and safe way for the person being cared for (which implies full respect for the client's life choices and values).

A properly established treatment plan will also avoid the ups-and-downs (also known as the "yo-yo effect") that mark in therapy the fact that we have misidentified or misjudged what we were facing.

It is important not to confuse the treatment plan which covers all the topics, events, relationships, etc. that will have to be subject of the therapeutic sessions, with the session plan which is the way to approach, during the session itself, the theme to be worked on today.

It is possible and necessary to re-evaluate the treatment plan according to what appears in the session. Sometimes, some materials only appear during the sessions and this may mean that the treatment plan needs to be reassessed.

Some information appears because the rapport - the therapeutic alliance – improves, or better when certain layers that prevented access to information have been resolved.

And sometimes we will have to reassess the session plan when some of these dikes break or other parts show up in the session.

One of the most important elements is to keep a comfortable working zone, avoiding as much as possible abreactions (painful emotional overflow) or their opposite, dissociations. Dissociation is equivalent to cutting oneself off from all emotional and physical feelings. There are several types of them (see below).

Summary of the treatment plan for complex traumas
- a) **Self and resources**
- b) **Present triggers**
- c) **Past events**

First element to be accomplished

Check the ability to make and hold resources. You can also start by installing a Safe or Calm Place.

Part 2: Advanced Clinical EFT

By "resources" I mean life events, situations, cognitions and thoughts, people who have been able to positively illuminate our life path, our experiences. We will prioritise resources related to the negative cognition, the negative belief that we wish to reprocess. We must therefore determine the negative belief and take the correct positive counterpart (positive cognition). As soon as it is done, we look for an event, a situation, a person who illustrates this positive cognition in our lives.

Detailed Resource Installation protocol (see the "Treatment plan" section above)

Resource follow-up

In the sessions following the resource installation, the therapist must reassess the installed resources to verify the effect of the installation on his/her stability. When the client is ready for the second phase of trauma confrontation, the therapist can begin the session by asking the client to select the resources (previously installed or new) he/she needs to deal with the trauma, and reinforce them in the TAT pose, by tapping (EFT, REMAP) or Self Emotional Balancing, among others.

We can strengthen them by tapping on acupressure points while revisiting the scene that illustrates them.

If negative elements appear during this tapping of reinforcement (negative thoughts, feelings, emotions), we deactivate them as we go along.

Another important element during the treatment will be to check whether this resource is still present and as strongly anchored. If not, we reinforce it by starting again its installation and reinforcement through tapping and visualisation.

If the person is unable to find one, or if the resources are not sufficient, the presence of the Self must first be checked.

1. The Self : definition

The Self is that space within us that is spontaneously serene and compassionate. It has no other intention than to Be.

According to Richard Schwarz's IFS model (*Internal Family System*, 1995):

The qualities of the Self are 8 (the 8 C's)

- **Calmness**: including appeasement, composure
- **Curiosity**: the ability to welcome everything, to hear everything
- **Compassion**: the ability to resonate with the other's experience without hyper-identifying with it
- **Clarity**: characterised by clear-sightedness, insight
- **Confidence**: confidence in one's own abilities and capacities
- **Creativity**: seeks alternatives, new solutions
- **Courage**: the ability to move forward, to expose oneself
- **Connectedness**: seeking connection with others and one's own internal parts.

The qualities of the Self are still there, even after multiple traumas. It may appear to be outside the body, obscured, even damaged, denied, repressed, but it is still there. All the knowledge, the skills are still intact and you just have to let the natural movement happen. It has a spontaneous motivation for health, it is a natural healer. And it is also the natural leader of the internal psychological system and creates harmony. Curiosity and compassion are especially useful to the therapist.

When we talk to the person, we always try to communicate with the Self.

If the Self is present, everything goes smoothly. Otherwise, another part of the psyche may appear and may block the process. We can then metaphorically ask her to put herself aside for a moment. In this process, the therapist asks the client to focus on his inner feelings and to report all answers to questions directly addressed to the parts present or appearing during this therapeutic process. For example, the client may become or feel sad or angry. The therapist directs his or her question(s) to the part(s) present (the sad and angry part in this example) to determine how to proceed to help resolve the internal conflict and resolve the problem.

The IFS key sentence to always check and validate if you are in connection with the Self is: **"How do you feel about this part?"** If the answer to this question includes the eight qualities of the Self (calmness, confidence, compassion, clarity...), it means that you are in connection with the Self. Otherwise, it is a part of you that reacts. Because if there is a particular intention to do something, to act or to expect something, it means that it is a part... and not the Self.[1]

If the Self is not clear or accessible enough, we will then have to go "temporarily" through the therapist's Self.

For if the rapport, the therapeutic alliance, is sufficiently built and solid, this Self will be the one by which the patient will be able to hear and recognise what he could have felt. And from this recognition or reconnection, the therapist will normally be able, little by little, to connect the patient to his own Self and from there, to resume the reconstruction and clearing of this inner space that we all have.

In practice, this means that the therapist will express from his Self what he feels for the parts of the client that are present and, in this way, will seek to reconnect the person being helped to his own Self.

This transition should ideally be temporary because the principle is not to risk a transference from the client to the therapist but to rely on this transferential link so that he can reconnect to himself. Through this exercise, the person being helped will be able to reconnect to his inner space of serenity: his Self.

If this does not happen, it is because first you need to check the good quality of the therapeutic alliance and work on it, strengthen it through better communication between therapist/patient, by using humanist tools such as the PCA (Person Centred Approach), the Rogerian approach, etc.

You can also suggest that the patient work at home between the sessions, using various self-help techniques or models such as self-hypnosis, Mindfulness, meditation or Energy Psychology tools. This work will also allow you to ensure or verify the proper resource installation and the presence of the Self. Because if the patient succeeds, it is because the Self is quite clear and present. And if the patient is not yet able to do so, it is

---

[1] SCHWARTZ R. C., *Internal Family Systems Therapy*, New York, NY: Guilford

Press, 1995.

because it is essential to check the Self and continue strengthening the resources.

When the resources are sufficiently strong and anchored, the client will begin to take better care of himself.

These are ways and means of controlling whether the treatment follows its course and whether the benefits of the sessions are well established in the client's daily life.

You can then move on to the third element and go back to the events of the past.

Because if, on the other hand, the Self and the access to it are good, you can directly continue with the search for a present trigger. First identify the negative cognition in order to be able to search for the useful positive cognition and counterbalance the negative. This positive cognition is usually measured on a calibrated VOC of 1 to 7 (see above). It will have to be installed or reinforced. Once this resource is properly integrated, you will pendulate between strengthening the resource and the desensitisation of the trigger.

Pendulating means that you first strengthen the resource with a few rounds of tapping and then move on to the present trigger you have chosen. I remind you to choose the right positive and negative cognitions (beliefs) in relation to each other.

When sufficient present triggers are deactivated, you can go meet the events of the past. Depending on the client's sensitivity, it is advisable to take past events from the lightest to the most difficult or reactive. If the Self and the resources are sufficiently present, then you can try to work directly on a more sensitive or difficult event from the past.

If you have doubts, first look for lighter past events in order to check the stability of the resources and the Self.

The treatment plan is therefore reversed compared to simple traumas.

If the subject is very sensitive, you can also use visual field treatment (REMAP, EMDR, IMO) to speed up or slow down the process and help you keep the patient as much as possible in the comfort zone and the working zone. This will avoid unnecessary discomfort for the patient and avoid having to deal with an abreaction or dissociation.

2. A few reminders on dissociation

If the client tends to dissociate or to mentalize, I advise you to first check for the presence of a Safe Place, the presence or the access to the Self... because dissociation is a defence mechanism. If the unconscious saw fit to place it, it was for a good reason. It is therefore necessary to act with caution and to ensure that the steps involved in verifying the Safe Place, the presence of resources or the accessibility of the Self are carefully followed.

Once these preliminary preparations are done, you can ask the client to tell his or her story well by trying to help him or her with your own feelings or with acting (acting or benevolent provocation), to reconnect the event and the normal emotions he or she should feel. Paul Gilbert, in his book *Compassion Focused Therapy* - CFT, advises to really play with emotions like in a mirror. These are entry doors that can facilitate reconnection.

When you observe that the client is reconnected with his or her own feelings, you check for the presence of negative feelings, emotions and cognition(s).

Be careful, if you have noticed that you are dealing with a complex trauma, it may be good to split and complete the anamnesis in several steps in order to avoid too much reactivation of the client.

In general, it is best not to stimulate acupressure points during this time. But sometimes, when patients tend to move from abreaction to dissociation, and vice versa, very quickly the stimulation will amplify the resonance effect and help reconnect while keeping the patient in the working zone that we need (cf. advanced EFT demonstration with Pamela, visible on YouTube : http://www.youtube.com/watch?v=WNVL5rbwtLU ,

or in REMAP and Provocative Therapy:

https://youtu.be/NGGkrrJ0JLA?si=ykmmLoZjHbr201nk

and its second part
https://vimeo.com/manage/videos/915311418/aff7933b6d/privacy)

3. And a few reminders on abreaction

Remember that after a trauma, we avoid asking the patient directly for details about the events, but we stabilise them first (by reframing, in particular: https://yves-wauthier.com/documents-ressources/)

https://yves-wauthier.com/wp-content/uploads/2014/06/acupoint-stimulation-feinstein.pdf

In phase two, we will integrate the memories using Energy Psychology tools such as Self Emotional Balancing, REMAP, EFT, TAT.

And finally, in the third phase, we work on the growth and development of the meaning of the event, in order to make sense of it and be able to propel oneself into the future again.

If the subject is so sensitive that at the slightest evocation of his situation the patient triggers a reaction that overwhelms him emotionally, then it is better to work directly on the Self, the Safe Place, the Container and the resources. The therapeutic rapport will obviously also guarantee that this comfort zone will be maintained.

There is a breathing and visualisation exercise which can be done regularly to strengthen our connection to the Self. This breathing inspired by the heart coherence will be reinforced by a special visualisation. You breathe in and out in five-second sequences. Five seconds of inhalation followed by five seconds of exhalation. You can help yourself by searching the Internet for mini-videos that present this exercise by a ball that goes up and down at this five-second speed. Enter the keywords "Breathing 6 times per minute YouTube".

When you follow this rhythm well, begin to visualise, while focusing on the following compassionate intention: when you inspire, you inspire all the suffering, all the negativity of the world. As soon as this cloud (to be represented by a negative colour of your choice) reaches you after five seconds, you visualise that it instantly transforms into a cloud of compassion of a healing colour of your choice, and you exhale it into the universe, the world, etc.

You can also add in the vision that you are sitting in front of yourself and that you are also inhaling and exhaling all the negativity of yourself, while sending to yourself and the universe all this compassion as you exhale.

This exercise, if you do it regularly and even up to three times a day for five minutes, will gradually lead you to reconnect with this naturally and spontaneously serene and compassionate space that simply *is*, without any particular expectation or intention.

In case of very strong reactions, immediately think of stimulating acupressure points such as REMAP (LI4, ST36, ear relaxation point, extra point 1 - I remind you that Large Intestine 4 and Stomach 36 are not recommended for pregnant women). Bring the person back into here and now, eyes open, bring his attention to objects in the environment, speak calmly and firmly. If necessary, do a reframing of the REMAP type (in 5 points).

F. Ideal reframing

1) **Even though** "sentence + specific problem"...
2) I love and accept myself completely **and deeply, more or less...**
3) **And it is normal** (natural, logical) **that I feel + "root" sentence** (recognizing the reality of the problem/the activated part)...
4) **And in reality**, "a true and verifiable element"... (Reframing >> anamnesis - ideally verified and certain!)
    and in reality (another reality), it's over
    I'm safe now
    it's not necessarily true anymore that XXX...
5) **I open myself to the possibility of "xxx":**
    Must be "open" (non-specific and non-directive)

    o being able to live, to feel things more easily, simply
    o experiencing things differently
    o taking emotional distance
    o digesting things more easily
    o finding a middle ground.

Also think about the fact that dissociation and abreaction are defence mechanisms that warn us to be careful and work cautiously. Get supervised if you are not trained or accustomed to accompanying this type of subjects or themes. Also, make sure to check the medical aspects carefully by advising your client to consult a doctor or mental health specialist if in doubt.

The passage through the Self is therefore essential because it will allow you to install or reinstall this Safety Place. It should be noted that in the case of children or adults who have suffered from early childhood trauma, the first thing to do is to stabilise and then build a Safe Place through the safe therapeutic relationship and alliance.

And as a last resort, remember that if you still do not feel comfortable enough with your "complex trauma" client, you should be supervised immediately or preventively. The other branch of the alternative is to refer the patient to a colleague who is more experienced in this area. Our main concern must be to support patients' requests in the most ecological and secure way.

Appendix 1: Dissociation

By Marco Di Tomasso - course on dissociation, Therapeutia.

I. Historical background

- Moreau de Tours (1845): dissociation as a phenomenon of psychological disintegration.
- 19th century: the concepts of dissociation of personality and dissociation of consciousness are used together.
- Pierre Janet (1907):"...a disease of the personal synthesis." "A form of mental depression characterised by the retraction of the field of consciousness and a tendency to dissociate and emancipate the systems of ideas and functions that constitute personality."
- Van der Hart, Nijenhuis & Steele (2006): it is "a lack of integration among two or more psychobiological subsystems of the personality as a whole system, these subsystems each having at least a rudimentary sense of Self".

II. Dissociative disorders

- Dissociative amnesia.
- Dissociative fugue.
- Dissociative Identity Disorders: DID.
- Depersonalization disorder.
- Dissociative disorders of movement and sensation.

A. The dissociation - a lack of integration

- Depersonalization: loss of sense of the Self.
- Derealization: loss of sense of the world.
- Non-presentification: loss of the sense of the present time.
- Inability to integrate the traumatic experience by alternating between feeling too much or too little (Janet, 1904/1911).
- High risk of dissociative disorders, due to lack of social support after terrifying events (Brewin, Andrews & Valentine, 2000).

B. Symptoms

Negative psychoform symptoms:

- amnesia;
- Alexithymia (lack of emotions or connection to emotions).

Positive psychoform symptoms:

- Schneiderian symptoms (auditory hallucinations);
- flashbacks;
- re-experiencing traumatic memories;
- (auto)aggressive impulses.

Negative somatoform symptoms:

- sensitivity losses;
- numbness, analgesia;
- unexplained paralysis.

Positive somatoform symptoms:

Appendix 1: Dissociation

- unexplained pain;
- involuntary movements.

III. Theory of the structural dissociation of the personality

- **O. van der Hart, E. Nijenhuis, C. Steele: *The Haunted Self* (2006/2010).**
- Differentiate between apparently normal functioning and emotional functioning.

Myers (1940) distinguished between:
- EP - emotional part of the personality, and
- ANP - apparently normal part of the personality.

ANP (Van der Hart and al, 2006, 2009) :
- oriented towards the survival of the species, the functioning of daily life;
- phobic avoidance of any traumatic content and emotional parts.

EP: systems of defence action against threats

Organised for individual survival:
- primary structural dissociation;
- secondary structural dissociation;
- tertiary structural dissociation.

A. Three types of structural dissociation

1. Primary structural dissociation

- *One predominant ANP and one EP; the latter is often neither very elaborate, nor very autonomous.*
- Simple types of acute stress disorder.
- Simple types of PTSD.
- Simple types of DSM-IV dissociative disorders.

2. Secondary structural dissociation

Appendix 1: Dissociation

- When traumatic events are increasingly disruptive or prolonged, an additional division of the EP may occur, while only one ANP remains intact.
- This *secondary structural dissociation* can be based on the failure to integrate various types of defence that have different psychobiological configurations, with different combinations of affects, cognitions, perceptions, and motor actions. The latter include positions such as freezing, fighting, running away, or being totally submissive.
- One predominant Apparently Normal Personality (ANP) and more than one EP; the EPs may be more elaborate and autonomous than in the primary structural dissociation, but they are generally less so than in the tertiary structural dissociation.
  - Complex PTSD.
  - Disorders of Extreme Stress Not Otherwise Specified (DESNOS).
  - Dissociative Disorders Not Otherwise Specified (DDNOS).
  - Borderline Personality Disorder (BPD).

3. Tertiary structural dissociation

- More than one ANP and more than one EP.
  - *Often several ANPs and several EPs are more elaborate and autonomous than in the secondary structural dissociation (including the use of different names and physical features).*
- Dissociative Identity Disorder (DID).
- ANP Division
- This *tertiary structural dissociation* occurs when unavoidable aspects of daily life become associated with past trauma: triggers tend to reactivate traumatic memories through generalized learning.
- When the functioning of the ANP is so poor that normal life itself is disruptive, new ANPs can develop.
- In severe cases of secondary dissociation and in all cases of tertiary dissociation, several parts may have a high degree of elaboration (e. g. names, ages, sexual gender, preferences).

B. Two different types of EP

- Controlling EP: fear of attachment, defensive actions,
- Victimized EP: desperate attempts to seek proximity rather than security.

This results in an insoluble conflict between

- The fear of attachment
- and the fear of losing attachment to the therapist (Steele and al. 2001, 2005, Van der Hart and al. 2006).

C. Dissociative disorders: problems

- Amnesia.
- Complete amnesia.
- Reluctance to disclose even known information.
- Shame.
- Beliefs: NC "if you really knew me, you wouldn't even want to talk anymore".
- Schneiderian symptoms (blaming voice).
- Transgenerational dimension of trauma.
- Fear of major desensitisation: increases the avoidance.
- Malfunctioning that has become familiar.
- The investigation of dissociative disorders is in itself destabilising.
- Often chaotic life circumstances: difficult to apply a standardised protocol.

Comorbidity

- Borderline Personality Disorder.
- Depression.
- Developmental Trauma Disorders.
- Other personality disorders: narcissistic, paranoid, etc.
- Delimitation with psychoses
- Long-term therapies: many external factors, difficult to control.

Identification of the dissociation

- Non-verbal behaviour during the session.
- Questioning.

Appendix 1: Dissociation

Non-verbal behaviour indicating dissociation

- During the session, tension and distress are visible.
- A state resembling a trance.
- Amnesia or brief absences.
- Does not hear the questions, has difficulty following the conversation, forgets the last question.
- Seems to listen and/or respond to inner signs, such as voices.
- Strange body movements or postures, inconsistent with the speech (putting their hand on the mouth to stop talking, fists closed while the patient is smiling, eyes moving in all directions as if they were looking for an exit while the patient is talking normally).
- Discourse with strange formulations, holes, inconsistencies, use of the third person when talking about himself/herself.
- Changes in voices or response styles (remember that the patient tries at all costs to keep control and show as few differences as possible).

Questioning the patient

- There are several standard questionnaires to diagnose dissociation, these questions can take several sessions.
- The questioning can inform us about the type of dissociation but also about the triggers.
- We will look at some sample questions:
- Feeling that a part of your body does not belong to you.
- Experience of not being in your body, that it seems anesthetized.
- Have you ever felt unreal?
- Do you feel that sometimes you are not really there, not completely present?
- Have you had the experience of being in a state of trance?
- Impression of looking at you from a distance.
- Looking at yourself from a point outside yourself.
- Looking in the mirror without recognizing yourself.
- Feeling that familiar people seem strange or unreal.
- Difficulties in recognizing your own home.
- Difficulties in recognizing a family member or a friend.

Questioning the patient

Identity problems

- ▶ Not sure of yourself or your desires and preferences.
- ▶ Confused about who you really are.
- ▶ Strong tendency to adjust to the expectations of others.
- ▶ Feeling that there is a struggle within yourself with strong feelings of ambivalence or conflict.
- ▶ Feeling of playing a role or a scene.
- ▶ Being told that others are surprised by (changes in) your behaviour.
- ▶ Feeling or behaving like a child.

Questioning the patient

Schneiderian symptoms

- ▶ Hearing discussions as if you were listening to voices or as if they were thoughts.
- ▶ Hear a voice commenting on what you are doing or giving you orders.
- ▶ Inside or outside?
- ▶ Can other people hear your voices as well?

D. Three-phase treatment

Phase 1: Stabilisation, symptom reduction and psycho-education.

Phase 2: Treatment of traumatic memories.

Phase 3: Personality integration.

1. Phase 1

- ▶ Stabilisation objectives
- ▶ ANP and EP
- ▶ Skills
- ▶ Mental energy
- ▶ Questioning
- ▶ Stabilization
- ▶ Stopping the dissociation
- ▶ CIPOS

Appendix 1: Dissociation

a. Stabilisation: objectives

- Stabilise at different levels.
- Reduce the frequency and severity of dissociative symptoms.
- Recover control over emotions, triggers, resources.
- Mobilise internal resources.
- Develop skills.
- Connect to external resources.

b. ANP and EP

- Determine which parts have important functions in the patient's daily life, and which ones disturb it.
- The distinction between ANPs and EPs is important because the priority in the treatment is to strengthen the ANPs and reduce EP intrusions, while still acknowledging their existence. For effective treatment, it is essential to know the mental actions of the EPs (e.g., their perceptions, feelings, memories, fantasies) and their behavioural actions, the action systems through which they manifest themselves, the conditional stimuli that (re)activate them, and their level of mental functioning.
- First interventions with the emotional parts blocked in traumatic memories:
- They take the past for the present and thus continue to act as a child or adolescent, they live in the time of the trauma. With these parts, the therapist's first objective is not the attachment itself, as attempts of immediate attachment will only trigger the defences even more.
- First of all, all parts involved must begin to feel safe in the present.
- The therapist "speaks through" the ANP to these EPs rooted in the traumatic past, encouraging them to look and listen to the therapist to find out if they feel safe.
- These parts can be encouraged to communicate with the other parts who have a relationship with the therapist and who are more focused on the present.

c. Skills

- Skills are the subject's ability to engage in the appropriate level of action, within the hierarchy of the action tendencies:

1) regulating action tendencies (affects and impulses), including the ability to manage one's own distress, to calm oneself and seek appropriate support and comfort around oneself, to regulate one's own social emotions such as self-loathing, shame and guilt;

2) enduring loneliness;

3) verbalising instead of taking action;

4) remaining in the present (mindfulness and presentification);

5) having empathy for yourself and others;

6) having social and intimate contacts with other people;

7) distinguishing between internal and external reality;

8) perceiving and understanding precisely the context and the concrete reality; distinguishing the past and the future from the present;

9) clearly perceiving and understanding the motivations and intentions of others and yourself.

Understanding how the patient works

- Examine particular situations in which the patient engages in symptomatic actions, including pathological alterations of consciousness, experiences that are too high or too low in the hierarchy of degrees of reality; physiological over- or under-activation; and other substitutive mental or behavioural actions, such as substance abuse, self-mutilation or the presence of inappropriate fantasies and beliefs.
- An early objective for the therapist and the patient is to identify precisely the desirable therapeutic actions that are now within the patient's reach, and to focus first on the achievement of these actions. It is essential that the patient is challenged enough to make progress, but not too early to face actions that require more mental resources than those available at the time. In this way, the patient's (often limited) mental energy can be conserved for feasible actions.

Appendix 1: Dissociation

- For example, he or she is first encouraged to learn to manage daily emotions and goals, before dealing with difficult emotions related to traumatic memories, because they generally require much more energy and mental efficiency.

d. Increasing mental energy

- Available and usable mental energy.

  - Reduce mental energy expenses (excessive work or activities).
  - Establish a sense of security.
  - Simplify the patient's daily life.
  - Reduce energy and time spent on the non-essential.
  - Set limits to overly demanding relationships.
  - Paying off debts.
  - Unaccomplished actions.

e. Stabilisation Profile questionnaire

- 1. Good daily performance
- 1.1 Basic needs: material and financial

  - Does the patient urgently need material/financial assistance?

- 1.2 Daily structure
  - Daily rhythm?
  - Does he/she have any daily activities?
  - How does he/she operate in these activities?
- 1.3 Health
  - General state of health?
  - Does he/she have any specific complaints?
  - Does he/she need medication?
  - Does he/she devote enough time to care and hygiene?
  - Does he/she have a balanced eating pattern?

- Does he/she have normal sleep habits?
- How does the patient use his/her resources?

▶ 1.4. Social environment
- Does he/she have contact with family/friends/neighbours?
- What availability?
- What kind of relationships does he/she have? Quality of contacts? Social skills?
- Can he/she set limits?
- Does he/she know how to ask for help?
- Can he/she handle conflicts?

▶ 1.5. Work environment / School
- How does the patient behave at work/school?
- Stress factor? Means of support?

▶ 1.6. Leisure - relaxation – sport
- Does the patient have any hobbies/recreational activities?
- What brings him/her relaxation?
- Does he/she exercise regularly?

▶ 2. Being safe and secure

1. With yourself
   - Self-injury? Risk behaviour?
   - Suicidal risk?

2. With the others
   - Is the patient safe from the perpetrator (partner, parent(s), stalker, etc.)?
   - Does he/she have secure contacts?

▶ 3. Feeling safe

1. In everyday life
   - When/where does the patient feel/not feel safe?

Appendix 1: Dissociation

      2. In therapy
- Does the patient feel safe with the therapist?

▶ 4. Internal strength
- Does the patient have enough self-confidence to be able to handle situations successfully?
- Is the patient sufficiently motivated?
- Is there an acquired helplessness?
- Does he/she feel in control?
- Does he/she have enough energy, enough strength?
- Does he/she know how to concentrate enough?
- Does he/she have personal opinions?

▶ 5. Hope
- Does the patient have any hope for a better life?
- If not, what is blocking hope?
- Can he/she imagine an improvement?
- What is his/her image of the future?
- Does he/she have any expectations about the therapy?
- Why therapy **now**?

▶ 6. Self-esteem
- How does the patient see himself/herself as a person?
- How negative is the self-image?
- Can he/she accept compliments or indicate something positive, strong in himself/herself?
- How permanent is the negative self-image?
- How realistic is the negative self-image?

▶ 7. Emotion management
      1. Recognition of emotion
- Is he/she able to feel emotions, recognize them, name them?

2. Tolerance to emotion
- Is the patient able to tolerate an emotion?
- How does he/she deal with emotions in everyday life?

3. Emotion management
- Can he/she manage to absorb a negative emotion?
- Is he/she able to make contact with a positive emotion?
- Positive experiences?
- Does he/she have a sense of humour?
- Is he/she able to make the transition from a negative to a positive emotion?

▶ 8. Attachment

1. With regard to the therapist
- How is the relationship between patient and therapist?

2. With regard to the inner child
- How does the patient relate to the inner child: awareness, empathy, rejection?

3. Exploring the patient's attachment

▶ 9. Double attention

- Is he/she able to stay here and now while thinking about the trauma?
- Does the patient get lost in the trauma?
- Is the patient unable to approach the trauma?
- Is there any confusion between the present and the past?

▶ 10. Identification of the triggers

- To what extent is he/she aware of the present triggers whose root is in the past?

Appendix 1: Dissociation

- How does he/she behave with the triggers?

f. Stabilisation methods

- Relaxation.
- Breathing exercises.
- Hypnosis, self-hypnosis.
- Imagination techniques - metaphors.
- Installation of EFT, TAT®, EMDR resources.

g. Resolution of the dissociative parts' phobia

- The therapist makes interventions at the level of the whole personality.
- The therapist will often have to remind the patient that all parts belong to one person and that they must all learn, in a timely manner, to find ways to communicate, understand, accept themselves and work harmoniously together.

h. Stopping dissociation during the session

- Give a strong signal from the outside.
- Reorient the patient in the here and now:
  - speak up;
  - have eye contact if possible:
    - look at me,
    - do you recognize me?
    - do you know where you are?
    - you're safe now.
- Try to give orders:
  - moving the body,
  - observing objects in the room,
  - changing places,
  - focusing on breathing.
- Self-interrupting by a sensation:

- squeezing an object in his/her hand (a ball, a stone).
- Touching the person (with their permission):
    - applying pressure, hand on the shoulder.
- Counting or other activities that stimulate the left hemisphere.
- Irritating the person:
    - giving false information;
    - mirroring behaviour.
- Using the body anchor to reorient:
    - feeling the floor, the chair.
- Clarifying the limits of the body.

i. Using self-distancing techniques

- The Cinema screen.
- The Train window.
- The Safe box.
- The Remote control.
- NLP.
- The Bubble.
- The Glass wall.

j. Self-soothing techniques

- Deep breathing.
- Progressive relaxation.
- Self-hypnosis.
- The Safe Place.
- The technique of the 5 senses (to calm each of the senses).

k. Strategy during crises

- Soothing:
    - focus on the here and now/the past;
    - calm your senses.
- Improving the present moment:

Appendix 1: Dissociation

- mental imagery: safe place, bubble;
- relaxation: muscle relaxation, massage, breathing;
- concentration on the body and sensations;
- encourage oneself.

▶ Using the emergency kit.

I. Emergency kit

▶ REMAP®.
▶ A reminding memo of:
  - the place to go to be safe;
  - the activities to do in order to feel good and be in the here and now:
    • physical exercise, walking, music, dancing, etc.
  - the stimulation of sensations:
    • hold some ice, take a shower, etc.
  - reinforcing spiritual and philosophical beliefs.
▶ List of names and phones of support people.
▶ Favourite music.
▶ Poems.
▶ Smells that give good associations.
▶ Dolls, clothes, bears, cuddly toys, etc.
▶ Photos of supportive people.
▶ Notes:
  - remember a crisis that ended;
  - think about the positive effects of distress tolerance, imagine how you will feel;
  - think about the negative consequences of not bearing the distress.

Bibliography and research

EMDR Protocols

DELLUCCI H., "The gearbox, navigating safely in therapy with people suffering from complex traumas", *EMDR Journal of Practice and Research, 2010.*

KORN D. L., LEEDS A. M., "EMDR Resource Development and Installation protocol", *Journal of Clinical Psychology, vol. 58, no. 12, pp. 1465-1487, 2002.*

O'SHEA K., *Reconstruction of Foundations, Reconnection to the Self - Preparation and Healing of Early Trauma and Neglect (0-3 years)*, EMDR Conference Istanbul 2006.

SHAPIRO F., *Manuel d'EMDR: Principes, protocoles, procédures*, InterEditions, 2007.

Provocative Therapy

CADE, B., O'HANLON, W. H., *A Brief Guide to Brief Therapy*, New York: W. W. Norton, 1993.

FARRELLY, F., BRANDSMA, J., *Provocative Therapy*, Cupertino Calif.: Meta Publications, 1974.

HALEY, J., *Uncommon Therapy: The Psychiatric Techniques of Milton H. Erickson*, New York: W. W. W. Norton, 1973.

WOLINSKY, S., *Trances People Live*, Connecticut: Bramble, 1991.

Energy Psychology

BOSTON UNIVERSITY, "PTSD associated with more, longer hospitalisations, study shows", *ScienceDaily, 28 March 2008*. Retrieved the 31 March 2008 from http://www.sciencedaily.com/releases/2008/03/080327172124.htm

BOYLE, S. H., KALEHZAN, M., SUND, B., FICEK, S. K. F., SCHATZBERG, A. F., "Hostility, anger and depression predict increases in C3 over a 10-year period", *Brain, Behaviour and Immunity, 21(6), 2001.*

BRADLEY, R., GREENE, J., RUSS, E., DUTRA, L., WESTERN, D., "A multidimensional meta-analysis of psychotherapy for PTSD", *American Journal of Psychiatry, 162, 2005, 214-227.*

BRESLAU, N., DAVIS, G. C., ANDRESKI, P., PETERSON, E., "Traumatic events and posttraumatic stress disorder in an urban population of young adults", *Archives of General Psychiatry, 48, 1991, 216-222.*

BROWN, K., "EMDR versus EFT versus wait list control in PTSD", *Clinical trial underway at Forth Valley NHS hospital, Britain, 2008.*

CALLAHAN, R., *Tapping the Healer Within: Using Thought Field Therapy to Instantly Conquer Your Fears, Anxieties, and Emotional Distress*, New York: McGraw-Hill, 2000.

CARBONELL, J. L., FIGLEY, C., "A systematic clinical demonstration project of promising PTSD treatment approaches", *Traumatology, 5(1), 1999, 4.*

CHURCH, D., *The Genie in Your Genes*, Santa Rosa: Energy Psychology Press, 2009, 223.

CHURCH, D., "The treatment of combat trauma in veterans using EFT (Emotional Freedom Techniques): a pilot protocol", *presented at the yearly Association meeting of Comprehensive Energy Psychology ACEP, Albuquerque, 17 May 2008, submitted for publication.*

CHURCH, D., BROOKS, A., "The effect of a brief EFT (Emotional Freedom Techniques) self-intervention on anxiety, depression, pain and cravings in healthcare workers", *presented at the American Academy for Anti-Aging Medicine (A4M), Orlando, 23 April 2009, submitted for publication.*

CHURCH, D., GERONILLA, L., DINTER, I., "Psychological symptom change in veterans after six sessions of EFT (Emotional Freedom Techniques):

an observational study", *International Journal of Healing and Caring*, 9 January 2009, 1.

CLANCY, C. P., GRAYBEAL, A., TOMPSON, W. P., BADGETT, K. S., FELDMAN, M. E., CALHOUN, P. S., et al, "Lifetime trauma exposure in veterans with military-related posttraumatic stress disorder: association with current symptomatology", *Journal of Clinical Psychiatry*, September 2006, 67(9): 1346-53.

CRAIG, G., *The EFT Manual*, Santa Rosa: Energy Psychology Press, 2008.

CRAIG, G., *EFT for Traumatic Stress*, Santa Rosa: Energy Psychology Press, 2009.

DAVIS, S., BOZON, B., LAROCHE, S., "How necessary is the activation of the immediate early gene zif268 in synaptic plasticity and learning", *Behavioural Brain Research, 2003, 142, 17-30*.

DAVISON, M. L., B., BERSHADSKY, B., BIEBER, J., SILVERSMITH, D., MARUISH, M. E., KANE, R. L., "Development of a brief, multidimensional, self-report instrument for treatment outcomes assessment in psychiatric settings: preliminary findings", *Assessment, 1997, 4, 259–275*.

DEFENSE HEALTH BOARD TASK FORCE ON MENTAL HEALTH, "An achievable vision: report on the department of defense task force on mental health", June 2007, http://www.ha.osd.mil/dhb/mhtf/MHTF-Report-Final.pdf. Retrieved April 24, 2008.

DIEPOLD, J. H., GOLDSTEIN, D., "Thought Field Therapy and EEG changes in the treatment of trauma: a case study", *Traumatology, 15, 2008, 85-93*.

FEINSTEIN, D., "Energy psychology : a review of the preliminary evidence", *Psychotherapy: Theory, Research, Practice, Training, 45(2), 2008a, 199-213*.

FEINSTEIN, D., "Energy psychology in disaster relief", *Traumatology, 141:1, 2008b, 124-137*.

FEINSTEIN, D., EDEN, D., CRAIG, G., *The Promise of Energy Psychology*, New York: Tarcher Putnam, 2005.

Bibliography and research

FELLITI, V. J., KOSS, M. P., MARKS, J. S., "Relationship of childhood abuse and household dysfunction to many of the leading causes of death in adults. The Adverse Childhood Experiences (ACE) study", *American Journal of Preventive Medicine, 4, May 14, 1998, 245.*

FELMINGHAM, K., K., KEMP, A., WILLIAMS, L., "Changes in anterior cingulate and amygdala after cognitive behavior therapy of posttraumatic stress disorder", *Psychological Science, 18:2, 2006, 127-129.*

INSTITUT OF MEDICINE, *Posttraumatic Stress Disorder: Diagnosis and Assessment*, Washington DC: Institute of Medicine, June 16, 2006.

IRAQ VETS STRESS PROJECT, "Energy Psychology therapists in the VA system", 2008. Retrieved April 10 from http://www.StressProject.org

LAMARCHE, L. J., DE KONINCK, J., "Sleep disturbance in adults with posttraumatic stress disorder: a review", *Journal of Clinical Psychiatry, Aug 68(8), 2007, 1257-70.*

LEDOUX, J., Synaptic Self: *How Our Brains Become Who We Are*, New York: Penguin, 2002.

LANE, J. "Wolpe not woo woo; counterconditioning not charlatanism: a biochemical rationale for using acupressure desensitization in psychotherapy", *paper presented at ACEP (Association for Comprehensive Energy Psychology) annual conference, Virginia, May 2006.*

MARUISH, M. E., "Symptom Assessment-45 Questionnaire (SA–45)", *in M. E. Maruish (Ed.), The Use of Psychological Testing, Treatment Planning and Outcomes Assessment (2nd ed.), Mahwah, NJ: Lawrence Erlbaum Associates, 1999.*

MOLLON, P., *Psychoanalytic Energy Psychotherapy*, London: Karnac, 2008.

NATIONAL CENTER FOR PTSD, https://www.ptsd.va.gov/professional/assessment/adult-sr/ptsd-checklist.asp. *Retrieved April 22, 2008.*

OSCHMAN, J., "Trauma energetic", *Journal of Bodywork and Movement Therapies, 10, 2006, 21.*

ROWE, J., "The effects of EFT on long-term psychological symptoms", *Counselling and Clinical Psychology Journal, 2(3), 2005, 104.*

SABBAN, E. L., KVETNANASKY, R., "Stress-triggered activation of gene expression in catecholaminergic systems: Dynamics of transcriptional events", *Trends in Neurosciences*, 24, 2001, 91-98.

SCHULZ, P., "Therapists' views on integrating Energy Psychology in work with survivors of childhood sexual abuse", in *P. Mollon, Psychoanalytic Energy Psychotherapy, London: Karnac,* 2008.

SWINGLE, P., PULOS, L., SWINGLE, M. K., "Effects of a meridian-based therapy, EFT, on symptoms of PTSD in auto accident victims", *a document presented at the annual meeting of the Association for Comprehensive Energy Psychology, Las Vegas, NV,* May 2000.

TANIELIAN, T., JAYCOX, L. H. (Eds), *Invisible wounds of war: psychological and cognitive injuries, their consequences, and services to assist recovery*, Santa Monica: Rand Corp, MG-720-CCF, 2008.

THAYER, J., "A model of neurovisceral integration in emotion regulation and dysregulation", *Journal of Affective Disorders,* 61, 2000, 201-216.

VAN DER KOLK, B. A., MCFARLANE, A. C., WEISAETH, L., *Traumatic stress: the effects of overwhelming experience on mind, body, and society*, New York: Guilford Press, 1996.

WEATHERS, F., LITZ, B., HERMAN, D., HUSKA, J., KEANE, T., "The PTSD Checklist (PCL) : Reliability, validity, and diagnostic utility", paper presented at *the Annual Convention of the International Society for Traumatic Stress Studies*, San Antonio, TX, October 1993.

WELLS, S., POLGLASE, K., ANDREWS, H. B., CARRINGTON, P., BAKER, A. H., "Evaluation of a meridian-based intervention, emotional freedom techniques (EFT), for reducing specific phobias of small animals",Journal of *Clinical Psychology*, 59:92003, 943-966.

WOLPE, J., The Practice of Therapy, 2nd edition, New York: Pergamon Press, 1973.

Other resources

FONE Helena, *EFT for Dummies*, UK Edition, 2008.

GILBERT Paul, *Compassion Focused Therapy, CBT distinctive features*, Routledge, 2010.

GILBERT Paul, *The Compassionate Mind: A New Approach to Life's Challenges*, Constable, 2010.

HANSOUL Brigitte & WAUTHIER Yves, EFT – *Tapping et psychologie énergétique [EFT – Tapping and Energy Psychology]*, Dangles, 2012.

KORN D. L. & LEEDS A. M., "Preliminary evidence for efficacy for EMDR: Resource development and installation in the stabilization phase of treatment of complex post-traumatic stress disorder", *Journal of Clinical Psychology*, 58, 1465–1487, 2002.

SCHWARTZ R. C., *Système familial intérieur : blessures et guérison - Un nouveau modèle de psychothérapie* [Internal Family Systems Therapy], Elsevier, 2009.

VAN DER HART Onno, Nijenhuis Ellert R. S., Steele Kathy, *The Haunted Self - Structural Dissociation and the Treatment of Chronic Traumatization*, Norton W. W. & co, 2006.

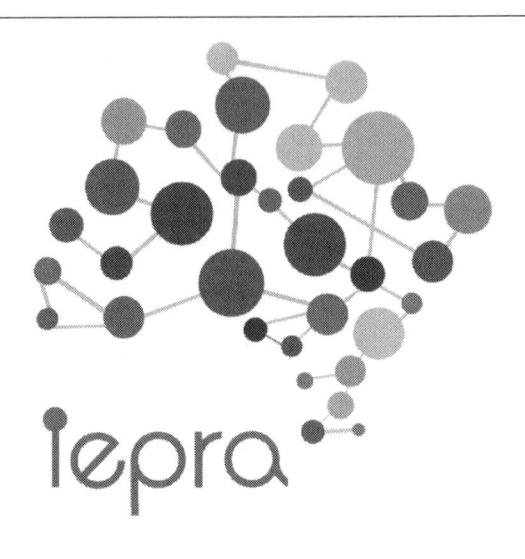

Training for professionals in helping professions
with clients one-on-one or in institutional settings

iepra
https://en.iepra.com/

Innovators in therapy, well-being, helping relationship and care
Integration of relational techniques and innovative neuroscience-based approaches

Our activities are of interest to you if …

- You are dissatisfied with your job and want to either (re-)create meaning and professional motivation, or to develop a complementary activity or start a new career;

Other resources

- You are already (psycho)therapist, coach, teacher, professional in care – social – public service sectors and, like us, you wish to work with cutting edge methods or continue to be enthusiastic about bringing the best to your clients;
- You are stuck in difficult thoughts or emotions, in superficial or complicated relationships and who want to learn to be lighter, happy and feel abundance and thrive.

iepra is anchored in a new dynamic view of (psycho-)therapy and care that is based on the knowledge of modern sciences and ancient traditions, and in a paradigm shift:

In the past, it was enough to have knowledge, today it is about knowing how to concretely use it to help us and others find a greater degree of freedom and choice, motivation and action, meaning and happiness.

Why train with us?

Because we have gone the way before you.
Because we are trainers – psychotherapists passionately integrating the latest discoveries in our field.
Because we want you to benefit from our engagement.
If, like us, you want, to be happy in your daily life, to be motivated in your job, to rediscover the initial meaning of your profession of care-help-service, or if you want to help others to change, to thrive.

Because with us you can work seriously and "seriously" have fun as well.

Who are we ?

We are psychotherapists and trainers, each with a whole universe of experiences, skills and personal "colors" who share a common passion: to help discover or rediscover the freedom of fully being themselves AND to experience rich and nurturing relationships.

Ulrike Weissenbacher

The paradox of life : I started out in life, barely escaping being aborted and that became the starting point for a lifetime of searching for the meaning of our existence...

Coming from a working-class family, prejudices "formatted" me from primary school on being labelled "unfit to study". To my good fortune, I was "saved" by a teacher who believed in me. However, a feeling of inferiority and self-doubt accompanied me and tinged even my best successes.

From my childhood I have known loving presence, connection as well as unbearable premature loss, the feeling of being alone and non-existent; constant aggressive arguments as well as great kindness and care; the paternal presence tinged with aggressiveness and alcohol as well as his joy of living. And the result? Others come first, be strong, do not feel, as well as a great sensitivity, compassion and interest in people and their stories.

Faced with this complexity, I sought to first get out of it by myself and then to want to save others. I "gulped in" psychoanalysis, gestalt, humanists, NLP... and then, in my quest for transcendence, the Vedic and Taoist teachings. Meeting spiritual masters and working on myself, more and more trusting the help I received, have transformed me in an ongoing process...

I chose to help others develop their full potential and I learned to love myself and calm the great expectations and demand from myself. Opening my heart and being present, helping to bring love, humor, the feeling of being satisfied, surrounded and loved to what is hurt inside the person is a source of joy for me.

The integration of knowledge and know-how of humanists, of clinicians, compassion and effectiveness of Energy Psychology approaches, is my great passion.

Other resources

And who knows, maybe it becomes yours too?

Yves Wauthier Freymann

Being human, existential questions, life, death, the meaning of life, nature, stars, mythologies, horses, martial arts, Japan, Judaism, Islam, religions, poetry, books, sports, books, fantasy, science fiction, science, humanities, books, humor, love, people...

These are some ideas that express the bulimic need to learn, to understand, to give meaning that have inhabited me from a young age on, in particular to fill a big emotional void... and, very quickly, I was attracted to offbeat humor, black, British, monthy python...

I was a very shy and hyper-sensitive child... Very early on, before I was 6, I questioned myself a lot about the meaning to be given to life and death... I was mistreated, without being able to understand the full scope of what I experienced and, even less, having the capacity to express it, to digest it. On the other hand, all this life experience and reflections have led me to favor and highlight humanist values and being human...

Quite naturally, this led me to become more and more interested in the functioning of humans inner workings, human systems, work on oneself through introspection, psychoanalysis, humanist approaches and, one thing leading to another, through my practice and my interest in martial arts, the qi and approaches mixing Eastern and Western human arts.

I then came to specialize in this new, particularly efficient current of trauma-work : energy psychology and psycho-physical approaches. Provocative heart-centered approaches, such as the work of Frank Farrelly, David Lake, Steve Wells complete this ever-evolving universe...

Other resources

ACEP
ASSOCIATION FOR COMPREHENSIVE ENERGY PSYCHOLOGY

Hereby Awards

Yves Wauthier-Freymann, DCEP

with the designation

Diplomate, Comprehensive Energy Psychology

This certificate demonstrates that this energy psychology practitioner has made a commitment to enhancing the profession by successfully completing all of the requirements of the certification program of the Association for Comprehensive Energy Psychology.

Robert Schwarz, PsyD, DCEP
ACEP Executive Director

Lori Chortkoff Hops, PhD, DCEP
ACEP President

Granted: 6/29/2009
Expires: 6/30/2023
Identification Number: 2117

Made in the USA
Coppell, TX
23 May 2025